IN
DAYS
TO
COME

IN
DAYS
TO
COME

A NEW HOPE FOR ISRAEL

AVRAHAM BURG

Translated by Joel Greenberg

NATION
BOOKS
New York

Nation Books
116 East 16th Street, 8th Floor
New York, NY 10003
www.publicaffairsbooks.com/nation-books
@nationbooks

Printed in the United States of America

First Edition: January 2018

Published by Nation Books, an imprint of Perseus Books, LLC,
a subsidiary of Hachette Book Group, Inc.
Nation Books is a co-publishing venture of the Nation Institute and
Perseus Books.

The Hachette Speakers Bureau provides a wide range of authors for speaking events. To find out more, go to www.hachettespeakersbureau.com or call (866) 376-6591.

The publisher is not responsible for websites (or their content) that are not owned by the publisher.

Print book interior design by Timm Bryson, em em design, LLC.

Library of Congress Cataloging-in-Publication Data
Names: Burg, Avraham, author.
Title: In days to come : a new hope for Israel / Avraham Burg.
Description: First edition. | New York : Nation Books, [2017] | Includes index.
Identifiers: LCCN 2017020692| ISBN 9781568589787 (hardcover) | ISBN
    9781568587974 (e-book)
Subjects: LCSH: Burg, Avraham. | Political activists—Israel—Biography. |
    Authors, Israeli—Biography.
Classification: LCC DS126.6.B87 A3 2017 | DDC 956.9405—dc23
    LC record available at https://lccn.loc.gov/2017020692

ISBNs: 978-1-56858-978-7 (hardcover), 978-1-56858-797-4 (ebook)

LSC-C

10   9   8   7   6   5   4   3   2   1

To my mother and teacher, Rivka Slonim,
and my father and teacher, Shlomo Yosef Burg,
of blessed memory.

For the loves of my life: Yael, Itay, Noa, Yuval, and Gal.
Roni, Ariel, Zev, and Ayal. Natan, Tamara Yang, and Lemoni.
Dan, Avital, Jonathan and Malachi, Noam and Noam.

And to Andrea, Anna, Azar, Bashir, Frans, Ghaida,
Hanes, Husam, Ivan, Lars, Leila, Martin, Mazen, Michael,
Ram, Sam, Shawki, and Yvette.

And to Gertraud, my Europe,
who opened all the doors for me and invited me in.

Birds born in a cage are convinced that flying is a disease.

ALEJANDRO JODOROWSKY

If there is no foreigner in my identity, I don't know myself.
I can be defined only through the dialectical relationship between
me and the other. If I am alone, with no one else, what do I understand?
I am full of myself, all of my truth, without dualism. . . .
I need heterogeneity, it enriches me.

MAHMOUD DARWISH

CONTENTS

PART II: LEARNING

AUTHOR'S NOTE

AS FAR BACK AS I CAN REMEMBER A QUESTION HAS accompanied me: what would your father say? Rarely is it the curious question of someone who really wants to know; mostly it is a taunt from someone who wants to win an argument without having a conversation. Many times, I ignore the question and the questioners, if only because they have no interest whatsoever in what my mother would say. Her comments were no less sharp and incisive than his. Our togetherness, she and he and a bit of me, brought into the world the baggage that I offer my children to adopt.

Between my parents, who have passed on, and my children, I am a link that awoke one morning a few years ago with great anger. It was during the bloody days of the second Palestinian uprising. A great silence and greater bewilderment enveloped the country. Death took its toll on both peoples, and we were its emissaries and victims. All the atrocities, killing, and bereavement had no meaning or purpose. Day after day. Terrorist attacks and retaliation, revenge and counter-revenge. That morning everything burst inside me. When I asked myself why, I realized that of all the people I was angry at, I was angry at my beloved and missed father most of all. He had been dead for a few years and the Palestinian uprising and Israel's responses were no longer his responsibility, and still all my arrows were aimed at him.

For weeks I continued the examination—why? Why the anger, and why toward him specifically? I reached the conclusion that I was angry with him because he, who was so important to me as a father and teacher, did not leave me anything written, no guide to the perplexed or a spiritual will about his conception of the roots of Israeli reality or its future directions. In our imagined conversations, I asked him again and again what he would have thought had he been with us. But from the book he did not write for me there were no answers.

In those days, I wanted to leave something for my children, wherever life may take them, and I began to write. I don't know what challenges they will have to face, and I have no idea what decisions they will make in the moments of truth in their lives. But wherever their winds take them, I want to leave them materials from which they can always stitch sails of thought and content that will fit their size. I have no property to leave them, just some insights as provisions for the journey of life, raw materials for shaping their lives. So that they will at least have an answer to the question: what would your father say? Despite the confusion of the times, do your utmost not to err like many do in distinguishing good from bad. And despite the nationalistic wave, which presents itself as the calling card of contemporary Israel, never forget the values of our home, the all-embracing humanism that is our safe haven. Never despair about the political and social reality. Fight it and change it. And never flee your inner truth, even if it means periods of loneliness and living as a minority. Because truth will out, and ultimately many of the truths of the minority became the majority's strategy for salvation. These are important and defining lessons that my parents drummed into me. But alas, they are not being passed on to the next generation, to Israel's grandchildren, who need them more than ever.

These days of the early twenty-first century appear to me as days of profound change against the background of global, local, and personal upheaval. That is why this book ultimately is a personal document, written at a stormy time as I perceive it, as an individual Israeli. Around the time of this book's publication, Israel, the region, and the international community will mark fifty years since the Six-Day War. That is a very long period in a person's life, but very short in the annals of history. There are few chapters of the past like this one, in which we as individuals and as a collective achieved so much, while making so many mistakes. Years in which greatness and folly were intertwined. This duality requires a great deal of soul-searching, of which this book is a part. I had the privilege of living and acting in this chapter of the history of my people, the Jewish people, and I have a few thoughts, insights, and reflections on the time, as well as about myself and others.

I've already written a few books. Each one has moved me a bit closer to the next, and given me another measure of courage to reveal myself to myself, and become almost entirely revealed to my readers. "Why on earth are you summing up your life? You're only halfway there," many people told me while this book was being written. They were right. I really did not try to write an autobiography. With all due respect to my public career, I'm not important enough to thread an entire period of history through the eye of my needle as a writer. All I wanted to do was to find and share the lost Israeli places between current affairs and history. Therefore, this is just a reflection and expression of what my eyes have seen. My personal experiences are just a means to help me decipher some of the riddles of Israeli existence. In this book I open parts of my personal life to the public in order to add another dimension of meaning to what is happening to us. Mine is an Israeli voice that tries to be different from the formal, shrill voices blaring from official Israeli loudspeakers. I'm trying to add another sound to the few heard from my generation, the generation that followed the establishment of the state and has not found enough expression, and the generation of religious Zionism that reshuffled the whole deck here and also is rather mute and very deaf.

I have anger and consolation, but I am not a prophet and do not come from a family of prophets. I just see history and current affairs as prisms through which I can prepare for the future. The following pages are therefore reflections of this sort, about current affairs that became history, and events happening right now, and those still to come. Brexit and Trump, the populist movements and the contemporary setback of liberal democracies are details, important but fragmentary. So here is my modest attempt to comprehend the larger frame, the "gestalt of

the zeitgeist," the way it is perceived through Israeli, Jewish, and liberal
lenses.

In Days to Come is the fruit of profound gratitude. First and foremost
to Noa Manheim, a friend and study partner, my Hebrew editor and
critic, and to Alessandra Bastagli, editorial director at Nation Books.
Many great thanks to the Bruno Kreisky Forum for International Dialogue in Vienna and to Gertraud Auer Borea d'Olmo, who gave me
a home and a fellowship, a social network and circles of warmth and
wisdom that few have the privilege of having in their lives. To the wise
Ivan Krastev and Anna Ganeva, who involved me in the activities of
the Center for Liberal Strategies in Bulgaria. Their invitation to the
Institute for Human Sciences in Vienna enabled me to broaden my
horizons and gave me time to write. To the Van Leer Jerusalem Institute, in whose quiet and enveloping library the book took shape, and to
the people of "Molad" for the lessons they have taught me.

And above all, my relatives who are around me and in me. To Yael,
my incomparable companion. To my wonderful children, their families, and Hillel and Talila, who are always with us. To Lucian and Ja-
nine, my parents-in-law. To my sister, brother-in-law, and my nephews
and nieces, who took the trouble to read, weed, and plant. They turned
the feelings into words and a melody. When I think about you, my parents gather in me and sing along with us the song of our life.

PART I

LIVING

CHAPTER ONE

MENORAH
OF BULLETS
(1955–1968)

T HE FIRST CHILDHOOD MEMORY I HAVE OF MY FATHER IS linked to the destruction of empires—the collapse of a world order that had once seemed eternal. Dad, whose life spanned nearly 90 percent of the twentieth century, was born before World War I. He spent his childhood in the seemingly stable but actually decaying reality of nineteenth-century Europe. From the window of his childhood home in Dresden, Germany, at Zerre Straße Nummer Zwei, he, the Jewish boy born in 1909, saw the revolutionaries calling for the overthrow of the king of Saxony. With his particular smile reserved for especially vulgar words, he quoted the Saxon king, with a heavy Saxon accent, lashing out at the rebels, "Mach deinen Scheiss allein" (Go deal with your own shit). A continent away, Mom's childhood was also shaped by terrible upheaval and destruction, wrought by the massacre of Hebron's Jews in 1929.

My parents' first and momentous memories are imprinted on me, while my own first memories are small and very personal, much like any child of my generation. The slats of my crib were already loose. My

3

crib was old. My parents bought it used, and then it served my sisters before it became my first bed. The three of us shared a room, and the furniture, like our clothing, schoolbags, and pencil cases, was all hand-me-downs. That crib is my very first memory, in which—like in many moments to follow—I was entirely alone. It was 1957, and I was a year-and-a-half, maybe two years old.

I squeezed out of the crib and walked around the house, beyond the permitted boundaries. I went from my room to my parents' room, which was a sacred space and not always accessible. In the middle was the tall kerosene stove, warding off the "draft" for Dad. A piece of beautiful cast iron, whose wick only Mom knew how to change and light without creating soot. A large pot with boiling water stood on the stove, to humidify the air and to prepare tea. And I, the fugitive from the crib, bumped into it with full infantile force. The boiling water spilled and scalded my tender back, the first burns of my life.

In those days, I probably attached little meaning to the crib slats and the escape, the fire and the water, the pain and the scar, the deposed kaisers and slaughtered Jews that launched me into the world. My childhood was mundane, not particularly heroic. I lived through twelve of the nineteen first—and last—sane years of Israel's existence, and although in those distant days of my childhood some vestiges of the excitement of 1948 still lingered, I didn't know we were making history.

In the sixties, from time to time, new children would join my class, from Morocco, France, or Poland. Children, not waves of immigration. I knew how to mock their foreign accents, but I failed to understand that I was being insulting and not welcoming. Aunt Bertl sent us packages from America full of used clothing that Tziona the seamstress altered for us on Mom's oversized sewing machine. For me, as I grew up, the Jewish Agency and the United Jewish Appeal were embodied in those packages my family received. Nobody even noticed that there were kids in class who did not have uncles and aunts in America, or uncles and aunts at all, and no one imagined that my worn and fitted striped American pants were actually the start of the social inequality gap. All these small childhood events flowed like tiny tributaries until they became, during the war that changed our universe, a big waterfall that has not stopped cascading since.

During the Six-Day War (June 5–10, 1967), I was neither a brave fighter nor an involved civilian—at twelve, I was barely a concerned citizen. I was just a little Jerusalem boy in transition from childhood to adolescence. Still without whiskers, but with some underarm sweat like the adults. I had a pair of Ata factory jeans and "a real cowboy's" holster belt and toy gun that Aunt Bertl had sent me in a package for Purim. In June 1967, I had long used up all the caps for my gun, but I still sat for hours on a punctured water tank left in the yard, riding bravely on the tin horse, galloping toward the enemies and driving them off. In that fashion, over many days, I saved Mom and Dad and my two older sisters, Tzvia and Ada, time and again. All by myself, like the cowboys and Indians who were both my father's childhood super-heroes and mine. Our daily routine, Mom's and the kids', continued as usual, but nothing was really in order.

Slowly, patiently, the tension grew and became stifling. Fathers went to the army, and vehicles we had never seen before—command cars, light armored vehicles, and other bulky trucks—were on the streets. Private cars were commandeered and covered with mud as camouflage. Occasionally a plane was seen overhead—despite the ban on flying over the city—and that caused a sensation. We, the Jerusalem kids, hardly ever saw planes before and never up in "our skies." Every day after school we took to the streets to fill bags from the piles of sand left by government and city trucks on every street corner. We painted car headlights blue for a blackout "like in London," adults said, recalling the blitzkrieg days of World War II. In Mr. Heller's grocery store Mom bought a little extra toilet paper and some canned food. But she said, "I'm not stocking up, because if they see me stocking up on food then everyone will think they need to prepare."

I was a sixth-grader in Mrs. Blumenthal's English class when, on a Monday morning, war came. It began just as they had explained it would: a siren, the lesson came to a halt, and we huddled next to the walls, under windows that looked like woven fabric, crisscrossed with the brown masking tape we had pasted on them with our saliva and little hands. Hundreds of children and a few dozen teachers—female teachers, to be precise, because almost all the male teachers had been called up to the army—waited tensely. Explosions reverberated through the city, Jordanian legionnaires fired sniper shots, there were explosions of shells and mortars from both sides, and the thunder of jets repeatedly broke the sound barrier as they headed beyond enemy lines. It was the first time that I had heard such sounds. The automatic machine-gun fire rang in my ears like a giant metronome. Then there was silence for a few minutes, as if the conductor of an orchestra had ordered all the musicians to stop playing and listen for a moment.

In one of those moments I drummed my fingers on the school's old wooden table. We all practiced different games to train our fingers to be nimbler. Who knows if it was just a game or an effort to release tension. Nothing I heard until that moment was as frightening as the shouts that followed. That petite and stern-looking teacher, Mrs. Blumenthal, took out her stress on me, venting the terrible anxiety I was protected from as a child, caused by the days of waiting in which we labored to fortify our homes and classroom and endured the absence of the men, including her partner. Poor woman, all her favorite disciplinary measures were denied her. She couldn't eject me from the classroom and endured because there was shooting outside. She couldn't send me to the principal because he too was sitting with us in the makeshift shelter. So she made do with a heartfelt groan: "How dare you? Don't you understand anything?" And the truth is that indeed I did not understand, though not necessarily the things she had in mind.

We went home with the mother of one of my classmates, Yisrael, who at that moment was for me the mother of all Israelis. As a young kid, I had no idea about defense systems, military powers, or diplomatic shields. She—this mom—symbolized for me, then, the fragile protection against the eruption of war evilness and the deepest of fears. We didn't walk on the main roads to avoid the fire from the Jordanian snipers in red-checked head-scarves who were posted at the top of David's Citadel. Suddenly everything that had been regularly forbidden to us became temporarily permitted. In those days, parental authority was supreme. A parent spoke, and the child obeyed. But in that moment the roles were reversed, and suddenly I became Yisrael's mother's guide. I told her "this way," and she obeyed. I showed her how to jump over fences, and she followed me silently. In those moments with her we were allowed to vault over roadblocks and go through courtyards that were forbidden to us all year. We passed through the Reform Har-El synagogue and the Baptist church on Narkis Street, which our parents and teachers shunned: the former because the Judaism practiced there was not ours, and the latter because of its missionary Christianity. But in that first time of trouble in our lives, everything was forgotten, and they—the Baptists and Reform Jews in the heart of Jerusalem—became our temporary refuge; the walls and fences of the church and Temple shielded us from the hostile fire, becoming the backroad safe way home, the one we hardly ever dared to take during peace time. That's life sometimes; places we find terrifying in times of peace can suddenly become safe havens in times of trouble and hardship.

We crossed the yard of the Ratisbonne Monastery, which was usually locked shut. I had always been haunted by the fear that if I passed by the place the priests in their brown robes and rope belts would seize me and send me to the Christian orphanage. But in the face of the demonic Arab enemy, the terrifying Jordanian Legion, everything unfit to eat became kosher, and all the fears became momentary security. The teacher, Yisrael's mother, and I did not know then that this was the essence of the Six-Day War for Israelis: turning the unacceptable into the appropriate, putting the stamp of approval on everything that was supposed to be absolutely forbidden, making it permissible and even sacred.

I arrived home safely. I clearly remember the sound of exploding shells falling in the yard and my sister's fear, as well as our surprise at the new, unfamiliar names the radio announcers peppered us with: Sharm el-Sheikh and Quneitra, Nasser and Hussein. Who are these terrible demons? Where are these hellish places?

On Wednesday, it was all over. After much shelling and bombing, endless rumors and news flashes, patriotic music playing on the radio, and families huddling together protectively, Dad returned home from his job at the government and said to Mom, "Get ready, we're going to the Kotel," the Western Wall. I didn't know exactly what this Kotel was. We were never taught at home to yearn for it. We didn't have a picture of it on the wall, not even a bronze engraving, as was common in so many homes at that time. The walls of Dad's large library were decorated with photos of Mom's family from the old Jewish community in Hebron that had been destroyed, and next to them was a lithograph of synagogues from around the world that were no more, from the Jewish diaspora that had been wiped out. But there was nothing to commemorate the Temple.

I will remember Mom's excitement until the day I die. She was wearing her blue pleated skirt. "Does this look all right?" she asked Dad, as always. "Very much so, Rivka," he replied, as always, and together they went to the road to board the military transport that had come to pick them up. A dusty, unshaven soldier helped them climb into the command car.

"I want to go, too," I wailed at the top of my lungs, crying heavy, salty tears whose taste I can still recall. It was the first great outburst of my childhood. Cries of longing and sadness, of fear and disappointment, of a parting much greater than myself. Perhaps I was curious to see the battlefields; perhaps I was just giving voice to all the fears that had built up inside me during those days. The cries of a young boy who was not ready to be left without the security and protection of his parents. But despite my tears, they left without me. When they came back after a few hours, my mother pulled out a small bag from her pocketbook and retrieved from it a few short, squat cartridges from an Uzi submachine gun. "I collected them at the Kotel especially for you," she said, as she handed the cartridges to me. She wanted to compensate for having left me behind, but she was also entrusting me with a little treasure.

In those last innocent days of the State of Israel, we all had to take a shop class at school. Once a week we left the gray, neglected schoolyard and walked a few blocks to the workshop of the teacher, Mr. Tarshish. In the faded apron of a craftsman from a bygone era, with a booming voice and a ruler he rapped against the table any time he grew angry, Mr. Tarshish taught us all the survival skills we'd ever need. How to fix a short circuit with a special iron wire, how to change a light bulb, how to sand down a rough board and polish metal. To this day, I don't particularly like manual work, mainly because I'm not that good at it. I am not just left-wing politically; I also have two left hands, far more left than my most firmly held views. I was also never good at conforming to the mold, or copying a template exactly and without variation. Even back then my spirit sought something else, something creative and original. The complete opposite of the strict, precise work ethic of the formidable Mr. Tarshish.

A few months after the war had ended, we prepared a surprise for our parents in honor of Chanukah: we made metal menorahs, the proud work of our own hands. We toiled for days, cutting the brass, bending and joining, shaping the frame and the branches. For me, the high point was taking the Uzi cartridges that Mom had brought me from the Kotel and attaching them to the menorah as candleholders. My souvenir from the remnants of the Temple is inextricably bound up in weaponry, violence, and bloodshed. I was not yet familiar with a Judaism of pacifism, but if I had been, I doubt I would have committed to it. In school, we had not yet read the biblical verse rejecting all violent

associations with the Temple and its altars: "And if you make for Me
an altar of stones, do not build it of hewn stones, for by wielding your
sword upon them you have profaned them" (Exodus 20:25). And thus,
the Jewish Kotel and the Israeli Uzi were melded together for me into
something new, inseparable.

T O THIS DAY, WE LIGHT THIS MENORAH EVERY CHANUKAH,
and I both love it and hate it. Each time my heart is pierced anew—
by longing for the childhood I once had and that is no longer, and by
lament for the great transformation that has come over all of us. I need
that particular menorah not just as a nostalgic link to those innocent
bygone days, but also as a tangible reminder of all those things that I
still want, and still need, to change in this world.

I always loved Chanukah, more than any other holiday. In the beginning, in my youth, it was because of the mystery of the darkness
and the small lights that banish it, and because of the modest little gifts
we always received from our parents. I loved those magic moments in
which Dad, Mom, my sisters, and I sat on the rug and played with the
dreidels, the spinning tops—one of the rare occasions when Dad came
down to our childhood level. Perhaps that's why dreidels became my
favorite collector's item, with thousands of them now decorating the
walls of our home. With time, I came to love Chanukah even more, as
a unique and special holiday in which Mom had a significant role. Not
just as the passive woman who says *Amen* to all the blessings, rituals,
and customs that Dad performed with flair, but also as the one who lit
the candles on the nights that Dad was not at home. I loved her in this
role—she inspired me to take on my first public position. It was during
Chanukah when I was in first grade. I was selected to play the part of
the *shamash*, the candle used to light all the others. Mother ironed
my white shirt, made me a cardboard crown with a paper candle on
top, and rehearsed with me again and again the line I was supposed
to recite in a loud voice in the class play. "To be a shamash is to bear

a great responsibility," she said to me, "and my son needs to be the best shamash there is." So I tried, for her sake. I wanted to be the best shamash there is.

Since Chanukah is always celebrated in the winter darkness, it is the Festival of Lights, similar to festivals of light in many other cultures, such as Diwali, the Hindu festival. We Jews, who do not worship nature in and of itself, have added more and more layers of religious meaning to Chanukah, as with many of our other holidays. The miracle of the jar of oil, the redemption of the Temple, the victory of the few over the many—the whole deal. Thus, we transformed a festival celebrating the shortest days of the year and the approaching lengthening of the hours of daylight into a religious holiday. Adam's sigh of relief, as his fears were alleviated when the winter nights stopped growing longer, was transformed into a great, spontaneous joy. The joy of the faithful over the redemption of the Temple in Jerusalem after the Greeks had defiled it with their pagan rites and their military conquest. The Greek empire issued religious decrees against us. Our benevolent God, the master of history, stood by our ancestors in their distress and granted them a "great salvation." As a sign of gratitude, and as a means of commemoration, the ancient Jews dedicated these eight days to giving thanks to the God who delivered them, and to praising His name.

It was never a holiday about wars and warriors. On the contrary, the mighty ones in the Chanukah story are the Greeks, not us. But that is something that no one told me before I ascended the tall chair of the shamash on Chanukah during first grade. In my black polyester Sabbath pants, which were secured high above my belly button, I sang my lines as loudly as I could: "In our time as in those days, God's Maccabee redeems always." I didn't know that in my cousin Moshe's secular school down the block, they sang the same song, but with a slight variation: "In our time as in those days, the Maccabee redeems always." For us, it was still a religious holiday with God at the center; for them, the holiday had already been appropriated by the steamrolling revolution of Zionist consciousness. God was cast aside, and the Maccabee took center stage.

The Zionist revolution dearly wanted to return us Jews to an active role in political history, and it grasped at every symbolic straw it could find. It is natural, therefore, that the heroism of the war and the struggle of the Maccabees became the most important port of call in the Zionist movement's voyage home. The return to the land and to our memories, to language and history, to the places that once were, and to the glory of the past. And we small children each were the best shamash there is, the caddies of this fantastic revolution. A decade later, in the mid-seventies, we in the army were singing completely different versions of those Chanukah songs. God had disappeared entirely from the holiday, and we marched in unison—left, right, left—accompanied by the hoarse loudspeakers:

> We carry lights
> Through darkest nights
> The paths aglow beneath our feet.
> We found no jar of oil
> No miracle but our toil
> We hewed the stone with all our might—
> Let there be light!

With rifles on our shoulders and heavy military steps, we trampled on any religious vestige of the holiday. From a Jew in my parents' home I became a new Israeli Maccabee. We, my Israeli friends and I, didn't rely on miracles. Not like all the weak, meek members of our parents' generation. We took responsibility into our own hands; we were the masters of our own fates. I was transformed from an anonymous little religious Jewish boy from Jerusalem into the conventional Israeli hero, whom none of my parents' generation or their parents before them ever had imagined.

This popular modern Chanukah song has become associated, in recent years, with the opening ceremonies for Israel's Independence Day on Mount Herzl in Jerusalem. The Hasmoneans (the ancient Jewish dynasty established by the sons of Mattathias the Hasmonean and encompassing Judea and surrounding areas) became retrospective heroes who were enlisted as the inspiration and model for present-day Israeli war heroes, those who "hew the stones." Through this marching song written for a Zionist Chanukah and played on Independence Day, Chanukah and Independence Day become inextricably intertwined in our consciousness. The modern holiday of Chanukah became a festival of heroism, rather than a festival of lights commemorating the rededication of the Temple. With each Uzi cartridge I fastened to our menorah—any of which may have felled someone near the Kotel in '67—I unknowingly fastened this new myth to our Israeli narrative.

"You have a holiday, again?" a non-Jewish friend asked me. "Which is it this time?" When I patiently explained it to her, I realized how hard it is to avoid the feeling that, for us, holidays and disasters are inevitably intertwined. It seems that there was always some disaster about to happen, always with a great villain involved, and we were always miraculously saved. That's why we have so many holidays and we celebrate happily with plenty of commentary and food. On Passover, we are threatened by the Pharaoh and we eat matzah as a culinary reminder of our ancient misery. On Purim, it's the wicked Haman, our classical anti-Jewish biblical antagonist, who was a vizier under King Ahasuerus (also known as Xerxes I), and we eat hamantaschen pastries, shaped like triangles to remind us of the evil one's ears.

One of my daughters asked me once, "What does the sesame on the burekas [poppy seed–filled pastries] commemorate?" One of my sons came home from kindergarten one day and asked, "Dad, who's the villain of Shavuot?" But the sesame is just sesame and the Shavuot holiday never had a "villain." In my childhood, Shavuot was a very low-key holiday but nevertheless quite a happy one. Though brief compared to Passover and Sukkot, it was heavily freighted with symbolism and meaning. On Shavuot, we went to the synagogue as Jews, as religious people. There we celebrated the giving of the Torah, according to our traditional customs. But on the streets and in schools, we were Israelis first, and as such we celebrated the other aspect of the holiday—the first fruits of the harvest.

As little children, we would march to the headquarters of the Jewish Agency in the Rehavia neighborhood, bringing first fruits. We wore white, put baskets of fruits and vegetables on our small shoulders, and walked slowly up the hill from the kindergarten to the Jewish Agency compound. The children of Jerusalem, festively dressed, trailed behind the kindergarten teacher, who carried a tambourine, her assistant with a triangle and cymbals, and all of us singing at the top of our small voices an old song of Levin Kipnis, the Zionist holiday poet.

That was our Zionist activity at its best. Blue-and-white youth in Israeli sandals—two brown straps and a hard leather sole—and white socks. In the streets, we celebrated the country and its districts, the land and its fruit, which we, the new Jewish generation, carried on our shoulders. And there I was, Avraham Burg, four or five years old, from 6 Ben-Maimon Street in Jerusalem, not my grandfather with the same name who is buried in Dresden. Me, the little Israeli, marching proudly in "our" streets and bringing the first fruits of the land—that is, fruit that Mom bought at the Mahane Yehuda market—to the headquarters of our new national institutions.

I was eventually elected chairman of those institutions, the Jewish Agency and the World Zionist Organization in 1995, when I was thirty-nine years old. The struggle to get elected to the post was long, difficult, and ugly, a global struggle that pitted the official representatives of the Jewish world who wanted me for the job against Yitzhak Rabin's more suitable candidate. (The officials were a mix of Jewish world leaders and philanthropists, and some Israeli political hacks who were concerned that my "young Turk" energy might put at risk the conservative stability of the organization.) It was neither the first nor the last time that I would face Rabin. A national hero when he was killed, Rabin was a man I intensely disliked and did not respect during his lifetime. In fairness, the feeling was mutual. He did not really like me, justifiably in his view. He was a famous military man and a war hero, and I was one of the founders of the protest movement against war. He was the embodiment of the Zionist establishment and I was not, and no longer am.

On my first day as chairman, I set out for work on foot from my parents' house. I walked through my old kindergarten, which is still standing, and walked up the street to the national Temple where we had brought first fruits as children. What was a difficult march for a three- or four-year-old was only a few minutes' walk for an adult. That day my journey took me across the phases of my life to that point. A leap across many years. A moment before I went through the door to assume my official appointment as chairman, I looked back down the street from which I had come. It was a quiet Jerusalem afternoon. I looked for little Avraham, but he wasn't there. I thought I was witnessing the closing of a circle, but I didn't know that nothing had been closed. Nothing. In fact, everything was about to open, and the path ahead of me was longer than anything I had ever experienced. The natural flow of childhood—with the naïve images of a national utopia as a way of life and the childish optimism that replaced the hardships of all the generations before us—changed in 1967.

The sense of relief and liberation after the Six-Day War was indescribable. Few wars end "well." Often the first days of the war are heady—mass enthusiasm and the bravado of leaders—but they end with great disappointment. I had read much about the high morale of nations going to war, and I had listened closely to the personal stories of German Jewish immigrants of Dad's generation (they would become the first members of the Israeli peace camp) when they talked about the enthusiasm that swept over them when they went off to fight in World War I. Like them and the rest of us, my enthusiasm in June 1967 knew no bounds. Like them, over the years and after gaining perspective, I would never feel the same way again. Since then, I have never again felt stirred or inspired by any of Israel's wars. In the first days of every operation, I'm always afraid, concerned, and critical. That is why in the closing days of each of these wars I am never disappointed, unfortunately, because the grim reaper always comes to claim his price. All wars have a dark, sad end, full of loss and grief. So many of my friends are buried in this soil that it seems to me that a very high price has been exacted for the hope that has yet to be delivered.

The Six-Day War began with fear and depression. During the three weeks leading to the conflict, we felt anew the terrors of the War of Independence and the losses of 1948—the six thousand dead, an incomprehensible number, 1 percent of the Jewish population in the country. (Today, that percentage would be equivalent to seventy thousand Israelis.) We repressed the memories of those incomprehensible losses for the first nineteen years of Israel's existence, despite the death and bereavement present in every house on every street. Suddenly the memories and emotions could no longer be repressed; everything came out with full force. The hardships of those three weeks seemed to us like the three weeks that preceded the burning and destruction of the Second Temple. There was a feeling of being in a new Warsaw Ghetto. But if the Six-Day War had begun with a grim mood, its ending was unlike anything that had occurred before (or since) in our long history. Many of us interpreted the quick and surprising end of the conflict as a miracle. In those six days, many chapters of Jewish and Israeli history were closed, and new chapters begun, quite different from preceding ones. We perceived those six days as the six days of creation, this time of a renewed Israel. In the six days of war, we erased the humiliation and shame of our past in the diaspora and gained a new sense of pride that countered the legacy of generations of misery.

Our generation completed what the founders of the state had failed to achieve: overcoming the exilic mentality of weakness. We were the first generation to fully express Jewish might.

The holiday of Shavuot, which came a week after the war, became something else entirely. Until 1967, we would go every year to Mount Zion and to the ancient compound revered as the tomb of King David. At the time, I was unaware of the industry of religious illusions that touts every local sheikh's tomb as a Jewish holy place, without much supporting historical or archeological evidence. In the sixties, I believed with all my heart that King David was indeed buried there, under the tombstone and its fabric cover. On holidays when my friends and I went to Mount Zion, within the small Israel of those days, adjacent to the ancient walls, we climbed the roofs of the compound and tried to see the Temple Mount, inventing yearnings we didn't really have. We greatly enjoyed the experience of being near the dangerous border and were addicted to the sensation of almost touching the walls of the mythical Old City. In those days, we also went to the Abu Tor neighborhood, a different viewpoint at the city frontier of the same yearned-for holy site, and from the corner lookout we barely managed, craning our necks, to see the southern corner of the Temple Mount. Whoever understood the explanations of the teachers and guides claimed that he saw even more: Absalom's Pillar and the Dome of the Rock, not gold-plated then and yet to become the symbol of Palestinian nationalism. All that was before that crucial war.

On the morning of the holiday, less than a week after the great catharsis, when the air was still rife with that mix of emotions that would never return—fear and pride, bereavement and victory, arrogance and wonder—throngs of people gathered in the square below my childhood home. A true pilgrimage: a mix of older people who had visited the Western Wall in "the old days" before 1948; relatives of the paratroopers, like Aunt Malka and Uncle Zeev, who longed not only for the encounter with the sacred stones, but to meet their mobilized loved ones, our heroes, the liberators of the wall; bereaved families fresh from their mourning period; and masses of young people like myself. A huge group of both regular and occasional worshipers who all felt a need to thank God as close as possible to his official abode. A long, seemingly endless column of frenzied dancers wound its way down to the Valley of Hinnom. Sweating men in prayer shawls, happy children like myself in holiday clothes, curious onlookers, and ordinary folks mingled together. I was short and got sandwiched between the man in front of me, whose shoulder I tried to reach, and the anonymous dancer behind me whose hand lay heavily on my back, pressing me down. This monotonous choreography went on for hours. Songs of religious faith rose from dry throats, and the hoarser the singer, the more righteous he was deemed. The human serpent entered the Old City through Dung Gate and danced up its alleys. I remember the rivers of sweat, the terrible thirst, the aching feet, but the ecstasy carried us onward.

In the afternoon, after many hours, I found myself again in the square below my home, at the starting point. "But where's the Kotel, the Western Wall?" I asked my neighbor. "Down there, didn't you see it?" No! I hadn't. Last week my parents didn't want to take me there and now, when I could have gotten there on my own, I had failed. The first time that I was allowed to visit the Western Wall, a remnant of the Temple, freely and not at the pleasure of foreigners, as a liberating owner and not as a Jew under occupation, and I missed it entirely. That first missed introduction seems to me the seed of the alienation I have felt since from the paganist cults attached to the place that have turned it into a repulsive focus of all that is primitive, primal, and aggressive in contemporary Judaism. When my intellectual guide, Professor Yeshayahu Leibowitz, the most important Israeli public intellectual of the first decades of the state, sarcastically labeled the wall and its cults the "disco-Kotel," many were angry at him. But I felt that he was describing precisely the defining experience that never, in fact, defined me in my dance to the vanished wall of 1967.

T HAT WAS THE POINT AT WHICH I BEGAN TO DIVERGE
from my parents' path. It was no coincidence that each one of us
encountered the Western Wall differently that week. In my view, there
is no objective sanctity of places, people, or things. I have no idea if
there is a God in heaven, if there is a Creator. Moreover, it is difficult for
me to believe—to say the least—that this God, whose existence is not
entirely clear to me, indeed announced something to one of us, or took
the trouble to designate by Himself certain places as more sacred than
others. It is all man-made and the fruit of our imagination, and I greatly
respect that. The only sanctity in my view is that which people attach
to things. If people appreciate, respect, and prefer a certain law, then it
is superior to other normative systems that people do not appreciate
and respect as much. For example, most people I know do not cross the
street on a red light; they respect red lights as part of a legal system that
protects the sanctity of life. Had there been traffic lights at Mount Sinai,
maybe they would have become sacred, if only because they guided
traffic at the foot of the mountain. Who knows? On the other hand, I
have trouble seeing any value in foolish laws. On my first official visit
to the British parliament I was told, in utter seriousness, that there is a
law that bans dying in parliament. I never checked whether this law actually exists. But such ridiculous laws can be found in many law books,
including our own scriptures.

The Bible and the five books of the Torah that it contains are for me a
wonderful human creation, complex, challenging, and valuable. I don't
believe that they were given by God to man, but I respect and therefore
venerate the devotion of the generations before me to these books and
their content. After all, they drove immense human movements.

My parents had much simpler beliefs, very basic and very traditional.
Every Saturday morning my father would choose one of the books he
would read and study during prayer services. His choice was always the
second book, because the first, which was always with him, was a Bible
commentary titled *Torah Temimah*, by Rabbi Baruch Halevi Epstein.
It was something of an iconic symbol of my father's perception of the

Jewish Torah as innocent of artifice and deception. In many respects the naïveté of my parents' faith and their way of life was a total contrast to the sophistication and wisdom that dominated other aspects of their lives. Dad—and Mom always at his side—could not have survived so many years in the Israeli political leadership, in so many Israeli governments, and particularly in his difficult and malicious party, had he tried to act with the same naïve and faithful honesty that characterized his religious belief. In practice, he maintained an emotional separation between religion and state, though unfortunately it was not the right separation. My parents separated their religion, which was simple and folksy, from the sophisticated, cunning, and virtually sacred state— "the harbinger of our redemption"—of which they were a part.

In the early eighties, I suffered serious back problems. I had been injured in a parachuting accident, and my battered back did not hold up under the strain I was subjecting it to. After many hospitalizations and treatments, it was decided to operate on the spinal cord and solve the problem once and for all. I vaguely remember the moment of opening my eyes after the surgery. Sedatives were still circulating in my body, but my eyes were open and I was conscious, waking up and trying to connect. Near the bed were my beloved wife, Yael, and Mom. The first words Mom spoke to me were: "Dad went to the Kotel to put in a note." I didn't have much strength in those first few moments, but what I wanted to shout still echoes inside me. What? My father putting notes in the crevices of the Western Wall, like the rest of the Jewish idol worshipers? I was taken completely by surprise, because this was so unlike him. Apparently, something hidden had emerged from deep inside him in the moment of crisis and overwhelmed his Germanic rationalism. I don't have anything like that inside me. I cannot imagine a situation, even one of extreme trouble and hardship, that would lead me to write a note and place it in the cracks of an archeological relic, built by flesh-and-blood people just like myself, and which had been destroyed by other human beings like me. I have never in my life prayed to God to come and save me. He (or she) is simply outside all my life's reckonings.

There was one other time, at least one that I know of, when Dad went to the Western Wall to try his luck with forces beyond his own. When my older sister became ill and was on the operating table, suspended between here and there, Dad went to plead for mercy in the place where Jews have always begged for mercy, at the Kotel. I don't know what he achieved there, because apparently his prayer was rejected outright. My sister passed away after great suffering, and yet he carried on with his cultish customs. There, on my sickbed, when I was still woozy, the next point of disagreement emerged, and with it a clear line of difference. The ideological abyss between us was our complete disagreement about the relationship between church and state. Much time passed before these small cracks widened into a full-fledged dispute, not only over the flawed religious arrangements in the country, but also over the essential clash between religion and state, God and man.

We talked very little about politics. From the outset, we understood that these disagreements are deep and unbridgeable, so why make the effort and fall into that yawning abyss. The danger of falling in was greater than the chance of circumventing the potholes and remaining in the circle of family love, whose flame was never extinguished. There was only one time when things came out into the open. During one of the election campaigns for chief rabbi of Israel, in the early nineties, embarrassing accounts circulated about sexual relations between one of the candidates and a very particular woman. "Did you hear the news about the rabbi?" Dad asked one Friday, as my children played with my wife, Yael, and Mom, while he and I were having our weekly father-and-son talk. With a thin smile, the kind that in our family serves as a prelude to the cynical understatement to follow, I asked: "Who do you mean, Dad, the rabbi of Tel Aviv and its suburbs?" At any other time, Dad would have relished the Hebrew double entendre: the word *bnoteha*, meaning "girls" of the city, and its suburbs, in modern speech—"daughters" in biblical Hebrew. But Dad, in atypical fashion, turned very red and lashed out at me: "How can you talk like that about the Rabbi? He is about to become the chief rabbi of Israel, our greatest achievement." His references to "our" almost always meant the party, the movement, religious Zionism. We did not discuss the issue again. Over the years, I became keenly aware that this is the main, essential difference between me and the legacy of my parents' home.

My parents were the children, and later the leaders, of religious Zionism. Mom imbibed it from her father in Hebron before the riots, and Dad was active in the movement in Germany between the two world wars, and became its leader at the height of his political career. For me he was just Dad. The best father I had, the best father I could have asked for: warm and wise, gentle and profound, hovering and touching, diving deep and flying high. All at the same time, all the time, in all matters. I loved him very much, and I miss him endlessly. To this day, so many years after his death, that feeling remains. I sometimes find myself near the telephone, wanting to call him and ask, "Dad, what is this . . . ?"

But to the wider public, as well as his colleagues in the movement, he was "Dr. Burg." Sometimes when people would ask me, "What's your father's name?" I would answer, "First name: Doctor, surname: Joseph Burg." The "doctor" was a public figure present in the lives of many during the first and defining decades of the establishment and existence of the state. They saw him differently, and I knew him through an entirely different prism. A multifaceted man. To his great credit, it should be said that he was just as large a presence at home as he was outside. That is why I couldn't help but laugh when my old mother, my sister and her family, my wife, children, and I were invited to the naming of a square after my father. Many political and municipal speeches were given in his memory, paying tribute to him, as is customary in such moments. One religious Zionist party hack outdid them all, saying, "Dr. Burg was the leader of a movement, so we thought that the most appropriate way to commemorate him would be to name an island in moving traffic after him." I saw Dad's beaming face floating in space and grinning with pleasure. Indeed, a traffic island, words that in Hebrew can also mean "non-movement." They had meant a sliver of land surrounded by a sea of vehicles, but he would have probably heard the pun like me. Because by the time he died his movement had become a vast nothingness compared to what he had dreamed and worked for his entire life.

The story of the rabbi and the lady represented something much bigger that divided us: not only the corruption of the hedonistic rabbi, but the spiritual corruption in the very existence of the institution of chief rabbinate.

"How can you not see," I asked Dad while discussing the case of the rabbi and the girls of Tel Aviv, "How can you not see where this is going? How religion is taking over the state. How the Jewish project is expelling the Israeli project from here. How even in your own movement the followers of the messiah and messianism are pushing you, the rationally religious, out of any framework of possible agreement?" But Dad did not see, because he was blind when it came to the movement, even when it changed direction and funneled the energy of religious Zionism in a direction completely opposed to his own value system. He saw delicate, balanced connections between religion and state, and I see terrible dangers in any overlap between them. He believed he could control the raging bulls, and I dearly wanted then, and even more so today, a restraining separation between these two systems.

The state I want to live in must be no more than a tool in my hands, in the hands of every citizen like me. I really don't want it to have its own content. I need it only as a tool by which we—the political collective living in it—will organize our lives. The state is a vital instrument to better the economy, improve education, defend our security, drain our sewage, and build and manage physical infrastructure. All the rest, all the baggage of my identity, must remain my sole responsibility. Because I'm not a lone wolf, but a social and communal animal, I will assert my identity within the realm of the existence and activity of my community. I want to live in a place where there is a full, defined, and clear separation between religion and the state. My religion, our state. I'm not bothered by, and even respect, people who organize for a politics of religious values, which they seek to enact in the public sphere.

That's what defines them. Provided, of course, that they don't exploit their democratic rise to power to enforce values that annul democracy. The minute the effort—by religious or secular people—is directed beyond promoting interests, and the state itself, the tool, takes on religious meaning, salvational or divine, I start to worry. A state that is defined by terms and content not taken from the world of government, that has goals that are not political, is something else. Ultimately at the end of Dad's life, one thing became clear. To my great regret, I was right and he was wrong; he was misled and he misled others. His partner-adversaries won a tremendous victory over him and us all. Israel became a country in which the Jewish-religious component is dominant, and the state does not control it.

Back to '67. After the war, I had my bar mitzvah, perhaps the first event in which the yawning gap between me and my parents received concrete expression. I loved them so much, I dearly miss them every day, all day, and still, I'm not sure I ever really understood them or whether they understood me and the realities of my existence. All my childhood companions celebrated their bar mitzvah, put on the ritual straps and scroll boxes known as *tefillin*, were called up to the reading of the Torah in synagogue, recited the traditional blessings, chanted a few verses, and delivered a sermon. Preparations for all this take several months. That's how it was with everyone else, but not with us. Mom and Dad stuffed all their former worlds, now destroyed and gone, into this traditional celebration meant to mark the transition from childhood to religious commitment, adulthood, and responsibility.

When I would come home from synagogue services I would chant loudly, like a cantor. I didn't know and didn't quite understand the words, and the tunes emanating from my mouth were hard to identify as the traditional prayer melodies, partially because of my paltry musical abilities. The results of my vocal embellishments were very different from those intended by the composers. My mother, who was endowed with a discerning musical ear and impressive, almost operatic vocal skills, took my off-key singing as a mortifying insult. In addition to which, the issue of "What will people say?" was constantly in the air. "What is going to happen?" Mom asked Dad in despair. "The boy will be called up to the Torah and won't know how to chant. What will people say?" That is the fate of the youngest son who was preceded by two sisters in the days when the role of women in religious ritual was blatantly unequal. The entire burden of our family history was thrust onto my back. "How happy I was when you were born," Mom would say again and again, "finally, someone who will carry forward the name Burg."

With such baggage on my young shoulders it was no wonder that preparations for my bar mitzvah began at age ten. A few times a week I went to a heder to study Torah and Rashi's commentary with Rabbi Yisrael Lev, an old-time Jew, a *Yerushalaymer yid*, as Dad would describe him. In addition to this, I went twice a week to the home of my own private tutor, Avigdor Herzog, one of the great experts of our time in the field of Jewish music. He survived the Holocaust as a youth, immigrated to Israel, and eventually laid the groundwork for Jewish musicological research. First, he established the Israel Institute for Sacred Music, and later the sound archive in the National Library. No one less than the leading Israeli expert on ethnic music was fit to teach such a failed talent as me. His patience, along with his ability to deconstruct every note and bring even me to sing it nearly perfectly, remains with me to this very day. He taught me the hidden secrets of the biblical tropes, the marks used to notate the chants sung in synagogue. Once I read somewhere that in addition to his being a musician from childhood, he was also a carpenter. Perhaps a master carpenter like him was required to teach a saw like me to produce melodies.

And as if all this was not enough for my parents, I crossed town time and again on my own on the way to the Hebron yeshiva, a stern ultra-Orthodox school in the heart of Jerusalem's ultra-Orthodox district. Dad wanted me to know about the existence of another Torah, different from our Zionist one. I sat there on the hard, wooden bench in my shorts and sandals, with my brash Zionist hairdo, an arrogant forelock. Around me yeshiva boys debated at the top of their lungs, wearing dark, shabby pants, black jackets, and sweat-stained white shirts, a uniform of neglected elegance. I don't know what I learned there; but aside from the physical, tangible gap between us, nothing from that period was impressed on my memory. There were several more private tutors who prepared me, but what was I actually preparing for? I don't know. It's strange, so many years have passed since then, and I simply do not know what all the commotion was about. I wanted a bicycle, because that was the bar mitzvah gift of that time, an expression of maturity, responsibility, mobility, independence, and ownership of property that mattered. I also expected to get a watch, and indeed I received one. I remember it well. "This is a Doxa watch," Dad told me. I had never heard that name. Michael got a Certina, and Yaakov had a Tissot, and there were a few more watches with familiar names. But Doxa? Who had ever heard of it? To my shame, the shop windows of the silversmiths and watchmakers downtown did not have even one such watch on display to show my friends. "Take care of it," Dad told me. "It's an important watch."

But aside from the meticulous preparations imposed on me and the exciting gifts I received, it wasn't my bar mitzvah. It was my father's bar mitzvah. In the fading photos of my childhood album there are virtually none of my friends, only friends of Dad, photographed endlessly. Menachem Begin and Levi Eshkol, ministers, VIPs, and rabbis. All the people we ran after for autographs in the streets of Jerusalem gathered to celebrate the "Burg Bar Mitzvah."

The climax of the festivities was my sermon. I took the stage in the banquet hall—not before Mom fixed my collar and brushed my bangs away from my eyes—and before the greatest orators of the Israeli parliament, I delivered my speech. I have no idea what I said, despite the many months in which I was compelled, despite my begging and protests, to learn the sermon by heart. "We don't read speeches," Mom decreed, injecting with that "we" my father's impressive rhetorical skills into my young life.

And indeed, it was a sermon that was entirely his. Meaningless Talmudic and halachic hair-splitting, a sweeping review of Jewish sources, setting up false disputes between rabbinic scholars of generations past and resolving them with one clever-sounding statement. This was a tribute to the world of classic Jewish argumentation, which sharpened the Jewish mind to the point that it became the signature organ of our existence. I understood nothing, and didn't want to understand anything about it.

Not long ago I found the yellowing pages of the speech, typewritten, full of corrections in my father's distinctive and unreadable handwriting. From a distance of fifty years I read the words that were supposed to mark the conclusion of my childhood, and lo and behold, nothing has changed. I still do not understand. Today I have no problem tracking the tortured path of the halachic argument, which dealt entirely with the relation between the prayer shawl and tefillin. But I have difficulty connecting with the message my parents wanted to convey to me on the most important day in the youth of a Jewish boy. What in fact did they expect of me? To become a young scholar like in days of yore? A brilliant and sterile debater? To grow up and become the Yankele of Yiddish songwriter Mordechai Gebirtig, the subject of one of the melancholy Yiddish lullabies that Mom sang to me at bedtime? It was a sad song about a little Jewish boy whose teeth have all grown in, and with a little luck—his mother dreams—he will go soon to the heder to study Torah and Talmud. "A *yingele* [the little boy] who will grow up to become a scholar." That yingele was me.

Where did they hide modernity, progress? Where was the new Israeli identity tucked away in the verbiage of that old Jewishness? Nowhere. It was simply not invited to my bar mitzvah. I think that my dear father and teacher celebrated himself on my birthday. He pictured a Jewish boy of the nineteenth century standing before the Torah sages of eastern Europe and impressing them with his arguments, his proficiency, and his sharp intellect. Riding the back of my bar mitzvah, he traveled back in time to his vanished childhood. He tried for a moment to revive yearnings that, in fact, had never really gone away. I was his atonement and replacement. Only when my children were born did I begin to understand. Along with my closeness to them, which has deepened over the years, I understand the unbridgeable distances

between Dad and me, between Dad and us. And I also understand the
foundations he laid for me, for the bridges across Jewish histories.

The gap between me and Dad was not age—the forty-seven years he
had reached in my year of birth. Dad was born at the beginning of the
twentieth century in a world that still followed the conventions of the
nineteenth century, the century of great changes and human optimism.
He grew to adulthood in Germany between the wars and reached his
personal and public pinnacle in Israel after the Holocaust. At least three
world orders stood between us. When I celebrated my bar mitzvah in
Jerusalem of 1968 he thought about his Galicia, Ukraine, Poland, and
Germany that went up in the smoke of the crematories. We spoke only
Hebrew, but he thought first in German. We, the first generation born
in Israel, were as prickly as cactuses, and he was as soft as a diffident
central European gentleman. When I reread that speech he wrote for
me, my heart went out to him for the yearnings from which he never
recovered, the spiritual limbs he lost and the place where he lost them,
which he anguished over, the phantom pains of spiritual worlds felt
long after they were amputated.

When I finished reading, I suddenly thought of that watch he gave
me. "Doxa" is a Greek concept that means "belief." The defining concept of modern religion, orthodoxy, was derived from it: "true faith,"
the right worldview. Dad had at least two watches. One that showed
the actual hours, shared by everyone, and a watch that beat and ticked
off Jewish time. At their bar mitzvahs all the boys received brand-name
watches made by famous companies—a watch in order to be on time,
to get to school on time, to not be late coming home in the evening,
to not miss the appointment with the doctor or the bus. I received a
Jewish watch—Doxa. While preparing for my bar mitzvah, my parents
revealed to me the hidden mechanisms operating this ancient watch,
the two elements it comprised: progressive and groundbreaking actu-
ality, and anachronistic conservatism with the most petrified customs.
"Take care of it," Dad said. "It's an important watch." And in my own
way, I'm still taking care of it.

CHAPTER TWO

A RAY OF LIGHT IN
THE DARK (1969–1977)

THE TRANSITION FROM ELEMENTARY SCHOOL TO HIGH
school in 1969 was not easy for me at all. Actually, it was terrible.
Everything that was stable, familiar, and loved fell away and vanished
all at once. My parents enrolled me once again in a boys' school. It was
the flagship of the religious Zionist movement, the Eton of the high
school yeshivas, but I, then as now, was never a brilliant student fit to
study in the finest educational institutions. But "people like us study at
the Netiv Meir yeshiva," I was told at home, and that ended the discussion that never began.

It was a yeshiva with a dormitory in the heart of Jerusalem. That
is, my house with my mother and sister—along with my toys and col-
lections, the yard behind the house, the hiding places and nooks and
crannies of the neighborhood—suddenly became a distant homeland.
A forbidden and unattainable home, beyond the pale of exile imposed
on me. At the yeshiva, we lived four boys to a room, and from the first
moment I felt alien. I was a persistent failure. My grades dropped, and
the good little boy became a rude and unruly teenager. I talked back, I
made friends with boys who were completely different from my former
friends, I learned how to lie to adults, I cut classes, went on long hikes

without permission, and never told my parents the truth about any of this.

I really didn't like the new me. A deep and grave sadness gripped me in everything I did in those four years. I didn't know what to do with my distress. Though I was born into this reality of elitism firmly established and arrogant in its religiosity and customs, I felt deep and frustrating alienation from it. Mom and Dad never succeeded in reaching beyond their circle of friends, who were exactly like them. Very good people, positive, delightful, full of good will, and enthralled by the Israeli enterprise that far exceeded their expectations. They were religious Zionists, a smug bourgeoisie, who at the same time had a sense of structural inferiority. Our home was the place I loved more than anything, and in its anachronistic way it loved me back.

At the same time, I never felt entirely at home in my parents' cultured household. For me, a boy looking for other pastures, their orthodoxy—with all their sensitivity, openness, and tolerance—was a coercive and compulsive system. I was a young Israeli looking for pastures that did not belong solely to "our" goats and to people "like us." During my army service, when my social circle was secular, Sabbaths became a source of deep discomfort. While my friends were hiking the trails of the Judean desert—boys and girls together, without any partition—I had to stay home either in my room or at the traditional rites. Each Shabbat in which I was on vacation from the army, my father would wake me with the loud call, "Avraham!" which meant only one thing: time for synagogue services—a time for men without women, a time of coercion. I might have been a different person had my launching pad to adulthood not been the Dickensian institution in Jerusalem's Bayit Vegan neighborhood. I will never know.

That social environment was mostly harnessed to the ethos of the yeshiva. The more I felt disconnected from the studies in the small and crowded rooms, the less I understood the Talmudic world of ancient Babylon and the ideas of its rabbis, the more I flourished outside of class and school. Together with other "naughty boys" like me, casual or temporary friends, I embarked on adventurous night hikes, imagining myself to be a mythical hero of the 1948 War of Independence. We crossed the Judean desert in solo hikes; twice we hitchhiked to dip in the beautiful streams of the Golan. We bragged about being students at the most prestigious institution. We failed to see and understand the way things really were: the moral corruption of controlling the life of others on behalf of "Jewish Values," the lack of religious tolerance, and the explosive potential of redemptive messianic politics. It sufficed for us that people said we were the best, that we were the latest embodiment of the ancient Jewish spirit. From this yeshiva and others, from the friends of my youth, from me and others like us sprang the new driving forces of Israel, those that changed and in fact slayed the original Israel. Our generation effectively eliminated our parents' generation and their heritage.

Those were the hardest four years of my life. I didn't understand a thing. I failed all my classes over and over, even gym. Everything I wanted was suppressed, and everything they—the rabbis and the strict educators—wanted depressed me. Boring archaic texts, demanding studies, no "spirit"; just memorization, meaningless religious demands, and enforced sanctimonious behaviors. I was alone. There were many classmates, but not a single soul mate. I barely had any real friends. The sad fact is that I now have no contact with the person who at the time seemed like my best friend. We swore, as teenagers do, to never part. We misbehaved and joked and dreamed together. In the end, he became an ultra-Orthodox rabbi with a long beard, and I was and remain an irrepressible liberal. I was disruptive in class, my parents were called in, I was reprimanded and punished. I wanted them to deal with my great despair, the frustrations, the slippery walls I wasn't able to climb, but the response of the system was different. I wanted to leave that place so badly. I wanted to go home, but "people like us don't leave such a school."

HAD TWO LOVES AT THE TIME. I LOVED MY CHILDHOOD sweetheart, who later became my wife and the mother of our children, and I was madly in love with the sports field. That's where I went when I got up in the morning, and I chose my clothes to match the games planned for the day. There I met my fellow sports enthusiasts, and there I was exposed to the lives of others. In one summer vacation I was accepted to a special camp for outstanding volleyball players. I wasn't that talented, but I wanted to be. My ambition made up to a small degree for the shortcomings and flaws I was born with. For the first time in my life I left the familiar closed circles of home, family, community, school, and encountered the world. Secular people, cigarettes, tentative talk about girls, international sports, and personal fulfillment. I learned more about life there than I had learned in my closed, stern, and tough yeshiva.

The effect was immediate. At the start of the new school year I joined a religious sports club that had a volleyball team. In order to participate in practice, I needed permission from the yeshiva to be absent once a week from afternoon classes. Secular studies, of course, because missing religious studies was inconceivable. I saw my dream coming true. I fantasized about rolls and saves. I jumped repeatedly to gain strength. I set up strange contraptions for myself with a ball and net to improve my spikes, serves, and saves. I was mentally ready, though my body wasn't built like the perfectly sculpted bodies of the superstars. But I so wanted it with all my heart and soul. Because then, like today, will was the strongest engine of my life. And then the worst thing happened to me. One of the rabbis, who wasn't even my teacher, forbade me to join the club. With a sickly sweet smile on his face he informed me that I couldn't play volleyball because it was "idolatry."

How scary, idolatry is one of the three prohibitions for which a Jew is commanded to sacrifice his life, to be killed and not transgress. Needless to say, that rabbi, his god, and his tradition lost me that day, at that precise moment. How could a boy be faithful to a good and beneficent god if this abstract and strange deity views volleyball as an enemy with equal powers, deserving destruction, and what's more, sentences me to death? If these are his enemies, how can you believe in him, this petty one who is supposed to run the world? I didn't know then that there is no real connection between the abstract god and his tangible charlatan rabbis. And now that I know, it's clear to me that some of them, maybe most, are idolaters who believe in the stars, astrological signs, and superstitions, against whom an all-out war is supposed to be waged at all times. This hostile train of thought, with my endless prayers for revenge against that unctuous man, was cut off by a terrible tragedy. One of his daughters was killed in one of the terrorist attacks in Jerusalem.

In those days—1978—of bereavement in Jerusalem I didn't really believe anymore in God, certainly not in the conception of God held by that rabbi: a kind of heavenly entity, a supreme accountant calculating every one of my actions with personal oversight, exacting prices and dispensing grants. And still, for a long time I couldn't stop obsessively wondering, was his God punishing him with cruel pettiness because of the many childhoods like mine that he took part in destroying?

A S THE YEARS WENT BY, TIME AND AGAIN I RECALLED that experience of understanding. The way that primitive rabbi saw me made it clear that this refined and noble ballgame was so sacred to me that it became the center of my being, taking up my entire reality. My shoes were volleyball shoes, my walk mimicked that of volleyball players I admired, though I don't even remember their names today. I always had a ball in my hand, the game was a constant subject of conversation. And when such a totality captivates someone, that rabbi thought, there is no room for God. So, he waged a religious campaign against me to eradicate the plague of idolatry from my body. A local exorcist, speaking in Hebrew and Yiddish and with a sanctimonious smile. Anything to make space in me for God.

Thanks to him much space was made; I lost both God and volleyball. I probably would not have become a real athlete, but thanks to him I learned a lesson in Jewish skepticism. I learned what I was not.

I am not him. In his wrong, violent, and self-righteous way he did me a valuable service, completely contrary to his original intention. He fought the spirit of sports that seized me in order to return God to the center of my being. And since then I have been fighting to push him away, because his absolute, zealous God is not my God. God is not a fact, just as she (yes, she) is not a ball. As a youngster, I felt intuitively what I can today easily express: God doesn't compete at volleyball because sports are sweaty and tangible, and God—if he or she exists at all—is far beyond the physical that can be detected by the senses. He or she is an idea, abstract, unattainable. And anyone who tries to conceptualize him will never reach him. In prayer services, we sang "He has no body or image of a body," and I remember pondering, the thought needling me, "Could it be that the rabbi's god is jealous of me for having a body?" The abstract Jewish divine is all that stands beyond the tangible, and the moment God is positioned beyond what can be comprehended with the human senses, a different, wonderful belief is born, completely different from the brutal faith of that gloomy teacher. The skeptical belief.

Maybe there is personal oversight and perhaps not, maybe this is our God and maybe he belongs to others, maybe he is male or perhaps she is female, maybe there is a Creator and maybe not. I will probably never know all these things. That is why I make do with my natural skepticism as an engine that is constantly working and helping me reach new thoughts and ideas. In the end, with time, my painful loss in those days became a very big gain, which shaped the foundations of my character. I gained two important things at the time: I learned to survive even while swimming against the tide, and I became a creative skeptic.

Those were sad, gray years. My oldest sister had already left home, Dad was busy and far away, somewhere at the height of his career, most of my childhood friends were immersed in the new religious enthusiasm—stirring, total, and all-encompassing. That's how they all were, similar boys from all across the country living the dorm life. And me? I didn't want to be absorbed and drowned in that sticky stuff, I didn't know that Freud had already invented psychology and that you have to talk about issues. So I internalized things and kept quiet.

"Er izt pushet hungarik" (He's simply hungry), Dad and Mom would reassure themselves when confronted with the mute anger of their youngest son and his adolescent problems. I was indeed very hungry, but for something entirely different. I read all the books by Hermann Hesse with avid interest. I became Demian and Steppenwolf, torn like them between contradictory and raging forces. Narcissus, the wise priest, and Goldmund, the creative and mending artist, were my real rabbis and advisors. My parents had sent me out onto life's path much too early, and the social and educational world was no more prepared for me than I was ready for it.

The years of my youth became a giant battleground between my soul that wanted to fly to freedom and the official jailers who did all they could to imprison me in the seductive place called "like everyone else." I had only one corner of human refuge at the time. My girlfriend, my partner in love, who was the one and has remained the only. Just then—right after the Six-Day War—she moved to Israel with her parents from France. I met her on her first Sabbath in the country, when she came to the local branch of our youth movement. I fell in love with her immediately, like all the boys. Foreign, pretty, new, and mysterious. I proposed to be her boyfriend near Falafel King, but it wasn't so simple. "Are you crazy? I don't know you!" she protested in her French accent, which was very pronounced at the time. More time and stubborn effort were needed, and ever since then she knows me better than anyone. And the craziness? It's still there.

We made furtive appointments on the streets of the religious neighborhood. I skipped classes to see her, even for a minute. She was the only ray of light in that darkness, and for those years of devotion I will be eternally grateful to her, to my last day. We were counselors together in the youth movement. One evening we returned home, and as young lovers do, we chose the longest and darkest route to walk, trying to take advantage of every minute together before she went back to her house and I returned home or to the dorm. After taking leave of the entourage of friends who went their separate ways, we wandered off in the dark in the narrow, wild paths of the Valley of the Cross. The large multilane road that now crosses the valley had yet to be paved. I can't remember if the new Israel Museum on the opposite hill was already lit up, but we sat on the dark and romantic slope and held each other with all the force and love and hopes of that age.

We were youngsters during the transition from the sixties to the seventies, and we wanted to experience some of the feelings and thrills felt by many of our generation in the West. Suddenly, out of the darkness, we were caught in a shaft of light. We were startled, scared; we had been caught. One of the young members of our youth group had pointed his flashlight at us. He shined a light, and we were plunged into deep darkness.

Overnight, we became easy prey for everyone. Self-righteous disapproval and institutional hypocrisy swirled around us. People demanded our dismissal from our posts as counselors. Some threatened to tell our parents, teachers, and worst of all, that the episode would be published in *Hatzofeh*, the official newspaper of religious Zionism. Were it not for the human and civic courage of the counselor in charge, things would have ended very badly. She, like us, was a religious girl on the brink of adolescence, on the cusp of modernity. She courageously backed us up, blocked our dismissal, talked with us, and calmed everyone down, both gossips and zealots. She turned that courage into a way of life. Many years later our paths crossed again, when she was one of the greatest supporters—with wisdom, experience, and resources—of the establishment of Israeli civil society. And that was the way she acted to her last day, which came prematurely and after great suffering. But then, in my early moments of youth, it was a great and tremendous embarrassment, too big for children. Real distress that only with time matured into broader insight.

In those days, we weren't actually taught anything about life itself. In class we studied Talmud, debating loudly. We were told that

Talmud develops the mind, and we felt that we were intellectuals and very smart. We meticulously parsed the details of religious law, we reviewed verses and commentaries, and we argued passionately about strange legal realities. We went through the motions of general studies, but they had no real importance in the hierarchy of yeshiva priorities. In our free time—of which we did not have very much—we were heavily preoccupied with utopias, repaired worlds, establishing settlements, and yeshivas. We sang patriotic songs and marched in paramilitary parades with deafening drumbeats and flaming, inflaming torches. We sang: "Let us spread the great light, the light of the Torah." We yelled at the top of our lungs: "God is the lord of vengeance," and we commanded him, "Lord of vengeance, appear!" We were not taught about the basic components of human life and human society. In the yeshiva, we were prevented from exposure to the existence of non-Jews in the world, to the existence of the secular world around us and its meaning, and more than anything, efforts were made to block out the very existence of women, girls, friends, and lovers. A world of boys without gentiles, secular Jews, and girls. And as a counterweight to this ignorance and restriction I was lucky; the sole stroke of luck of my youth was that I had a girlfriend. She was the one who led me through that gloom, gave me a hand, and had faith in me in the days when I didn't have any faith in myself.

That ray of light in the darkness of night led to my first public crucifixion, shedding some light as well on the sanctimoniousness that permeated our Bnei Akiva youth movement and our entire generation. The debates that divided us then were so naïve. Mixed dancing or not. Western dancing or only hora dances. Nylon stockings and makeup for girls—heaven forbid. But this didn't last long; the questions were replaced with answers, and the question marks became unequivocal and one-dimensional exclamation points. The circles of boys and girls were consistently moved farther and farther away from each other. The girls' skirts grew longer and thicker. My mother and sisters never routinely covered their hair. Today? Woe to the woman who walks uncovered and with her hair showing in a religious neighborhood, in a settlement, or on the city streets. Woe to the young woman who still lacks the modest head-covering of marriage. In general, modesty has become one of the obsessions of this community, a loaded and somewhat sick term, trying to limit and restrict the most complex human relationship—between the sexes.

All the signs of illness of those days have become complete madness in recent years. Excluding women from public spaces, members of parliament seeking to ban female performers from official ceremonies in the Knesset, neighborhoods with separate sidewalks for women and men, buses with places reserved for women (in the back, of course). Soldiers and commanders of military units refusing to hear the sound of a woman singing because "a woman's voice is nakedness," religious decrees prohibiting women from running for parliament because that would violate modesty restrictions, and even a prohibition on participation in parlor meetings "because these are immodest public events"—these things no longer surprise anyone. After all, "this mixes men and women like salad."

When I read the writings of these religious and ultra-Orthodox moralizers or hear their sermons—in Judaism and other faiths—I feel that these are sick people and a community of followers and believers who are no less ill. The preoccupation with rules of modesty, sex, and sexuality is itself a kind of permission to engage in pornography in reverse. There's something demonic in their attitude toward women. They feel so threatened by their very presence, as if women were sex machines endowed with nothing other than seductiveness. That is why they are thoroughly obsessed with every exposed and covered inch of a woman's body. As if their whole purpose in life is to hide the witch inside her. "Mom, are you a witch?" I once asked my mother after a synagogue lesson on the phrase in the Sayings of the Fathers: "The more wives, the more sorcery." "No, yingele," she replied. "I love you, and witches can't love." I calmed down.

We were never allowed to ask the questions raised by this approach to the world. I had a girlfriend who introduced me to the great spirit of women. Together we got to know ourselves and our relationship, and that was enough for me. From a distance, I can draw some distinctions between those who had girlfriends in their childhood, a sweeping, permitted love like mine, who became committed to sexual and gender equality, and many of my friends at the time, who unlike me learned the laws of marital relations in distorted theory books, primitive volumes of Jewish law, from a ritual bathhouse attendant and bridal counselors provided by the rabbinate. They became blind zealots, following a Judaism of discrimination and exclusion.

So it is regarding women and secular Jews, and even more so when it comes to conversation with anyone who is not Jewish. I think that until I was seventeen I hadn't set eyes on a real gentile (I don't mean a local Arab or one under occupation, which somehow fits in a different category, but a gentile like Dad's gentiles and his friends from "there," the perished Jews of Europe, with their colorful Jewish stories). In 1972, I traveled abroad for the first time in my life. I landed at the Amsterdam airport on the way to Munich and the Olympic Games. On the way from the airport to the city there was a small traffic jam, and the bus came to a halt. By the side of the road local laborers worked at laying a pipe in a ditch they had dug. Every so often the blond head of one of the workers would pop up from the ditch, and I stared at him as if I were hypnotized. A blond laborer? I had never seen such a thing at home in the Israel of the fifties and sixties. We didn't have many blond people at all at the time, and all the workers I had seen until then were black-haired and dark skinned. I think he was the first gentile who made an impression on me.

My experience in later years taught me that precisely conversations with those who are not like me, not like us, are the most enriching. As a collective, we sanctify the stultifying narrative of "a people that dwells alone," clinging to any manifestation of anti-Semitism as a justification for our isolationist existence, talking only with ourselves about ourselves, completely unaware of the great missed opportunity of our life: the wonderful richness of conversation with the other, someone different.

I N THE MID-NINETIES, I WAS INVITED TO VISIT JAPAN. IT was the first time in my life that I spent a few days outside the boundaries of monotheistic civilization. Until that trip anything I knew about the world was processed through Jewish, Christian, and Islamic tools. I wasn't aware that far beyond the monotheistic half of the globe there is a parallel world, no less deep, complex, aesthetic, ethical, and wise. The pain I felt during that visit surfaces every time I encounter the limited thinking of an interlocutor who is not prepared to genuinely recognize the truth and beauty of the other, of someone who is different. These are the limits of the victim of monotheism. The blind followers of the one God are systematic problem-causers, because in a place where believers can entertain only one truth, making room for only one God and only one brand of faith and commandments, there is no room for others. Ultimately it comes down to "yours" or "mine." In the eyes of the religious monotheist, there can't be room in heaven or earth for two or three Gods: Elohim, God, and Allah together. Therefore, the potential battle between them is constantly joined, until Armageddon and the victory of "the true God."

In distant Japan I was exposed to a different approach. We were a group of Israelis from several walks of life. In Kyoto, in a very old traditional tea house, we had a meeting with an elderly Buddhist monk. We all sat around a low table, very close to the floor, kneeling and waiting for the traditional tea service, as is customary. After five minutes my knees were about to collapse. I writhed, asked for a chair, got up, sat, walked around, and got back down on my knees before repeating the process. Very undignified and disrespectful. And he, the old monk, sat there calmly, gaunt and erect. Not a movement. He had translucent skin and a soft smile on his face. We talked, through an interpreter, about everything, but mostly about faith and its principles, about the traditional way of life and the customs derived from it. About human duty and duties of the heart. I sensed that I was having a conversation with a partner who understood me. At that moment, I wanted to leave everything and stay there with him as long as he was alive.

During that entire sensitive meeting, a phrase from the Jewish morning prayer flashed deep inside my head: "to understand, to learn, to listen, to study and teach." I wanted to know much more, to understand and to learn. I was avidly ready, there of all places, to listen, to hear and learn from someone older and wiser than me.

At the end of the evening, the Buddhist monk gave me a book of Buddha's sayings in Japanese, with English translation. The book was wrapped in delicate silk paper, in the finest origami style. I felt like my hand had been scalded. "Idol worship, idol worship," all my rabbis from that narrow-minded yeshiva shouted at me from my inner darkness. All the epithets hurled at the New Testament, at the "idolatry" of other faiths, scorched my palms. Three times a day we would all pray devoutly, "they bow to nothing and pray to a god who will not save them," and the stricter ones among us would spit—during prayer—on the floor while saying these words.

Once we went, as a group of children, to one of those places that were called "missionary," a distribution point for Christian missionary messages. We asked them, as a complimentary gift, of course, for copies of the Bible and the New Testament bound in one volume. Each one of us received a copy, and together we went to one of the empty lots in town and used their profane pages to make a large bonfire. We didn't know then what burning books meant. We hadn't been taught that Jews had burned the philosophic wisdom of Maimonides, and we had not learned about the burning of the Talmud in the Middle Ages. And we had no idea that only a few decades earlier the Nazis built a large bonfire in the bustling center of Berlin, in the opera square, before its name was changed to Bebel Square, and burned tens of thousands of books, the finest world literature written by Jews. Because the great Heinrich Heine was a converted Jew, no one bothered to expose us to his wisdom written more than a century before that conflagration, to wit: "That was only a prelude; where they burn books, they will in the end also burn people."

All those hidden flames burned my hands. During the entire visit to Japan I could do nothing with that book. Disposing of it would have been inappropriate, because it is a book revered by many of my hosts. Reading it was out of the question, if only because of the heavy burden of the prohibitions of my childhood. So, I dragged it around in my bag like a useless object until the flight back to Israel, which lasted almost twenty-four hours. At night, half a world away, having difficulty sleeping, I began reading Buddha's sayings. Until then, to my shame, I had not read any holy book aside from our Bible. Neither the New Testament nor the Koran. And here in the high spiritual place, literally between heaven and earth, I discovered to my surprise, and perhaps even to my dismay, that I understood many of these sayings that were written far beyond Judaism and its younger sisters, that I recognized and identified with them.

Then came long days of thinking. For the observer in me, that visit to Japan opened a window to entire worlds that were inaccessible to me from childhood: the wisdom, experience, ethics, history, and culture of other peoples and nations. On the emotional level I again felt that sense of missing out, a sourness that dogged me all the days of my youth. Life inside a plugged-up bottle. The dense air, the breath fogging up the glass and preventing any eye contact or access to the external world. The profound feeling that someone is fooling me, deceiving and blinding me. Amin Maalouf had not yet written then about the clash of identities, and that "identity [is] the sum of all our allegiances, and, within it, allegiance to the human community itself would become increasingly important, until one day it would become the chief allegiance, though without destroying our many individual affiliations."*

---

*Amin Maalouf, *In the Name of Identity: Violence and the Need to Belong*, trans. Barbara Bray (New York: Arcade Publishing, 2001), 100.

When I opened myself up to this wonderful and complex Lebanese author, I learned from him, from someone who is supposed to be my official enemy, a great piece of wisdom: identity is not necessarily the constant and destructive need to choose "either/or," either God or volleyball, either modesty or a girlfriend, either a Jew or a gentile. Either Elohim, or God, or Allah. A rich identity can be all of these and contain many elements even if they are contradictory. There is great serenity in containing such contradictions. Why not study Talmud with the wisdom of Buddha? Or understand Maimonides along with the Islamic scholars who influenced him? Or think about the commentator Rashi in the context of the Crusader period and the Christian theology of the Middle Ages? Seeing Jewish works as a constant conversation with all the cultures of the world, as integrated histories, is openness. Forbidding me to play volleyball, turning my love for my girl at the time into a torturous web of prohibitions and guilty feelings, deliberately blurring the identity of secular people and blocking the light emanating from other cultures—this is the worst of ghetto culture. And there, in one of the alleys of the renewed Jewish ghetto in the State of Israel, I spent those years.

M Y GENERATION WAS THE BRIDGE ON WHICH THE ISRAELI Jews crossed from Athens to Sparta. We experienced firsthand the mechanisms that made possible this shift from the soft, warm, and inclusive parental home to the hardened and tough nation that grew up here seemingly unnoticed.

In our house, as in many religious homes, there were two appliances meant to get us through the Sabbath safely: the electric hot plate and the hot water dispenser. Every Saturday they were there, long before most of the Judeo-technological inventions, which were meant to deceive God according to Jewish law—the Sabbath timer, the Sabbath elevator, and all the rest of the strange and embarrassing deceptions.

In our home the bluffing didn't reach such high levels. On the contrary, the hot plate was just a plain hot surface, with no thermostat, on which the food being cooked for the Sabbath was placed, and beside it was a tall water container that in the early years stood above the Jerusalem single burner on which my mother cooked. When the water in the dispenser ran out, Mom added more so "that there won't be too little if guests arrive." She improved the food on the hot plate as she saw fit: a bit more water here, a stir there, or the addition of missing ingredients. When the water got low in the dispenser we tilted it toward the small faucet at the bottom to use up what was left, and when it got in the way of the strict order in Mom's kitchen we respectfully moved it to a less intrusive place. No one talked about strictures and prohibitions. We made sure to observe the Sabbath according to the tradition in our house, a tradition very similar to those of other homes but not exactly the same. Every home had its customs, every family had its heritage and traditions. The Jewish chain was extended, as always, from generation to generation, in all our homes.

On one Sabbath, Judge Haim Cohen was invited to give a lecture in the synagogue. He was "one of ours," a German Jewish immigrant with a high forehead, a heavy accent, wonderful Hebrew, and a matching sense of humor. He talked about the relationship between his parents. His father was a stern-faced rabbi in Frankfurt, and his mother managed both him and the house with a flourish. Once, he said, a Jewish woman came to the house on Sabbath Eve and asked his father for a ruling on whether the slaughtered chicken in her basket was kosher. The rabbi's wife brought the chicken into the father's room, and he carefully examined it and ruled—not kosher! The rabbi's wife came out of the room and returned the chicken to the Jewish woman. "It's kosher, you can go," she said, wishing her a good Sabbath as she accompanied her to the door. "Why did you say that to her?" the young Haim Cohen, then still known as Herman, asked his mother. "Dad ruled differently." "Yes," his mother replied, "Dad saw the chicken, but I saw the widow." I'm not convinced that it was a true story, perhaps it was just a fable. But I remember how Dad told it to Mom when we returned home, and they both drew their conclusion: "Nu, of course it's obvious."

In 1969, when I was fourteen, it all ended. Myriads of children like me, almost an entire generation, were disconnected from home and exiled to other places. No longer did we grow up according to the customs and flexibility of home and natural, understandable compromises. We shifted to life "by the book." The strict, absolute books of Jewish law became our operating instructions for the correct life. All at once, the day-to-day shrewdness of the Jewish housewife was gone, and Dad's eyes, not averse to overlooking things, were closed. The forbidden became absolute, and less and less was permitted. Everyone became uniform, like assembly-line matches. A body of wood and a head either on fire or scorched. And everyone had the same operating system. From a child of my parents I became a robot of my rabbis. Colors were erased, different shades disappeared. Home lost its magic, its authority, and its role. Other institutions took its place and kneaded our young consciousness like soft dough, the consciousness of the first religious Israeli generation ever.

There were mediators for the transition from home to the new institutions. In my case they were the rabbis, known as the *Ramim*, our yeshiva teachers. They were always to be addressed in the third person: The Rabbi. The Rabbi thinks that . . . The Rabbi, I have to go to the bathroom. The Rabbi said that . . . Most of them came from the ultra-Orthodox world, graduates of the adult yeshivas of the Lithuanian Torah tradition. I don't know why they came to us. Had the yeshiva world already produced more graduates than the ultra-Orthodox community needed to sustain itself, and we received the surplus? Perhaps it was a strategy of ultra-Orthodox infiltration behind the lines of the religious Zionist enemy in order to defeat it from within? Or perhaps just unexplained coincidence. Either way, I again encountered the ultra-Orthodox world that I got to know in the heder classroom of Rabbi Yisrael Lev and the bar mitzvah preparatory lessons in the

Hebron yeshiva. Again, the rabbi as teacher, and me as the pupil. Again, they are the carriers of Jewish historical knowledge, and I am an empty ignoramus who is supposed to be filled from their reservoirs. I was hostile to them all from the start, except one.

There was something fake about every one of them, almost fraudulent. One of them invited us once to his house, and to demonstrate that he was with it, young and plugged in to our reality, he showed us the television hidden in his clothes closet, somewhere between his folded ritual fringed garment and his wife's blonde wig. He tried to communicate openness, and I sensed hypocrisy. Another one spoke pompously about values and ethics, but time and again deceived us with double messages, half-truths, and absolute lies. A third was cruel and wicked, venting his frustrations on schoolboys. And the most prominent among them, the head of the yeshiva, a mythic figure in our circles, turned out to be a weak and hollow prisoner of his controlling wife.

The one I genuinely liked was Reb Nissan. This is the appropriate place to thank him for his wonderful role in my life, which at the time wasn't so wonderful. He knew how to smile, tell a good joke, share experiences of his youth and his dilemmas at important junctures of his life. He invited me over to his house several times, even in later years when he was no longer my teacher. Simply a good man. But he was the exception. In those days, religious Zionism did not have enough of its own Torah scholars, and its rivals gave it no quarter. The ultra-Orthodox criticized us as ignorant boors, empty like secular people but much more dangerous because we pretended to be something we were not. "You," they lashed out at us with zealous fervor, "are not the followers of venerable Jewish tradition." And they would conclude with the most terrible criticism: "You are Reform Jews." On the other side were the secular Israelis who denigrated religious Zionism with no less intensity. "You're not really pioneers, you're not really settlers, you don't really bear the burden of the country's security." This was not only an abstract ideological argument; it was an almost daily experience.

One of the main sites of our childhood experiences was the "branch." The branch was the center of activity of our youth movement, Bnei Akiva. The location of the historic Jerusalem branch was at something of a midpoint. The direct route from home to the branch went along King George Street and passed by the secular Hashomer Hatzair youth movement center. We wore Sabbath clothes, they wore the blue shirt, their youth movement uniform. We had neatly parted hair, they had hair that covered their ears, we were full of awkward hesitation between boys and girls, they spent time together naturally, we ate sunflower seeds, they smoked cigarettes on the Sabbath. Beyond the branch, down the street, in the Mea Shearim quarter, lived, then as now, the most powerful and fanatical concentration of ultra-Orthodox Jews in Israel. Sometimes one group provoked us, sometimes the other threw stones at us, or vice versa, and sometimes both. On the way to the branch, we got it from the Hashomer Hatzair kids; on the way back, from the ultra-Orthodox members of the Neturei Karta sect. One thing never changed: the branch was always torn somewhere in the middle, between the Zionists and the ultra-Orthodox, between the extroverted freedom of the former and the antiquated conservatism of the latter. All those years that's how we were, children of religious Zionism, playing second fiddle to the two other large orchestras.

Some strings were pulled taut, almost to the breaking point, by apologetics directed at the ultra-Orthodox, the strictly observant fanatics of God who seemingly never compromised and would never give up their total belief. Their religious absolutism stood in complete contrast to the compromise that characterized all aspects of religious Zionism. We were a little bit of everything, but there was nothing totalitarian that characterized us. We very much wanted to be like everyone else, so we weren't fanatical about anything. We tried to dance to the tune of pioneering Zionism. We left our shirttails out, and we wore khaki pants manufactured by Ata, folded very short. We wore simple one-strap "biblical" sandals, and the daring ones among us grew moustaches. We learned how to build structures with wooden poles and tie knots "like the kibbutzniks." We wandered the paths of the country like the greatest hikers. We sang the songs of the youth movements, and we knew the war songs by heart. We admired the bearers of their culture, Meir Har-Zion and the heroes of the paratroopers, the pioneers of tower and stockade, the illegal immigrants, and the fighters of the Palmach militia. They were all theirs, and not a single one was ours. We didn't have even one personal and intimate hero of our own, until 1967.

Only then did we finally have our own heroes. Our leaders were born, and at long last we had our own dreams. Only we spoke about reviving the monarchy, and only we had a plan to conquer the country, the whole country. It took a few more years for this potential to burst forth, but from the start the writing was etched on all Israeli walls: this is our time, the youth of religious Zionism. The storm of 1967 ripped all the old doors from their hinges. Nothing returned to the way it was after the cease-fire. Everything had been thrown open, breached, and made possible. From a small country surrounded by narrow and oppressive borders we became an expansive empire.

The new wide-open spaces of the Holy Land opened before us. Here was Hebron and Bethlehem, ours and King David's. There was Jeroboam's Tirzah and Gideon's Ofrah. We almost climbed our forefather Jacob's ladder, whose legs were planted in Beit El, and our heads touched the sky. It started with trips. We youngsters wandered here and there around Jerusalem, and the older ones "went down to Sinai." We knew by heart the Tombs of the Kings, Kidron Valley and the necropolis adorning it, and we meandered through Tzofim Stream and the burial caves carved into its banks. Sometimes we climbed on foot from Lifta to the tomb of the prophet Samuel. We went down to the Givon pool and imagined ourselves as the heroic biblical fighters led by Yoav Ben Tzruya, defeating Avner Ben Ner and his fighters there—establishing the young Kingdom of Judea with our very hands. Jews unwittingly vanquishing the Israelis of the Israelite kingdom. Sometimes we were taken to Kfar Etzion to see the renewal of Jewish settlement there. A religious Zionist revival in the place where both settlers and the young Israeli army were defeated and humiliated only nineteen years earlier, in the War of Independence.

On Sabbaths, we went to the Western Wall. We prayed at the Chabad House. We came back home with dusty shoes after we descended into the depths of the four synagogues in the heart of the destroyed Jewish Quarter. We got to know all the steps and climbs on the walls of the Old City of Jerusalem. We walked there with heads held high. We hid in the nooks and crannies of the wall when we were searching for some romance mixed with identity and meaning. In all these places, we met only children and youths like us. There were virtually no secular children in all these new places. Most of us belonged to the same youth movement, Bnei Akiva. We were members, counselors, or graduates of the movement. Our parents came from various distant diasporas. They had other accents, old-fashioned clothes, customs and mannerisms from worlds that had existed but were now destroyed and vanished.

And we were so proud of our uniformity. You've seen one, you've seen them all. If you listened to one of us, you knew all of us. We wore plaid shirts over white T-shirts. Khaki pants, definitely not jeans. We wore our ritual fringes under our clothes, and we all had knitted skull-caps. Our sisters or cousins knitted our head coverings. For the happy ones among us, they were gifts of love from our girlfriends. Yael knitted me a skullcap, or *kippah*, and I made her a keychain of olive wood, on which I pasted the symbol of the youth movement, committing us all to "Torah and Work." Ultra-Orthodox youths weren't there, either. All the *shababniks* we had seen in massive demonstrations on Sabbaths in Jerusalem were absent from the new Garden of Eden. Greater Israel became our stage, on which we could suddenly break out and express ourselves.

My early childhood was restricted by walls. Fences around houses and communities. A fence along the borders. Fences across the whole country. Independence ringed by coils of barbed wire, and it was

natural and understandable to everyone. Near the old City Hall, bus
number 15 had to make a sharp left, because Israeli Jerusalem ended
with a high wall covered with rusty metal sheets topped with barbed
wire. There was a no-man's-land fence under the Yemin Moshe neighborhood and the whole scary area beyond the new zoo. All these fences
came down at once. I felt this way only one other time in my life: when
I watched, along with billions of people around the world, the fall of
the Berlin Wall. I felt the tremendous catharsis of Berliners. I thought
to myself then that only Jerusalemites, Berliners, and Irish residents
of Belfast could understand the momentous declaration of President
Kennedy: "Ich bin ein Berliner."

We grew up in a city with a wall through its heart and we witnessed
its collapse. We collectively skipped over the wreckage and rubble and
went out to new places. Here and there people were already talking
about settlements. Renewing the Jewish community in Hebron hovered in the background in our home. The Hebron settlers compelled
the Israeli government to appease them. The blood of those murdered
in the 1929 massacre of Hebron's Jews was their most powerful argument. And to this argument, Dad, the moderate minister, partner
of Mom, a survivor of the riots, had no response. He also employed
the Zionist rhetoric, that building and settlement are our ways of revenge, and did not understand that this path leads to many more wars
and bloodshed than any local massacre. Those were years of great arrogance. We had defeated armies, we had struck a resounding blow
against the bombastic Arab leaders. Daring David had struck multitudes of Arab Goliaths. We had the privilege of being born in a generation that completed what the mythic generation of 1948 had not
succeeded in doing: liberating Jerusalem and lifting the siege ringing
the reddening and thickening Israeli neck.

A few days after the '67 fighting died down Dad went on a ministerial tour of the territories. I don't recall if we called them "occupied"
or "liberated" at home, but we felt very good about them, with "our
Hebron" and "our Shchem," or Nablus. My father was the ultimate
charmer. There was not a person on the Jewish earth that he could not

engage in conversation, communicate with, and endear himself to. He remembered many people and their personal histories. He memorized thousands of family trees. He knew human and Jewish history and the annals of hundreds of communities and multitudes of figures. When he was told something he never forgot it. Faces were forever engraved in his phenomenal memory. And on these strengths, he was able to always draw associations, make conversation, create a connection.

We all traveled in his giant official vehicle, a vintage American car, to Nablus, Ramallah, and all those places that just a moment ago were beyond the pale. On Mount Gerizim, we met the high priest of the Samaritans, and for the first time I saw my father dumbfounded. Dad wore a European hat with a wide brim, and the priest came toward him with a head covering that looked like a mix between a fez and an Arab head-scarf. Dad was clean-shaven, and the priest had a wild beard. My father in a tailored suit and matching tie, the priest in a white *jalabiya* robe reaching to his ankles. Dad spoke many languages fluently, and the latter understood neither Hebrew nor Yiddish. Oy, he couldn't be humored with a good joke, and he hadn't even studied the biblical commentary of Rashi. A European Jew facing a Samaritan—neither Jew nor Arab—and the foreignness of the territories struck us mercilessly in our first encounter. Faced with this new reality—half of which was old and identifiable, and the other half new and strange, embodied in the figure of the Samaritan high priest—even Dad was left speechless. Today, when I reflect on that moment, I see his loss of words back then as a symbol of far greater losses.

From there we went on to the Golan Heights. I had my picture taken near the Banias Fall, a twelve-year-old boy with a pioneer's hat, holding an Uzi submachine gun. My head is tilted jauntily to one side like a tough fighter, as if I were a war hero of those days. With all these places, people, images, and experiences, my spirits soared sky-high. But Dad, it seems to me in retrospect, gradually shrank. On the way back he asked Mom a question that has remained unresolved since: "What will we do with two million Arabs?" But he and his colleagues never made any genuine and committed effort to find a real answer.

Those who had survived the destruction of their childhood, the destruction of the thousand-year-old Jewry of Europe, those who had the strength to save those uprooted by the Holocaust and were part of the founding of Israeli society, reached the great struggle for the Israeli soul weary and exhausted. Dad surrendered almost without a fight to the rising forces in his movement. The messianic youngsters bested him and dragged him against his will to be one of the builders of the new settlements in the territories, and, as a result, one of the main destroyers of the original Israel that he had established and loved. Today it is clear to me that in order to return to the path from which we strayed so dramatically, we have to destroy as many as possible of the failures of Dad and his partners gracing every hill and mountain in Judea, Samaria, and Jerusalem. Actually, all of them, and return to the path Dad had meant to take were it not for those messianic hijackers.

Like stampeding goats, they stormed his generation, the young against the old, Israelis against diaspora Jews, pioneers against the establishment, radicals against conservatives. It was an epic battle that ended in resounding defeat. Not one of his political maneuvers worked. How can you make a deal with fanatics? What can really satisfy totalitarian people? Nothing. Dad's worldview was the path of compromise. A complex man, he was able to understand and contain all sides of a dispute and always serve as mediator and problem-solver. But they were simplistic people who saw only one side. They were not interested in anyone but themselves, and took no one else into account. They wanted it all and immediately. All of the promised land, the redemption. Power and rule. He battled in smoke-filled halls and rooms, and they were fighters on the hills and mountains. He escaped by the skin of his teeth from "there," from the Holocaust, and they won the Six-Day War and liberated the Holy City. They connected directly to convenient parts of the myths and ethos of the early days of Zionism and Jewish settlement and scorned him and his learned, universal sources of inspiration. They stole the symbols and content of the Labor movement and took them to new and bad places, showing arrogant contempt for those who established the state for them. They adopted the external trappings of secularism and loaded them with different, new Jewish content that had never been here before. The same huge moustaches, the same creased sandals and hands, the same coarse and meager language. But inside they burned with the fanatic fire of doctrines of redemption and the end of days.

The most significant public-opinion molders of the time, a mixture of Labor Zionists, Revisionists, writers, and poets, launched them; people like Nathan Alterman and Moshe Shamir, Haim Gouri and Rachel Yanait Ben-Zvi. The younger Rabbi Kook gave them a blessing for the road, and they have never looked back. Traditional conservatives, the religious Zionists, joined with nationalist conservatives, led by Menachem Begin and the Likud movement, along with economic conservatives to embark on their paradoxical path: revolutionary conservatism. I was with them in their first moments; I was born from the womb of religious Zionism. With the insights I gained over the years, I grew very distant from them. We were together in the first chapter, in which Israel was secular, socialist, a budding democracy, whose organizing idea was state authority. Today, when they are at the height of their power, I see them as nothing less than a real and present mortal danger.

In 1977, the first ever right-wing government was formed in Israel. With this political upset and the rise of the right to power, I went my own way. They became the entrepreneurs of the second Israeli chapter and partners to it, and since then they have made Israel less democratic and more nationalist, capitalist, brutal, and religious. Territory, the complete and sacred Land of Israel, replaced the state for them as the ultimate organizing idea. And I did my best in the opposing political bloc, moving from protest movements to the heart of the establishment. Our movement was in completely opposite directions. They went far to the right to the extreme fringes, and I was becoming more of a peacemaker and working for the separation of religion and state. I was becoming a pluralist, a feminist, opening up to a great degree.

Today, many of them are doing what they can to move Israel to its third chapter. In the second decade of the twenty-first century, when religious winds are blowing throughout the region, Israel is also growing from the chapter of Greater Israel, with all its associated ills, to the chapter of the Temple and its myriad dangers. For many, too many— nationalists, secular people, and many of my religious relatives—the idea of erecting the Third Temple is the yearning that organizes all political activity. In this chapter of theirs and of a profoundly changed Israel, two things are becoming clear to me. One is that they have gone from being political rivals to bitter enemies, and that bloodshed, a real civil war, is no longer inconceivable if the Temple movement indeed becomes a political reality. The other is that without a complete humanistic, egalitarian civic doctrine that will fight them and replace them and their rule, Israel will be lost.

In the beginning, the outlines were unclear; the lines separating us blurred. Our general feeling of euphoria lasted a few more years. We called the Arabs names, laughed at their powerlessness and the primitiveness we attributed to them. The "them" and "us" always ended in our favor, and they always accepted the result, which for them was no more than zero. "Arab work," "Arab army," or just "Arab" were the most common derogatory terms. Who knew then that this good feeling does not necessarily indicate good health, but is rather a sign of serious illness, the racism that has eaten away the Israeli body and soul? Very few. I wasn't one of them.

I T WAS 1973, AND I WAS PREOCCUPIED WITH OTHER anxieties. The culmination of every yeshiva high school student's educational experience is the matriculation exam in Talmud. I couldn't sleep. I had been absent from so many classes over the years that I didn't have the slightest idea of the material. The little I knew, I didn't really understand. I was a long way from the Talmudic exchanges between the great sages Abayey and Rava. They were discussing *gittin*—Jewish divorce documents—and I was dreaming of my love, Yael. They were debating the laws of Shabbat observance, and I just wanted to be back home for my mother's chicken. To this day I sometimes wake up in the middle of the night in a panic because "tomorrow is the matriculation exam in Talmud," and I don't know anything. A mix of castration fears and performance anxiety that never leaves you.

Over the long course of those days of study, each of us tried to pave his own way to his future. Many went to continue their studies together at the college-level yeshivas and in the army units comprising mainly students from the same yeshiva. This was a special arrangement, known as *hesder,* for religious young men, combining the yeshiva and army settings. And I, as in all the previous years, continued without them—alone and lonely.

Over the course of my final year of study, my rabbi, the one with the television in his closet, tried to persuade me to enroll in a college-level yeshiva instead of signing up for military service. He held out lots of sticks, and a few carrots. The sticks were the destiny of the Jewish people and my own personal responsibility as the scion of an elite religious Zionist family. He assailed me with all this during every one of our conversations. Like everyone else in those days, I was always trying to stay fit. I lifted weights, I did push-ups, and I hoisted myself up again and again over the chin-up bar. But this weight was already too much for my fragile religious frame.

The rabbi's biggest carrot was my final grade on the matriculation examination considered most important of all—the exam in Talmud. This grade was calculated by averaging the final exam grade with that given by the school, which assessed and weighed my accomplishments during all my years of study. "If you will go on to yeshiva, you'll get a very high grade. And if not . . . then not," he kept repeating to me. Obviously, I wanted the highest grade, and over the course of that year I led him to understand that his wish would come true, and I would indeed continue my Torah studies. I gave him what he asked for in order to get what I wanted. But it was an empty promise in exchange for a hollow grade. Most of my friends didn't hesitate about the decision at all. They planned to continue learning Torah at the various institutions suggested to them. Only a handful of the 120 in my grade informed me, with heads held high, that they intended to go into the army as soon as they finished their studies. The majority simply went with the flow.

It was strange that, despite the constant presence of the army in our lives, and in spite of the crowns of glory and the miracles we associated with the Israel Defense Forces (IDF), they—the various governmental agencies, educators, and army recruiters—did not prepare us at all for army service. It always loomed before us, but we didn't exactly know what it was about. Our rabbis and educational role models put tremendous pressure on us to continue our studies in the college-level yeshivas. From their perspective, it befitted their pedagogical efforts, their investment in us. They sent us for a "yeshiva week" in various institutions of higher Torah learning in order to give us a taste of the intellectual paradise they would offer us. That was the last thing I needed, more of that terrible thing that had destroyed all the beauty of the last few years. But to say that aloud also was the last thing I needed, because it would come at the expense of my final grade.

Quietly, almost clandestinely, I began the official process of enlisting in the army, like most other Israelis my age. I had no one to consult. My parents didn't know anything about the subject, my schoolmates were in the thrall of another world, and I didn't really have other friends. And so, two parallel channels were dug beneath the puddle of my life. The rabbi dug his, and I dug mine, and they were heading in opposite directions. His, the rabbi's, was heading toward my yesterdays, and mine was heading toward my own tomorrow. The army officials, in those pre-computer days, the days of copy paper and pencils stuck behind the ears of bored clerks, didn't notice that I was registered on two lists: the rabbi's, which was for a deferral of army service, and mine, which was about immediate enlistment.

Signed up on both lists, I walked into my exam. Two stern-faced rabbinic examiners sat with my rabbi and asked me a few questions. I didn't fully grasp their questions, but suddenly there came to my aid—for the first but not the last time in my life—my father's prodigious memory. Until that moment, I hadn't known that I had inherited this quality from him. I began quoting extensively and flawlessly from the text in which the concept they were asking about appeared. They spoke out of deep understanding, and I spoke in quotations; they asked learnedly, and I responded by rote. But I passed the terrifying exam, and with a high grade, which they told me then and there. "One last question," the examiner said to me, when my hands were already pushing against the door. "What are you doing next year?"

It was a moment of truth, a decisive moment. "Next year I'll be a paratrooper," I responded forthrightly with the answer I had not even given myself yet. It was as if the clouds of the last four years had suddenly parted to reveal a sun that shone right on me. The sun shone in one place, but night fell in another. It gave me pleasure to see the shadows pass across the examiners' faces, and my rabbi's face, livid. He yelled at me, "But you said you were going to yeshiva—otherwise I would not have given you such a high mark. You would have scored much lower!" But it was too late.

CHAPTER THREE

SOLDIER IN WAR, ACTIVIST IN PEACE (1973–1982)

I T WAS THE SUMMER OF 1973, THE LAST SUMMER OF MY innocence. The Yom Kippur War broke out in the autumn. A pin burst the balloon of my pride that had steadily inflated those last six years. People I knew well, peers, friends from my youth movement, others who were in my year at school, counselors, and other acquaintances, were mobilized, were wounded, were killed. Almost every home was touched by death. One friend from our synagogue, like me the son of German parents, was taken captive, and for many days we did not know what had become of him, until the relatively good news arrived that he was a war prisoner in an Egyptian jail.

I spent the Yom Kippur War far from home, at a kibbutz in the Beit She'an valley. I was there for nearly two months, preparing with other young men and women for the Nahal infantry brigade. During those years, my beloved brother-in-law, who never judged me and always accepted me as I was, helped me find an entirely new social circle where I could try to reinvent myself. I didn't know anyone, because all of the friends with whom I'd finished school a few months earlier had gone

elsewhere. Some to yeshivas, some to the army, and many to the combined service of the hesder yeshivas. I didn't want to go with them. I
wanted a clean break from those dismal yeshiva days. They went their
ways, and I went mine. And suddenly, out of the quiet of the holiday
and the debilitating heat of the Beit She'an valley, another war broke
out. Unexpected and unplanned. And this time—just six years after
the Six-Day War—I was no longer a little boy seeking shelter behind
his mother's pleated dress.

I have only scraps of memories from the day of my induction, which
came just a few weeks after the official end of the war. Years later, when
my own children were inducted into the army, I wept bitterly. I wept for
the end of their childhoods, and for my own childhood that had been
abruptly cut short. I wept for the accursed fate of the Israeli parent,
who has to ascend with his child to the national sacrificial altar, and
who is expected—as I was expected—to do so with pride. As each of
my children enlisted, other forgotten aspects of my own enlistment
floated to the surface of memory. I don't remember where my mother
was, but for some reason only my father was there as I left home and set
off on my way. He wasn't fully dressed. He walked me to the door and
said goodbye. No hug or kiss. Not even a word of advice or a parting
blessing. I know that deep in his heart he was terrified for me. And I
know, too, that he loved me, but that he didn't know how to give hugs
or kisses. I felt the great, heavy door of my parents' home close behind
me, and in that moment, I did not know that it would remain closed
forever. My father, who did not understand me while I was a schoolboy,
was not able to take leave of me when I went off to the army. If he had
known what to say, he would have spoken to me; if he had known how
to hug, he would have wrapped his arms around me. If he had kisses
on his warm, smiling, wise lips, he would have kissed me goodbye. But
he didn't know how, and he didn't have them. With the closing of that
door, my childhood came to an end.

I was in the first round of basic training following the Yom Kippur
War. My base was at Pardes Hanna, the mythic Camp 80, in the center

of the country. The first army joke I heard—and after that I heard many others, none more tasteful—was, "Who will stop the Syrians on the borders of Camp 80? The Egyptians." What was going on? Moments ago, I was a self-assured young man fresh out of high school, who could never be defeated or humiliated, certainly not by those Arabs. Now I was a soldier in the midst of defeat and degradation, of a resounding, painful blow, the humiliating Yom Kippur surprise of 1973.

Maybe that was the reason why I loved the life in the barracks. Coming out of my failure in my teenage years I learned how to run. I returned to my body, which had withered and been struck dumb when my love of volleyball was stifled. I was a good military recruit. I tried to be all that I could be: disciplined despite my rebellious spirit, diligent despite my natural laziness, orderly and organized despite my inclination from birth to be messy. I wanted to succeed, to escape that feeling of being a loser all the previous years. I felt the tremendous power of the army as a place that socialized, democratized, and granted wonderful opportunities to all those who had missed out on life until that point. I didn't quite feel at home, but I felt good about myself, and about my uniform and my dog tags and my rubber-soled boots and my heavy gun.

I had planned to continue on the same track with the friends who had enlisted with me in the Nahal unit, to combine kibbutz life with the best of the paratrooper tradition, but that war upended everything for me. Even before the end of our basic training, some of my comrades and I were put under tremendous pressure from our superiors to go to noncommissioned officers training. Many junior commanders in the IDF had been killed or wounded that past autumn in the Yom Kippur War, and the army, like every army, needed to replenish its ranks. We needed to take their place. I was happy. Finally, I was being recognized for my achievements. The noncommissioned officers course was the continuation of my basic training, but with new people and more substance. The training program included the first take-away lessons from the war. Our direct commanders had been in the war and thus had far more authority than their official ranks would indicate.

In the middle of the grueling course we were granted one Saturday night off. I had waited a long time for it. It was not as sweet as a furlough, but it was a calm evening on the base before the exhausting week that lay ahead. In the lecture hall, they screened *The Graduate* with Dustin Hoffman. I had never seen movies like that, so explicit—at least as far as movies dared to be back then. I sat there fascinated and aroused in the darkness, pretending I was indifferent and experienced when from time to time they turned on the lights to switch the film reels. Then suddenly, in the middle of all the excitement, there was an announcement: "Company A, attention! Fall out in ten minutes." The movie lost its magic, and we returned to life with a sweaty scramble. I never saw the end of the movie because we were catapulted into another movie—the movie of our new Israeli lives—whose end, too, was not yet known.

The officers checked our helmets, ammo belts and weapons, and the water in our canteens. First aid bandages, identity cards, dog tags. They didn't make their usual jokes, and they didn't hassle us just for the sake of it. We could sense that this was real, more than just a routine exercise. "In five minutes, everyone's on the military vehicles—we're out of here." No one knew where to. Silence hung in the air. Maybe another war? Maybe this was it? Fear and anticipation. Just before dawn we arrived at a place we had never been before. There was a lot of commotion all around us. They had us assemble in the far corner of a parking lot. We were ordered to leave our weapons and ammunition belts. One of us was appointed to guard the weapons and the equipment. The rest of us were given wooden clubs and a quick briefing: "We're going up there by way of the mountain. When we get to the site, we will evacuate everyone who is there." It was not clear to me who "everyone" was, and where "there" was, but we set off.

At sunrise, I found myself in an open field at the top of the hill, in the middle of a confused jumble of people. Cries, dust, and struggle. Soldiers and police officers dragging people who were clinging to boulders, hugging trees, lying beside one another and screaming. The dawn slowly dispelled the darkness and the picture became clearer. Those who were doing the evacuating were in uniforms—like me—and those being evacuated were wearing kippahs like me. We pulled, dragged, schlepped, and beat. One after another. And they kept returning, like an obstinate boomerang.

As the sun came up, there was a bit more light, and there was Yosef lying at my feet, his tefillin straps wrapped around his arm and head. Just a few months ago we had played volleyball together in the schoolyard. His cheeks were no longer smooth—they had started to sprout a wispy beard. The kippah on his head, too, was larger than usual.

He wailed bitterly, "Burgie, don't beat me." I didn't beat him.

"Yosef, what are you doing here? What's going on here?"

"We're returning to Samaria, to our land. We're renewing Jewish settlement here." I didn't understand what he was talking about.

"Who told you to come here?" I asked.

"The rabbi," he answered and pointed. On the other side of the site, students, police officers, and soldiers surrounded the venerable Rabbi Tzvi Yehuda Kook, son of the elderly Rabbi Abraham Isaac Kook. And then I understood.

"The rabbi," in their circles, is always Rabbi Kook. I knew him—not personally, but I knew very well who he was. In the past I would sometimes go to his yeshiva in Jerusalem. Once, in order to witness the spiritual experience that had swept up so many of my friends, and sometimes to visit those same friends, and occasionally to sit and learn with one of my older cousins who studied there, I heard the rabbi teach. My friends and relatives who studied with him spoke of him and his teachings with the highest praise. Now the rabbi was on the other side of the huge courtyard, Yosef was lying on the ground, and I was standing over him. He was lying there in the dust, and I was the oppressor. He was the Jew, and I was the Israeli.

"Burg, why are you just standing there?" my junior officer shouted at me furiously. "Take that religious guy and throw him out of here, to hell with him. Clobber the kippah!" he went on, more explicitly. And

I stood there torn between Yosef and the officer. Here was my friend, here was my officer, and me—where did that leave me? "Burg!" Together my officer and I took hold of Yosef and removed him. In that moment, my youth was over. The last thread that had connected me to the world of my childhood was severed. Between the rabbi and the sovereign, I chose the sovereign. Between man and land, I chose man. Since then, I've never changed my mind, though at that moment I was merely an enforcer for the majority, and today, often enough, I'm in the most remote corner of the minority.

As I later learned, the place they had brought us was the old train station of Sebastia. Hanan Porat and his associates had dragged the members of our generation, my childhood friends who revered them, to the hills of Judea and Samaria, carried on the winds of that same rabbi, that prophet of the modern redemption. In loud voices and with shofar blasts they railed defiantly from every hilltop against the entire social order as we knew it. Within religious Zionism they proposed an alternative to the passivity of my father and the rest of their leaders. Their knitted kippot banished the diasporic black kippot of the movement's strongholds of power and influence. The macho moustaches defeated the chubby cheeks, and their rough hands bested those that learned classical music in their youth. They took advantage of the emotional, political, and ethical weakness of Yitzhak Rabin and Shimon Peres in order to topple the entire old Zionist structure. Instead of the "heavy black cloud" of Israeli despair, which covered the sky since the previous Yom Kippur, they proposed a "white sail on the horizon," which signified a complete renewal of all ideas and symbols. They drew an imaginary, demonic line from Hanita, a kibbutz founded before the state, to the West Bank settlement of Elon Moreh, from the early "tower and stockade" settlements to Kfar Etzion. From the despair of the war that had just ended to the hope of conquest and fulfilling their vision of redemption in "our" Greater Israel. The first violins of religious Zionism took center stage for the first time and played their solo. The rest of the Zionist orchestra fell silent, muted almost entirely.

Dad had no more strength. The same door was also shut in his face. Only when he was near death, in his last words to me, he admitted, "Avraham, I'm worried, who will take care of the Jewish people?" On that last day, I hugged him with all my might until his end. But by then the hour was too late on our Jewish Israeli clock.

S OMETIME AT THE START OF MY MILITARY SERVICE, RIGHT after the cease-fire agreement with the Egyptians, we were taken to guard facilities and airfields on the other side of the Suez Canal, in "Africa." I spent night after night in the foxhole I had dug for myself. The desert night was beautiful as always, very bright stars, endless skies, and I, alone in the world. Our orders were to stay on alert, awake all night, to guard against a planned infiltration by Egyptian commandos and to "report any development immediately." I had not ever, and not since, known such fear. Surreptitiously, against all instructions and orders, I took a small transistor radio with me to the foxhole. I put in the scratchy earphone and tried to get through the night terrors, to listen to news from home and understand the reality spinning me like a leaf in the wind.

One night, a broadcast carried the deep voice of Egyptian President Anwar Sadat promising his people that he is prepared to sacrifice another million and a half Egyptian soldiers in order to redeem the occupied lands of Sinai. God, a million and a half Egyptian soldiers against me? Avraham Burg, the yeshiva boy from Jerusalem? What did I do wrong? What did I do to him? What's going to happen? My fear only increased. The memory of friends killed just a few months before in the Yom Kippur War still hovered in the air. The army was beaten and hurt, and the commanders continuously reminded us of their painfully fresh experiences. Large cracks appeared in the Israeli structure and threatened to bring down the whole house.

In the end, the Egyptian commandos never came, disengagement agreements were signed, and my military service eventually came to an end. I began my life, and Israel went back to its new routine, the routine of post-trauma of the collective after battle and failure. In the years after my military service all my friendships were new. Friends from the army and other friends who all came from the social circles of my then-partner and later wife, studies, and service. The new friends brought other new friends. I experienced great joie de vivre. I got up in the morning with a smile and went to sleep happy. I was 100 percent "me." In the yellowing pictures from that time I'm still thin, with flowing hair, a torn T-shirt, ragged jeans, a hand-woven belt from the Far East, and a strange hat that was part stylish, part replacing the kippah. I pursued African studies and dreamt of far-away countries. I sat in anthropology classes and gained a completely different understanding of the stories of Genesis. I took a tour guide course and hiked, guided, and taught those who came after me. I had many dreams in my head, but none of them approached the realms of politics. I knew that I would not be a public figure, that I would not be well-known, that my children would have a full-time dad, not sharing his time with countless voters and other pesky nuisances.

Four years went by, and the same Sadat of my youthful fears came to town. The transition from war to peace, from existential fear to great hope, carried me away as it did everyone. We ran after his convoy and yelled at the top of our lungs, "No more war, no more bloodshed," over and over.

The Jerusalem of this twenty-three-year-old Israeli never looked more beautiful and optimistic. I had already lived through three wars, two of which I could actually remember (the Sinai Campaign of 1956 was not engraved in my consciousness as an influential experience, because I was only a year old), and here was one peace in return.

I believed that the cliché every parent recites here to his or her child, "Son, when you grow up there will already be peace," was coming true for me and my friends. I sensed the potential of changing the Israeli vocabulary, replacing words of siege and war—"the whole world is against us, and it's us against the whole world"—with a completely different lexicon. I sensed how a new conversation, beautiful like a butterfly, was emerging from the cumbersome chrysalis. One whose syntax was established by Anwar Sadat—the Pharaonic visitor whose car I ran after, rushing like a serf of old behind the chariot of a venerable king—and Menachem Begin, who was at my bar mitzvah, and in half a year would be invited to my wedding with Yael.

"Begin will bring us the most beautiful gift," we said dreamily to each other, "peace." Though I had never voted for him, I very much wanted him to succeed; how naïve I was. I believed Begin, and I didn't listen to completely different voices that did everything they could to divert the course of Israeli policy from the path Begin wanted to pursue. Four years, that was the entire extent of the chapter that could have been the most important in the annals of Israel. For four years Israel moved forward toward peace and normalcy. Away from the siege mentality, from the sense of a tightening ghetto, from endless combativeness with no purpose. We did not know then that the day in which it would end was so close.

When Begin and Sadat made their heaven-sent peace in 1978, Yael and I decided to make our connection official and get married. It was the perfect time to create a new family—we would raise our children in a world in which all would be well. The wars started to grow more distant, terrorism was muffled and far away. The leadership turned failure on the battlefield into a peace with "our biggest neighbor." Years of considerable and heedless optimism lay ahead. Dad and Mom invited all their friends—and there were loads of them—to the wedding. My parents, with their eminent friends, and us, surrounded by the circle of our friends, dancing to distraction, to the heights of optimism. Like all Jewish weddings, this one ended with the breaking of a glass.

A year later, Prime Minister Menachem Begin appointed Dad to head the negotiating team on autonomy for "the Arabs of the Land of Israel." I understood that literally, and understood nothing. I had no doubt, as I was taught in the army, that Dad had been given a mission—to solve the troublesome problem of the occupied territories, which he had mentioned to Mom when we came back from the big trip after the Six-Day War—and that he would carry it out successfully. I was convinced that this talented, peace-loving man, whom I loved and respected so much, would finally bring us the longed-for chapter of our existence—peace for Israel. I believed that his clever statement he used so often that "history is the politics of the past, and politics is the history of the future" was guiding him to his proper place in the history of the Jewish people.

I knew nothing of the schemes and plots hatched by the pair of brothers-in-law, Ezer Weizman and Moshe Dayan, against him and Begin. The "deceased," as Weizman would call Begin in crude jest. I hadn't noticed the micro-politics that members of Dad's party wielded against him. And above all, like many others, I didn't understand Begin's malign and masterful maneuver. Dad was the "queen" in his chess game. And Begin, in a brilliant gambit, sacrificed the queen in order to save something entirely different. Begin was ready to sacrifice the Sinai Peninsula, with its flourishing Israeli settlements, bountiful oil wells, and huge security hinterland in order to save the apple of his eye—the historic core of the Land of Israel, the mountains of Judea and hills of Samaria. Begin appointed Dad to this post so that he would fail. I don't know if they had discussed the move, but Dad effectively carried out the mission with significant lack of success. The fact is that there is no peace for his children, grandchildren, and even great-grandchildren.

For most of his life, Dad was not a diplomat, but an uncynical politician and scrupulously observant. Begin could be sure that my father would do everything to avoid giving up the Promised Land and at the same time would not be easily broken, while Hanan Porat, the young charismatic settler leader, and his colleagues were dancing and jumping in defiance of him on the West Bank hills and in the central committee of the party. And Begin was right—my father failed.

I remember his stories about the foolish ideological debates he would have with his foreign partners in the negotiations, who came from Egypt and the US: President Carter, the Baptist Christian, Foreign Minister Boutros-Ghali, the Copt, and General Gamasi, the

Muslim. In those moments, he was at his best, in his element. The Talmudic polemicist, protector of Jewish sacred sites against the representatives of other faiths. I always listened to him carefully, and I tried to imagine the meeting, the atmosphere, the details. As a byproduct of the surprising mission he was charged with, I also became a momentary student, tutored in the advanced Israeli school of diplomacy and politics. I first understood then what today I know so well—that in politics and diplomacy you usually have to put up with a lot to obtain a kernel of something nourishing.

These rituals repeated themselves over and over again. Dad traveled, Dad returned, he traveled again and returned again. At home, he amused me with jokes and riveting anecdotes from behind closed doors, and outside the papers reported the growing impasse. The gap between the stories I heard at home and the diplomatic, political, and media reality widened and deepened. And in my heart, I already predicted the missed opportunity. At one point I instinctively felt that everything was going to be lost. That Israel, through my father as the public servant of Menachem Begin, was missing the great opportunity offered by Sadat: to replace the talk of war, which flared time and again in 1956, 1967, and 1973, with a conversation about peace and reconciliation.

"How can you travel to Egypt and have all these silly debates?" I asked him.

It was a direct question that was not customary in our home. It came after a long and detailed description of what he had told "them," the Americans and Egyptians, Christians and Muslims. And what they told him, and what he told them. And over again, right up to the polemical knockout he dealt them: "I told them that Jerusalem is not mentioned even once in the Koran, while it is mentioned in the Bible 656 times."

And I was angry. "You don't understand what war is! One bullet from a machine gun whizzing near your ear and you would have already forgotten all these hair-splitting arguments. And they're also stupid. They should have told you that Jerusalem is not mentioned even once in the Torah. Are you traveling there to hold an international Bible contest?" I ridiculed him, the man who during his life was most identified with the national trivia game as its head judge for thirty years. We didn't continue the conversation because I had crossed the line between intellectual debate and respecting one's parents. But I knew that he had heard me; he felt the sting but kept it to himself.

THE ISRAEL OF THOSE DAYS WAS AMBIVALENT ABOUT THE sudden and unwanted peace thrust upon it. Just two days before Sadat's visit, the army's chief of staff at the time, Mordechai Gur, warned against another Egyptian conspiracy. Because "Sadat, in his youth, was a member of a pro-Nazi youth movement." Begin's right-wing camp and the right flank of religious Zionism tried furiously to destroy the prospects of this auspicious turn of events. The Peace Now movement was founded during the 1978 Israeli-Egyptian peace talks between Israeli Prime Minister Menachem Begin and Egyptian President Anwar Sadat, at a time when the talks looked like they were close to collapsing.

Three-hundred forty-eight reserve officers and soldiers from Israeli army combat units published an open letter to the prime minister of Israel in which they called for the Israeli government not to squander the historic opportunity for peace between the two nations.

How strange that it was established to support Menachem Begin, the quintessential rightist, in his readiness to evacuate the Sinai Peninsula, though in short political order it would aim all its arrows at the same Begin himself and everything he represented.

From the first moment, I felt that this new movement is my true political expression. I didn't have the privilege of being one of the founders of the movement and signers of the letter appealing to Begin, but I was so happy about the new political home being built before our very eyes. A movement and not a party, a message and not interests. I went with my friends to Peace Now meetings in a studio apartment behind the Smadar theater. I felt like I was in a youth movement, but one that fit me much better, both politically and socially. I went out with my new friends to demonstrations and gave out leaflets and stickers on the streets. Because of my intimate knowledge of the country and its landscapes, and my love for the tangible aspects of the homeland, I literally felt physical pain every time I put up the sticker "Peace is better than Greater Israel." Precisely because of that love, I reached the full-blown understanding that in this space there are only two possibilities— either to live in partnership or to die together in war. Propelled by that understanding, I broke my remaining ties with relatives and friends who had become either complacent right-wingers or gluttonous settlers. Often the windshield of my car would be smashed because of the stickers, but it was worth it, because in the clear-cut choice between the Land of Israel of my former friends—the land of the hikes of my youth, the domain of identity, the land of awakening religious Zionism, of Joseph on the soil of Sebastia—and the peace of Sadat, reached between him and the young soldier from the foxhole in Sinai, I preferred peace.

This historic and unique peace process was completed and destroyed in April 1982, four years after Sadat's historic visit to Israel. The evacuation of the Sinai settlements was painful and traumatic. Young people barricaded themselves on rooftops. Some of them would soon become my parliamentary adversaries. The settlers greatly increased their resistance, honed in many struggles on the mountains of Judea and hills of Samaria. But the government of Israel was determined to evacuate them and honor its international agreements. Earlier that year, Menachem Begin said in parliament, "We are fighting today for peace. How fortunate we are to have this privilege. Yes, there are difficulties in peace, there are pains in peace, there are sacrifices for peace, but they are all preferable to the sacrifices of war!" And with Begin the rhetoric was always loftier and more important than reality. His readiness to make sacrifices for peace lasted for only a few more weeks.

CHAPTER FOUR

THE PUBLIC LIFE
(1982–2001)

I N JUNE OF 1982, IT WAS ALL OVER. THE LAST STEP OF THE peace with Egypt was immediately followed by the first step of a long war in Lebanon. This is how the war mentality annihilated the hopes for an expanding peace. Egypt first and the rest of the region right after. No sooner was the last stage of the agreement with Egypt—the painful evacuation of the settlements—completed than we embarked on the path of war. We will never know if Sharon—then a controversial "bully" and deceitful minister of defense—misled everyone, including PM Begin, or if Begin knew. Anyway, the end is known and very painful: Ariel Sharon kicked over Menachem Begin's bucket and spilled both the water and Begin. In June 1982, Israel invaded Lebanon.

Could it be that Begin and Sharon's sense of having made a great concession over the expanses and settlements in Sinai required emotional and territorial compensation somewhere else? Did Begin understand, with his sharp political sense, that after the evacuation of Sinai it would be the turn of the West Bank mountain ridge and its settlements? Because if evacuation is possible in one place, it is possible elsewhere as well. Could it be that he thought that the only way to thwart the autonomy of "the Arabs of the Land of Israel"—his euphemism for the Palestinians—was an all-out war against them in their place of refuge in Lebanon? I think so. Begin no longer trusted the maneuvering ability of Dad and his team and instead decided to join Sharon, adding his own kick to the diplomatic bucket to make sure not a single drop of peace was left. Inside him there were at least two Menachem Begins, the statesman and the militarist. We witnessed with our own eyes what happened when the first weakened and the second grew stronger. At the decisive moment, the statesman in him, the democratic man of peace, surrendered to the man of challenge and war.

When that war was declared, I didn't imagine that because of it I would eventually find myself a public figure, a member of parliament and filling high Israeli and Jewish public posts for decades. I was still a young student then, and we were a private and happy family: a father, mother, and two small children. Like many of my friends, my daily routine was essentially a kind of long hiatus between one stretch of reserve duty and another, from the distant Sinai to the heights of Mount Hermon. And in between we were called up for training and to brush up on our skills.

The only thing I liked about all these "soldier games" were the parachute jumps. I exploited every opportunity to do them. I liked to take to the skies, stand first at the door of the plane, gaze into the distance, control the fear, and jump into the enveloping silence. I parachuted dozens if not hundreds of times in my life, always with the same intoxicating enjoyment that swept me away. Until I was injured in training. A few meters before hitting the ground, the wind direction changed. And while my whole body was poised to roll forward, "calf, thigh, right shoulder," to soften the impact of the hard ground, the wind carried me in a "reverse glide." I was dragged along on my back for hundreds of meters, battered by the stones, until one of my fellow paratroopers grabbed the wind-filled parachute and stopped the drag. For many months, I walked around with back pain, refusing to give in, until the lower part of my body was almost completely paralyzed. The hospitalizations and operations became inevitable. In the spring of 1982, after two years of treatment and recovery, my body was still in a cast. I used a cane, and I was being treated in trauma, pain, and rehabilitation clinics. I was a disabled army veteran trying to resume the normal trajectory of life for a young man.

On the Sabbath before the Lebanon War, we—Yael, Itay, our first-born, and little Roni, who was born only two months earlier, and I—were visiting friends up north. Without any warning a duel between artillery and Katyusha rockets began over our heads. An Israeli provocation meant to unravel the cease-fire agreement with the PLO in southern Lebanon. In the kibbutzes, people went down to bomb shelters. City streets were deserted, and we turned back and returned home, driving alone on the roads going south. In the opposite lane were long convoys of tanks, armored personnel carriers, and artillery guns. Again war, again the old fears. And again, mobilization of all the relevant nationalist rhetoric. When we reached home, I called my parents to report, as always, that we had returned safely.

"Dad, do you know that there are army convoys heading north?" He didn't know.

"Surely, it's just skirmishes," he reassured me. My eyes saw one thing, and my ears heard him saying something else. I wasn't aware of the contradiction developing between my eyes and ears, my information from the ground and his government, which was deceived by Sharon and deceitful with the Israeli public. A few more days passed, and one evening a call-up order arrived at my house. I kissed Yael and the children and went off to war, disabled, limping, in a cast, and mobilized.

"You can go home, it's a mistake, you're injured," the commander told me.

"Forget it," I replied in typical Israeli fashion, "I'm with you."

On June 6, 1982, we crossed the border into Lebanon. Soldiers equipped with ammunition belts, guns, and self-confidence, and me, with a cane and a cumbersome metal brace to stabilize my back. The first week of June is deeply symbolic—on June 6, 1944, the allied armies invaded Normandy; on June 5, 1967, the Six-Day War broke out; and here we were again in the week of wars. This symbolism likely did not escape the keenly aware Menachem Begin. He was a man of symbols and gestures, the greatest Israeli gestologist of all. He may have wanted to go to war on that date in order to erase the humiliation of the Yom Kippur War waged by the hated Labor Party with his own glorious campaign, which was supposed to evoke the victorious war of June 1967.

I was away from home for many days. We moved a bit and camped a bit. We fired a little and were fired on. We were shaken by thunderous artillery and saw the contrails of jets. We heard loads of rumors: about friendly fire by our planes on our forces, about comrades killed, about other forces at the gates of Beirut. Here and there civilians would give themselves up to us. I photographed children emerging from a pit in the ground with their hands raised.

"Like Warsaw," someone said.

"Only the opposite," someone else said, "this time it's not us." And everyone laughed. There was talk of a battle that went wrong on an adjacent route. Something didn't work out. They—PM Begin and his Ahitophel, Sharon—said forty-eight hours and it's been a few weeks already. They talked about forty kilometers, but who's counting? The radio broadcast certain things, and in reality, other things happened. We excused it all as the "fog of war." In the end, we were discharged. I remember only a few details: Fatima Gate near Metulla, the cold pizza in Kiryat Shmona in the middle of the night. But actually, it was all erased, because the minute I entered the house, my parents' home, Mom's scream pierced the air. She, who never lost control, who never got too angry or too happy, gave a full-throated yell. A great and liberating shout of a mother's joy, the likes of nothing else. And my mother, who wasn't with me when I was inducted into the army, and did not understand so many of the twists and turns of my life, was with me when I returned from the war. My heart goes out to her even now, when she is no longer alive, and to that special moment like no other. The moment in which a mother was born to me, and I was born again, differently, to her.

Later we met friends and friends of friends. Everyone told a bit of the story and a big picture started to form. A giant picture. The government of Israel knows nothing about the war it declared, and which Ariel Sharon is waging on its behalf. At home Dad is talking to me about forty kilometers and forty-eight hours, and we are already deep inside on the Beirut-Damascus road, with no departure on the horizon.

"We ordered the army to stop at the forty-kilometer limit," he tells me authoritatively.

"The guys are many kilometers to the north of this imaginary line. We are already in West Beirut," Alon tells me, the son of Yehiel Shemi, the sculptor from Kibbutz Kabri.

"IDF vehicles are moving on the Beirut-Damascus highway," Nahum Karlinsky, the pilot, tells me.

"We were given a briefing with maps," Dad tells me at night in a call from the government meeting room.

A great many contradictory reports move through our human network, which played an organizing and decisive role before the PC and Google, before WhatsApp groups, faxes, and speedy email. Despite all the fog and deception, the denials and deceit, everything became known and exposed. The government is lying, and my comrades are killing and being killed—just like that, as if it were nothing.

One by one I brought my friends to Dad, people the likes of which he had never met: secular, young, direct, and blunt. So different from Isi Eisner, Eugen Michaelis, and Yaakov Tzobel, his dignified and serious German immigrant friends. Secular Israel—which had never been in our house, and which we did not learn about in the yeshiva, and which we did not get to know in the youth movement—came in to stop that war, the first war of the Israeli right wing.

Minute by minute I was drawn in. I broke all my oaths in terrible anger. So many times, I had sworn to myself that I would never be like my father, that I would not get involved in politics. And now, facing the enemy—the government of Israel—I was sucked in by forces I could not resist. We began collecting signatures, we created a movement called "Soldiers Against Silence," and in the process, we discovered that we were not alone: soldiers, in mandatory service and reserves, came without fear, added their signatures, and organized demonstrations and meetings. We traveled around the country and tried to persuade people. Unwittingly, my small cog meshed with the large machine of real national politics. Without noticing, I became an active, full-time politician.

After a few weeks of rallying support, we requested a meeting with Prime Minister Menachem Begin. We wanted to personally present him with the soldiers' signatures. To our surprise, we received a positive answer. On the appointed day, three of us arrived at the prime minister's office: Alon, a veteran of the elite Sayeret Matkal unit, Nahum, a pilot, and me, a limping paratrooper with a cane. For the first time in my life I entered that office. The prime minister's room is small and modest relative to the grand offices of important people and world leaders. Begin was lying on the couch. I seem to recall that a few days earlier he had slipped in his bathtub at home and broken his hip. His large glasses further magnified his vacant eyes. In some moments, I had the feeling that he was not with us. We gave him the signatures and explained to him what was happening on the ground, that he was losing the support of the soldiers on the battlefield.

Instead of answering us directly, the prime minister got up with difficulty and leaned on his cane, hobbling over to a wall with a map of the Land of Israel. We also rose, I with my cane. "I see that we have something in common," he joked with me. He waved a limp hand and pontificated with a weak voice, the voice of the exhausted, a faint echo of his vanished demagogic powers and rhetoric about the Land of Israel. We had come to speak to him about Lebanon, but he was preoccupied with issues of Greater Israel. We talked about war and the senseless sacrifice, and he was busy with unrealistic dreams and fantasies about kingdoms of Israel, the one that was, and the one to come. While he was whipping himself up into a frenzy near the map, I went over to the

adjacent bookcase and took out a Bible. I opened it and quoted the
resounding verses from the book of Ezekiel (33:23–25):

> The word of the Lord came to me: O mortal, those who lie in
> these ruins in the land of Israel argue, "Abraham was one man, yet
> he was granted possession of the land. We are many; surely, the
> land has been given as a possession to us." Therefore say to them:
> "Thus said the Lord God: You eat with the blood, you raise your
> eyes to your fetishes, and you shed blood—yet you expect to
> possess the land! You have relied on your sword, you have com-
> mitted abominations, you have all defiled other men's wives—
> yet you expect to possess the land!"

Begin, with the remaining lucidity he could muster, said, "Well, if
you're going to the Bible, let's return to the couch." We returned.

As if on a director's cue, the door opened and the prime minister's
shrewd media advisor entered and whispered something in his ear. "Of
course! Of course! Bring them in," Begin blurted out. Three women
entered the room. Their dresses were long, severe head-scarves hid
every hair on their heads, and they wore sickly sweet smiles. Three
stereotypical settlers. The weakened Begin did not even get up to greet
them, and they, in keeping with Jewish purity customs, did not shake
his limp hand.

"We wanted to bring the prime minister signatures of thousands of
Jews who support him, the government, and the war." They concluded
with a few words about the lands of the biblical tribes of Naftali and
Asher, liberated in the north of the country as part of the "Peace for
Galilee" war, and about the yeshivas and settlements they intend to
establish there with their husbands, sons, and daughters.

"Did you see them?" Begin said with pleasure after they left. "So de-
mure, so . . . chaste, so supportive. Well then, you are not alone," he said,
banishing us from his consciousness before dozing off for a moment.
The media advisor, who was in the room, tried to hustle us out before

there was further embarrassment. When we got up, Begin opened his eyes and said, "How can I stop now, when eighty-five saintly fighters have already been killed?" and ended the meeting.

Outside the office, still stunned by the weakness of the most powerful man in Israel, we agreed with the media advisor that the meeting would remain undisclosed. I was not yet familiar then with the power-plays and deceit of that office. In those days, it was very difficult for a young citizen to be cynical about his government. We believed in the wisdom of the government and its integrity. Though we were blunt, we didn't doubt. And government offices, as they have always done, invested much of their energy in deception. Sometimes the deception is meant to camouflage big moves, and sometimes it was meant to cover up small mistakes. But at that time, the whole government of Israel was mobilized to hide from the people the fact that there was no leader at the helm. Who knows if Begin was manic-depressive or just depressive. Who knows whether it was the medications he took or the burden which had become too much for him. Maybe the truth had struck this honest man and stunned him. We will never know. One thing is clear: In those days Israel had no prime minister, and everyone did what they liked. Ariel Sharon did many things, and it is doubtful if even one of them was honest.

We, as young patriots, people whose belief in the state and its institutions and love for the place and its fate were stronger than any other public feeling, kept our meeting with Begin secret—as we had promised. But it didn't last long—the next day the meeting was disclosed in a headline in one of the morning papers. Overnight I went from being an anonymous Jerusalem youngster to something between a media ploy and a new political prospect. Even though I was supposedly born into politics, I wasn't ready for it. Actually, my life until then had flowed in the opposite direction. I lived in the deep anonymity and privacy that were made possible by the walls my parents had built between the public and the private. All the strings I had tried to cut between the trajectory of Dad's life and the life I planned for myself came together, as if on their own. As soon as the lights went on, I was on center stage. The media and the public could not ignore the strange combination of someone wearing a kippah being a leftist, an injured paratrooper being a pacifist, and especially an activist in a protest movement against a war waged by a government in which his father served.

It was now my turn to negotiate the space between public and family life. I did this with caution, searching for a way to be true to myself and to the mission I had partly pursued and which had partly been thrust on me, while maintaining the warm ties with my parents' home, with my small children, with the wonderful friendship between my wife and my mother. Those days marked the start of atonement for all the pain between us during previous years. Dad said almost nothing, and whatever was important for him to convey he conveyed through Mom. "They're using you," she said, meaning the sudden interest of cynical politicians and the media, and she was right. But I also used them, and I was also right. Standing one day on the long and narrow porch at the entrance to my childhood home, Mom told me, "I don't know why you need all this 'Peace Now.'"

"Mom, I want to leave my children a better country than the one you left us," I told her, and her reply surprised me very much: "This country is not the country we founded." They really lived in the classical Jewish world of two Jerusalems, heavenly and terrestrial. They loved the utopian, idyllic, and perfect Israel of their imagination, and lived in it within their protected and insulated environment. They hardly knew the reality outside. They knew of its existence, but they never got near it or rubbed shoulders with it. I, for my part, repeatedly hurled terrestrial Israel at them, which they refused to see or get to know. Our disagreement was a familial microcosm of the Zionist rebellion against mother Judaism. Between those two entities, theirs and mine, one the object of dreams, the other embattled, is where the Israeli struggle is playing out to this very day and will continue for many days to come.

I was very careful to maintain respect for Dad just as I was making every effort to damage the standing of his government. The forty-eight-hour war we were promised had been going on for three months. On Rosh Hashanah of that year, 1982, the year of Sharon and Lebanon, a terrible massacre occurred in the Palestinian refugee camps of Sabra and Shatila. On the morning of our holy day, when Dad and I were standing beside each other in our small synagogue, the Christian Phalangist fighters, Sharon's allies, completed two days of slaughter and bloodshed in the helpless and defenseless Palestinian refugee camps. The Phalangist fighters left the camps, and that's when the horrific news began to arrive.

When my friends came into the synagogue to tell me about the massacre, I whispered to Dad, "I can't go on, I'm going home," and in my heart, I literally shouted for a response to the day's prayer to "remove the wicked government from the earth." Yael was sitting in the synagogue's women's section with our little Roni; our firstborn, Itay, was with me. We met outside the synagogue and went home. In the square between the synagogue and my parents' home, the police were already trying to disperse demonstrators with tear gas, and we all breathed some of it. Those were really Days of Awe. At home, we didn't talk much about politics, and in public we didn't talk at all—my father and I—about one another or with each other. We never planned our joint moves, or more precisely our non-moves. But our deep and intimate knowledge of one another produced, seemingly spontaneously, a deliberate decision never to be on the same public stage, not on radio or television, not in the press or in any political encounters.

In those days someone, probably one of my friends, spray-painted a huge graffiti message on the wall of my parents' home: "Burg, learn from your son." Time and again the municipality asked my parents if they wanted the writing erased. "No!" Dad said. The large inscription stayed there, gradually fading, until a few years after his death, when it disappeared entirely. Until his last day, Dad was very attentive. Not always understanding, not necessarily agreeing, but wanting to be updated and very curious. His personal example, his open-mindedness and readiness to learn from anyone, which he always accompanied with the old Jewish saying, "A person is jealous of everyone except his son," was a motto that enabled me to be a partner, pupil, and friend of all my children.

During those months after the Rosh Hashanah of Sabra and Shatila, the pattern of relations between me and my family, as well as between me and the Israeli public, was set. Until the massacre in the refugee camps, the Israeli political system treated us—the protest leaders—with expedient hypocrisy. Everyone benefited from our public work, and few were willing to really pitch in and help. There were a few thousand soldiers who had been in actual combat in Lebanon, and who came back home and said, "No more," and "The emperor is a liar." The right needed us in order to sic its mob against someone. And who better than the "well poisoners," "traitors," and "backstabbers of the nation," who are all satanic leftists? Begin and his followers had a long tradition of double-talk. Lofty declarations about the unity of the people and despicable acts of goading and incitement. And the opposition to Begin, the Alignment Party, didn't exactly know what it wanted. Some of them refused to meet us, others met us and then issued denials. And the rest simply didn't care, because they were going about their business. We were killing and being killed, protesting and struggling, and they were in the Histadrut labor federation, in the party or party branch or municipality. Only the massacre in the refugee camps managed to unsettle them and force the entire political system to take a stand. Completely against their will, even the smooth and evasive operators among them were compelled to become retroactively courageous.

On Saturday night, September 25, 1982, retroactive activists like them streamed to Malchei Yisrael Square with hundreds of thousands of people. People shocked by the massacre and opponents of the war, veteran peaceniks along with the begrudging presence of opposition members. Leaders were swept along, led by the masses who were much more honest and ethical than they were. The square was packed with people. It was hard to believe that sight, unbelievable that a few young men in Jerusalem—honest, yet simple soldiers coming back from the battlefield—had generated this tremendous human movement, or more accurately, were active partners in extracting the cork from the bottle in which the spirit of all these people was trapped. For the first time in my life I was on the stage, any stage. All the bigwigs spoke, Rabin and Peres and many more. I was the eleventh speaker. I stood off to one side. I didn't know any of them. They appealed to the crowd with rousing, impassioned calls that set off waves of applause, trying to compete with their rhetoric against the hypnotizing oratory of PM Menachem Begin, the king of city squares.

I went up to the stage, hobbling with my cane. I had the feeling that utter silence had descended on the world. Before me were notebook pages on which I had written the first speech of my life. Hiding under the stage, where the traditional theater prompter would be, was Haim Bar-Lev, the general secretary of the Alignment. In his slow cadence, he whispered, "Two minutes and fifty seconds left, two and a half minutes . . . " How in heaven did we get to a situation in which the acclaimed former army chief of staff, who had avoided any affiliation with us and our argument, became a hidden whisperer in this defining demonstration? And what the heck was I doing up there, in the three minutes allotted to me? I said what I said, ending with the words, "We believe in a Judaism whose ways are pleasant and all of whose paths are peaceful." I think there was applause. I'm not sure. My stomach was knotted with excitement and I couldn't stand up straight because of the momentousness of the event. I didn't know that this was history, but my body apparently understood that something was changing at that moment in our existence. The demonstration dispersed, and I walked, bent over, leaning on the shoulders of my dear father-in-law Lucien, who never wavered in his opinions, and with whom I attended many more demonstrations, gatherings, and memorial days.

When I got home I called my parents, as I always did until their last day. I hadn't told them that I was going to that demonstration, but they likely already knew. We talked about how the Sabbath had gone, how the children were doing, who had visited whom. As if it were weekend business as usual. At the end, a minute before we hung up, at that moment, in his first and only reference to my political activity, Dad paid me the highest compliment, correcting the pronunciation of the biblical quotation I used in my speech. I'm not entirely sure that I mispronounced it, but if there was such a mistake, in a verse that I had chanted and sung so many times since childhood, then it was the best mistake I had ever made. So much was folded into that sentence of his. All the mannerisms of the German immigrant, all the politics, all the appreciation, and all my upbringing at home. He basically told me without spelling it out: I know you were at the demonstration, I know you took care not to use the stage to harm me. I know that your words were well received and different than the words of others. I'm glad you used Jewish tradition as a basis for your political argument. But you have more to learn, because it's important to be as precise as possible in citations and quotes, and not to fall into the abyss of ignorance threatening many pundits in Israel. So meticulous was this comment, so European in its understatement, and so him. Only time taught me the meaning of his pithiness. In his conciseness, he was saying to me: I know how to recognize your inner truth among your layers of verbiage and rhetoric. He knew, because he was like that too.

It took me many years to understand the secret of his conciseness. On the day of my marriage to Yael he called me into the kitchen. "Sit down," he said. I sat down with great embarrassment. He chattered in a roundabout way and finally told me, "Look, according to Jewish tradition, I have to prepare you now for the wedding and marriage. But I fear that regarding some of the subjects, about which our Jewish forefathers would talk with their sons at this moment, you know more than me. I'll make do with one word: Gently." It's hard to describe the degree of my astonishment, my sense of insult, the feeling of emptiness. Finally, for the first and perhaps last time in our lives that we're sitting down to talk, this is all he has to say to me? Today I'm leaving his house and establishing my home, and that's it? For a long time, I carried this searing pain in my heart; so little, almost miserly.

Over the years that anger gave way to a wonderful insight. And when my children were married, this is how I blessed them: "Between today and tomorrow, with the rays of the sunset, we will send you off on your way, as is customary in our home, with the blessing of Grandpa, of blessed memory: 'Delicately.' Continue your enchanted beginnings delicately, set the pace delicately, take flight to the sky delicately, and with the same delicacy go deep into hearts. With the delicacy that typifies only you continue the legend so that it will never stop."

Because that lesson of gentleness was the essence of my parents' lives and the basis of all the relationships between me and all my loved ones, the members of my household. Sometimes one word is etched in memory more than an entire speech. That's how it was when I was sent on my way in life on the day of my wedding, which was his day of happiness, and that was his summary of my first experience on the public stage, the correction of the verse which in "his language" was an absolute recognition. I cherish and fondly remember all these words of his with longing and in a renewed search for meaning. Lucky, in fact, that he didn't say more, because then I would have enjoyed it at the time without retaining anything for all the moments in the future that await me.

THAT MASS DEMONSTRATION, WHICH WAS KNOWN LATER as the four-hundred-thousand-people protest, was a defining moment for me. It cemented my place in the public consciousness and reorganized, for the better, the whole fabric of relations between me and my parents. Our political differences improved and our relationship deepened. On the one hand, we understood each other much better. Contrary to the past, we now started to talk in the very same language. We loved and appreciated the same people, and the list of people we didn't particularly respect was almost the same. I thought that one was a liar, and my father sarcastically commented, "Not at all. He lies only to stay in shape." About another he claimed that "he lies even when he's silent." And about one of our common adversaries he had this to say with feigned affection, "He's a man of principle. Principle number one: opportunism." On the other hand, the deep differences between us on issues of religion and state, policy and political alliances were so significant that we didn't have to confront each other about them. It was obvious what our positions were, and we saved ourselves a great deal of time.

Still, my point of entry to the political atmosphere was not easy for him at all. Two weeks after that demonstration I received an invitation from Shimon Peres's office. He was then the leader of the opposition, who had already lost a few elections to Menachem Begin. We met in the ornate lobby of a hotel in Jerusalem. "I heard you speak at Malchei Yisrael Square two weeks ago and I was very impressed," he said. "I would like to offer you to join the Labor Party."

"What does that mean, exactly?" I asked, surprised.

"Just join the party, and I'll see to it that you will become a member of the central committee."

I didn't know precisely what the central committee was, but this institution still radiated great power at the time, the source of energy of the historic Labor Party.

"And what will I do there?" I wondered.

"What would you like to do in public life?"

"I want peace, and I want the separation of religion and state," I said, reciting the two pillars of the doctrine of my teacher and guide, Professor Yeshayahu Leibowitz.

"Excellent. So you will be the chairman of the platform committee for issues of religion and state," he said, concluding his offer.

Despite my surprise, I responded, "Thank you. I accept, but I ask that you give me a few days before making it public, so I have a chance to discuss it with my parents and tell them. So they won't hear it elsewhere first."

"Of course, of course. Give my regards to your parents, especially to your special mother."

"Thank you. I will call you after the Sabbath, after I speak with them."

The next day, very early in the morning, even before the hour that people from Germany thought was the polite time to call, the phone rang. On the line was my dad, literally crying, sobbing and swallowing his words. It turned out that immediately after the meeting with me, Peres went to the Labor Party branch in Jerusalem and publicly announced that I was joining the party. His announcement was reported in one of the back pages of the mythic labor movement *Davar* newspaper. It is doubtful if anyone saw it aside from my father, who was very hurt, not by the political decision but by the way he had found out about it. And he was right.

A few months later, the committee I was promised to chair convened. I arrived in the room, twenty years younger than the youngest member there. I had gotten ready for this meeting over many days. I had prepared my remarks and the committee agenda. I had intended to propose a process for adopting new and fundamental decisions on an issue that had not been dealt with much until then. I wanted to sit in the chairman's seat, "mine," and discovered it was already taken. Shimon Peres had already promised it to someone else, older, more aggressive, and far more experienced. He had arrived a half hour earlier and had taken the seat. That's how you create facts in the Labor Party. Needless to say, Peres was not there to resolve the complication created by his empty promises. The committee room was filled with people who had received promises from Peres that he had forgotten to keep.

Within the space of a few months I had met personally with two of the most significant figures in Israel, the prime minister and the leader of the opposition. Begin was an honest but weak man, surrounded by a coterie of admirers who protected him in every way possible, and who were not averse to deceiving the public for that purpose for many years, up until he resigned, worn out and feeble, in September 1983 with the painfully truthful statement of an honest man: "I can't go on." Peres was neither one nor the other, neither weak nor honest. There was only one thing they had in common: the need, the unquenchable thirst for popularity. Begin flirted endlessly with his audiences, and Peres, who was rejected as different, an "other," and was unloved for most of his career, bore his cross through all the stations of the Via Dolorosa until his popular redemption in the presidential residence in the twilight of his life. I still preferred Peres and his path over Begin—because of his path. At the time, I still believed that Peres was indeed a man of peace, and the rest was less important to me.

In the mass demonstration I described previously, a process began that culminated in the establishment of the state commission of inquiry into the massacre at the Sabra and Shatila refugee camps. The committee submitted its conclusions in the winter of 1983, the grimmest of winters. The government of Israel was very hesitant: to accept or not accept the report? To adopt or not adopt its conclusions? The report recommended dismissing Ariel Sharon from the post of defense minister, undoubtedly a great achievement for our unequivocal public demand. But Sharon, in true Sharon fashion, refused to resign.

In February 1983, masses of protestors took to the streets again. This time we asked to receive the report and its recommendations. A demonstration left from Zion Square in Jerusalem to the government complex. It passed for a few kilometers downtown, in my childhood neighborhood, all the places I knew and loved in the city when it still had some remnants of intimacy: Atara Café; the Hatik leather store; the Maoz HMO; Badihi's Falafel King stand, where I asked Yael to be my girlfriend and was rejected; Benny's Fish restaurant. This time the walk had no romance. It was one long, violent scene. Incited supporters of the government, rightist street thugs, repeatedly broke through the thin line of police that was supposed to protect us. In the moments of truth, during the event, I had the constant impression that the police were part of the rioters, and not a defense deployment against them. Spitting, tearing of clothes, shouts, curses, pushing, and actual blows. In the end, we arrived at a place across from the prime minister's office.

Upstairs, the government was meeting to discuss the commission report. They were up and we were down below, they in power and we in the street. We raised our voices, hoping to penetrate the sealed windows and deaf ears. I thought then that Begin, who for so many years had been in the opposition, would understand the meaning of the street protest more than his colleagues in the cabinet. We raised placards, speeches were given, and we sang the national anthem. There's always a very special pause between the end of such an activity and the return to private routine. A minute of transition from the adrenaline high to everyday ordinariness. A moment when everything stops. This is the time of calm between all kinds of storms. Into this special moment, right at the end of the last strains of the hoarse "Hatikva" that crackled from the makeshift loudspeakers, burst an unmistakable sound—the explosion of the detonator cap of a hand grenade. My soldiering instinct, still imprinted in me, counted off in my head by itself: "Twenty-one, twenty-two, twenty-three. Boom." Grenade! Somewhere on my left a deadly hand grenade had been thrown out of the darkness, and like all my colleagues who were there we became participatory witnesses to the first political assassination of our lives, in which Emil Grunzweig, a friend and a devoted peace activist, was murdered by Yona Avrushmi, a right-wing zealot.

The large crowd began running in all directions. Someone fell next to me. And another. I bent down and began giving first aid. I don't remember any thoughts going through my head as I hunched over the wounded person at my feet, just lots of legs, shoes, socks, and cuffed jeans in the style of that time. Nothing aside from the silent vacuum that always prevails in pressure situations. Thoughts disappear, leaving only the operating system in automatic mode. Tourniquet, calming down, tearing a shirt, and dressing the wound. A large vehicle, a Volkswagen van, arrived out of nowhere. I carried someone in my hands, and then another person, and we hurried together to the nearest hospital, Shaare Zedek. When it was all over, someone said, "Avrum, you have a hole in your coat and blood on your back." I took the coat off, and I discovered that I had been hit by a fragment from the grenade and hadn't even felt it.

In seconds, everything took on an entirely new dimension. From being a responder I became a casualty. I was laid down on a bed in the emergency room. They stripped me, then cleaned and dressed the wound. And all around there was a big commotion of doctors, police officers, photographers, peace activists, noisy rightist thugs, and ordinary busybodies who always gather in emergency rooms. I felt a great weariness. The entire load of the recent months and the changes in my situation landed on me at once. Unable to sleep, I asked to call Yael, who was at home with the kids. A short time later I sensed movement on the other side of the curtain that separated patients from the large space of the emergency room. The curtain was pulled aside, and my father stood there. He had left the fateful cabinet meeting, gone through a transformation, and was again my father.

Something between horrible worry and liberating relief was etched on his face. I was so happy to see him. I loved him so much at that moment. The whole world went quiet around us. Searching for the picture that would frame the event, a quote, a gesture, or an expressive face. And we felt as if it were just the two of us in the world. I drowned myself in his kind eyes. And he too leaped through my eyes directly into the depths of my soul, and I immediately knew that all the bad years between the two of us were behind us. But I didn't know that all the bad years for Israel still lay ahead.

CHAPTER FIVE

AN ALIEN
IN THE KNESSET
(1988–1992)

I WAS ELECTED TO PARLIAMENT, THE KNESSET, IN 1988. I
was thirty-three years old, quite young to be a member of the Knesset, maybe too young. Were I elected today, knowing what I know now, I would be a better member of parliament, serving my constituents much better. In my first years, I wasn't sharp and precise enough. I don't want to unpack my long career from the limited perspective of that youth who saw through the old and foolish emperor's new clothes, nor as an active and involved player whose nakedness was also exposed, but as a somewhat distant observer with considerable experience. At a certain moment, I realized that I was part of the empire, the government, and the kingdom. That's life. Youth is lost, and the empire is almost always naked even when you are part of it. And when there is nakedness, your private parts are also exposed.

Reuven Rivlin, a close personal friend and now the state president, told me, "My father used to say that the higher the donkey goes up on the ladder, the more his backside is visible." It took me a very long time to understand the essence of the Knesset: where the ladders are, and who sees what of whom. When I understood, I didn't always have partners for conversation and action on the basis of this understanding, and I wasn't always an appropriate partner for others.

It began badly. In the past, parliamentary correspondents would summarize in the press the first plenary session of the new parliament members, an attempt of sorts to predict who is a flash in the pan and who is made of long-term parliamentary stuff. At first I didn't know to which category I belonged. No wonder, therefore, that my activity was summed up this way by one of the more malicious reporters: "Avrum Burg is wandering the corridors of the Knesset like an alien connected to his beeper and waiting for a message from another planet." This is a quote whose accuracy I didn't bother to check in the archives. It was engraved in me verbatim, like a searing brand that will never be forgotten. It's difficult to describe my shock when I read those words, the insult and fear of the terrible failure I faced. And worst of all—he was right. I watched haplessly as my colleagues were making their mark in the media and being appreciated, legislating, joining debates in the plenum and committees, and expressing opinions in faction meetings, while I remained mute at best, inarticulate at worst. I invested my energy in gimmicks and blunt statements in order to get some media attention, but as someone told me in an off-the-cuff comment at the time, "You won't get anywhere because you're not hungry for anything." He too was right, and my spirits were very low. I needed fame, but I wasn't hungry for it—because I was already a bit famous. I didn't pursue unimportant legislation just to get into the Knesset statistics books, and I didn't try to rack up as many speeches and parliamentary questions as I could on patently marginal issues.

I wanted to deal with the pure issues for which I had entered the public meat grinder. I wanted to deal with history and substance. But to my chagrin, I discovered that I had come to the wrong address. In the main public arena, the Israeli Knesset, there is virtually no activity dealing with the central issues of Israeli society. It is a junction where all interests meet and collide, like a very busy street market. A real arena, with struggles, violence, and all the rest. A lot of tactical realities, but surprisingly little strategic substance. Religious people of various shades don't meet in synagogue but in the Knesset, where they fight and quarrel with the full force of their beliefs. Jews and Arabs don't encounter each other anymore on city streets or in places of work because ethnic separation is very effective here. The same goes for new immigrants and longtime residents, the city center and the suburbs, the bourgeoisie and socialists, religious and secular people, and so on. For all these groups, all that remains is the Knesset plenum, and therefore the friction there is sometimes violent to the point of physical altercation. The Knesset deals with many day-to-day matters, and usually it suffers from a huge and unnecessary load of minor current affairs and pettiness. Knesset members live in their own tree and don't always see the Israeli forest, with the demons and wild animals prowling it.

At that time, I had two sails propelling my political boat forward. The sail of separation of religion and state, and the sail of peace, both powered by the wind of one person—my teacher and guide, the late professor Yeshayahu Leibowitz. From my childhood to the day of his death, his figure was like light and shadow, part of my life. Today's Jerusalem is almost empty of its original children and packed with immigrants from the West—especially from the United States and France—with their luxury apartments. In the early days of the Israeli enterprise when I was young, the city was much smaller, but its people loomed large. Martin Buber and S. Y. Agnon, David Flusser and Marcel Dubois, Miriam Yellin-Steklis and Zelda, Israel Eldad and Yeshayahu Leibowitz walked the streets like ordinary people. You could approach them on a street corner. You could often see people buttonholing one of these celebrities and launching into long-winded debate or a discussion of current events. Leibowitz was always there—a long-legged intellectual with a crooked back, gangly with a spring in his step, carrying a battered leather case and wearing a thin-brimmed hat, his expression half enigmatic and half curious, watching the world and criticizing it.

Over the years, I had the privilege of getting closer to Leibowitz, studying with him and learning from him, so I considered myself the representative of his values and path in the Knesset. Then I still lived an Orthodox life and I ignored the structural contradiction at the root of his worldview, the contrast between his wonderful openness and the rigidity of Jewish law to which he was committed. From time to time, I found issues in the Knesset that I took up, but most times I returned home sad, depressed, and with a sense of missed opportunity. The amendment to the "pork law"—whether it could be permitted to import pork to the Jewish state, something that was "unheard of and un-thought of" according to the common coalition hypocrisy—was a sad example of how matters proceeded. In my view the original law, like the proposed amendment, was pure religious coercion. A prostitution of religious values for the sake of rabbinic interests, the work of kippah-wearing religious thugs. The law was characteristic of the religious establishment's cynical use of its political power. It stood in stark contrast to my view of the desired relationship between religion and state.

In my vote, I wanted to apply what I had imbibed in Leibowitz's home on Ussishkin Street in Jerusalem when I was young—complete separation of religion and state. But the Labor faction imposed factional discipline, because, as always, the fate of the coalition depended on this vote. "If we don't stand together as one, the religious parties will withdraw," "the ultra-Orthodox politicians will be angry," and "Rabin and Peres may go back to quarrelling with one another" or, God forbid, fall from power. And any rookie Knesset member knows this: power is not the main thing—it's the only thing. I abstained from the vote and felt like a spineless, gutless rag. And there were many more such votes.

In my first term, 1988–1992, the media published several stories about mistakes by ritual circumcisers or medical complications caused by neglect during circumcisions. As was customary in parliament, I immediately submitted a bill to regulate the entire circumcision realm. It kicked around the corridors, got reasonable media coverage, and in the end, did not receive a shred of support in the ministerial committee for legislation. I still wanted to raise the issue for a Knesset vote, and suddenly the pressure was on. Ministers and directors-general, the prime minister himself and his lackeys became overnight experts on the cutting-edge subject for Jewish newborns. It turned out that, again, the resilience of the always-fragile Israeli coalition was hanging by a thread. And, again, as usual, the ultra-Orthodox parties threatened. And, again, as usual, the leaders of the country were scared and scrambling. Meetings were arranged for me with current and former chief rabbis, with representatives of the ritual circumcisers and of the Israeli Medical Association. They all made pilgrimages to me, made promises and broke them, deceived me, threatened me with fifty shades of threats, and in the end, as expected, the coalition easily survived. The bill was defeated in deafening silence.

A large majority was mobilized against my vote and the votes of a few assertive members of the opposition who happened to be in the plenum. The ritual circumcisers continued to work without medical training and supervision, and all the promises I was given were ignored. And on the other hand, at the same time I managed to pass an amendment to the law requiring the leashing of dogs. The lesson couldn't have been more bluntly clear: I can legislate regarding dogs, because they have no rabbinate and party hacks, they have no power in the coalition nor the ability to make threats or break promises. But God forbid I should touch the tip of a newborn baby's penis, because on him rests the future of the entire Jewish people, or at least that of a few politicians who claim to represent it. From that point on I virtually stopped making the effort to pass bills and legislate just for the sake of statistics and unimportant laws.

These disappointments and many others compelled me to look inward, deeper, into the essence of being a parliamentarian. There are two possible models. The first is the vanishing breed, the public servant, who in addition to his personal urges is motivated by a real sense of mission. The second, proliferating like weeds, is nothing but a public scarecrow or political technician. When I recognized this crossroads, I knew what I did not want to be. I didn't want to grow old in the temple of democracy and become a tired priest, like that venerable member who told me at one faction meeting, "I was always against the war in Lebanon." And I, who remembered every one of them and their evasive excuses, didn't quite recall his resolute stance. At the height of that war of lies I had requested a meeting with him, when I was still a young activist, and I had a different recollection of his position.

"Really?" I interjected. "I don't remember."

"Of course," he said. "I even wrote an anonymous poem in the *Maariv* newspaper against the war." I didn't want to be a poet like him.

Parliamentary life is very intense, especially when you're finding your way like me and running around all day in search of yourself. It doesn't leave any time for reflection and thought. Long days at the Knesset and other days, just as long, of politics, voters, party branches and institutions, recruiting support, and endless conversations with constituents. In order to preserve the family and sanity, and to recharge, we strictly observed certain guidelines at home. Friday and Saturday were always devoted to the children, and the annual vacation was greatly anticipated and a source of strength and renewal. At the time, we liked to travel down to the Sinai Peninsula, not only because of the soothing wide-open spaces, but also because of the message to the children— you can travel abroad by car. We wanted them to know that the Israeli reality is not only a siege wall on all sides; it also has breaches of peace, like the southern border crossings. Precisely there, as far as possible from the commotion in Jerusalem, from the tension, from the brutal competition and scathing criticism, I gained an understanding of the new reality I was living in.

We were on a hike in the high mountains of Sinai, along with friends, Bedouin escorts, a few camels, and the expanses of creation. For many hours, I walked behind a camel and thought. An irrepressible mental association ran an old Talmudic saying through my head again and again: "One who sees a camel in a dream—death was decreed against him from heaven and he was saved from it." I thought about the gap between the negative Jewish image of the camel and the great love, dependence, and appreciation felt by the Bedouin for their camels. There are those who think that the camel is an expression of what is bad in the world and others think that it is the source of vitality in the world. And the camel? He's the same camel, what does he care. So why do I care so much about what certain people or others think of me? I'm a camel walking in the desert. Sometimes I drink, sometimes I'm thirsty. All I lack is the camel's patience. To walk slowly and go far. That was one of the two times in which I altered the pace of my life. I returned changed from that vacation in Sinai. I was done with ingratiating myself, and I let go of much of the drivel associated with exclusively media-directed behavior. I had searched for and found part of myself.

I N THOSE DAYS IN THE EARLY 1990S, THE LABOR PARTY was mired in another one of its deep crises. The years-long partnership with the conservative Likud Party in coalition governments had effectively eliminated the existence of an opposition as a vital supplier of alternatives in Israeli politics. My party had simply given up its role as a genuine alternative, surrendered, and committed hara-kiri. We were treated as a venerable old lady, sometimes respected because of her past, and sometimes a barely tolerated nuisance. We occasionally provoked anger because of our inability to let the Likud govern without helicopter parenting. Fatigue had spread throughout the system, and another election defeat seemed closer than ever. And this in the wake of a searing and painful failure in trying to unseat Prime Minister Yitzhak Shamir by means of a not particularly successful political maneuver. "The stinking maneuver," Rabin called it in his dry, colorful language. Gloom settled over us. Together and as individuals, we had reached a low point. And we didn't know then that there were even lower ones ahead.

On the eve of Yom Kippur in 1991, I left a meeting of the Knesset
Finance Committee with Haim Ramon, a veteran Labor lawmaker and
the architect of "the stinking maneuver." Ramon's face reflected reality—pale and desperate. "Avrum, we're lost," he told me. I was, at the
time, a political novice, without much understanding of loss and success. I sensed that I had an opportunity to connect with politics with
the tools that I knew. Like that camel, walk slowly but go far. "Haim,
I have an idea," I told him. "Let's draw up a position paper with all
'our' issues and go for broke. Against the old folks, against the establishment, against all the disgusting people, come what may. At worst,
we'll die standing tall and not like dishrags." This collegial discussion
led to a document of principles that was original and novel in the political landscape of the time. We recruited our immediate friends and
a few pillars of the party and presented the party convention with "the
Document of Ten," a statement of principles on behalf of ten parliament members and central party figures that offered a good alternative
to the moldy ideology of the Labor Party. We intended to employ all
our political energy to promote these principles at the coming party
convention.

The statement of principles endorsed the immediate reform of the
Labor Party's corrupt linkage with Israel's organization of trade unions
as well as with the unions' health service organizations. Our statement
sowed the first seeds of the Oslo agreements, and it was the beginning
of the change from socialist hypocrisy ("Bolshevik," we called it among
ourselves) to a much more contemporary social-democratic worldview. That party convention was eventually convened and was cast in
advance as a generational struggle. Our young political group against
the old, worn "rest of the world." I'm not convinced that anyone in the
future will ever consider those days historic. But there was something
like it then.

Haim Ramon gave a wonderful speech at the convention, where he
described the fading labor movement as a whale committing suicide.
He portrayed the Labor Party as a whale swimming to shore to die

there, and how he, Haim Ramon, with his "meager resources" was trying to save it from its suicidal fate. I was in the audience and was very moved. It's not often that you have the privilege of being present at a public birth, the birth of a leader. Then Yossi Beilin took the stage and presented our political thesis. It was worth living through the previous decade, from the Lebanon War up to the decision by the convention, to feel with all my soul that we were moving the wagon that was stuck. We were agents of change, and we had influence.

In the afternoon, it was my turn. The time had come for discussion of issues of religion and state, and I had the honor of raising the subject on behalf of our group. None of my colleagues remained; political solidarity doesn't always function perfectly. Few of my partners considered the subject important, and none of them believed that it was really possible to change anything in this area. The atrophied religious status quo was the comfort zone where everyone felt good hunkering down. The fact that I had come from another place—religious Zionism— with the public status I enjoyed gave me a perspective that was a bit higher and broader, and I could see the sickness of the system with my own eyes. Everywhere I went I felt religious extremism: in my family circle, in the fiery speeches in the synagogues, in the size of the kippahs and women's head coverings among my former friends from my yeshiva past, in the length of the ritual fringes, in the condescension and resentment toward secularism and secular people, and the disconnection from family that the missionaries of return to religion had imposed on their victims. I identified the breaches that religious and ultra-Orthodox politics were going to open in the Israeli body politic. On the other side, I could already hear the beating of the tom-toms in the secular jungle, the hatred of the ultra-Orthodox, which would soon produce the Shinui Party with the hostile, almost anti-Semitic and blunt agenda of its late leader, Tommy Lapid.

I thought that our proposal for separating religion and state was a complete structural alternative that could save Israel from the one issue that has the real potential of causing bloodshed: internecine strife and

civil war over issues of the identity of our undefined state. "I don't entirely agree with you," one of my partners told me, "but go for it, anyway, it doesn't have a chance." I spoke, I thought, persuasively. I felt that
the audience was listening to me, that it was thirsty and yearning for a
totally different message on a subject that, while not at the center of political reality, stirred anger in everyone encountering it. My speech was
over and well received, a few other comments later and the chairman
of the convention counted the votes, and lo and behold, our "gang of
ten" proposition won the majority.

It is difficult to describe the uproar that erupted in the convention
hall. Loud applause. Hugs along with cries of distress. The industrious,
hard-working party hacks summoned the mythic heads of the party,
Rabin and Peres, and all the rest of their comrades. The chairman, a
consigliere for dirty jobs with a clean image, requested another vote.
And I tried to again persuade those who had just joined the debate.
The scene played out again, and again I won the vote. It was a great
moment, perhaps the highest point I had ever reached in public life. I
was practicing the politics of values and meaning, and I was happy. For
a few hours, I experienced all the excitement of power and influence,
and all in the name of ideas and the mission that I believe in to this day.

I didn't know that precisely at that moment my public position was
in jeopardy. Greatness and smallness were apparently intertwined
when they were brought into this world. The main headline of one of
the important papers announced, "Avrum Burg put a gun to the head
of the Labor Party." And the subhead sharpened the message: "And
he pulled the trigger." In another paper my dear father was quoted:
"Avrum has lost his chance to be elected to the next Knesset." And
Dad, who understood old-style politics better than anyone else, really
thought so. I wasn't really insulted, because his voice was part of a huge
chorus that was trying to understand what had happened. I was part of
a reshaping of the Israeli conversation. He and they were still stuck in
the past, and I was already in the new era, which ultimately responded
completely differently than he had expected.

The next internal elections of the Labor Party were held in 1992 for the first time ever as a primary among the party's members. Hundreds of thousands of them. To the surprise of all, I came in first place. Shimon Peres and Yitzhak Rabin were hysterical. In my heart, quietly, I reassured myself: What do they know about religion and state? Give them the army and soldiers, deniable atomic bombs, settlers and political operators, and they will prove their buoyancy and swimming skills, two world freestyle champions. But just confront them with something that has to do with the essence of Judaism and Israeli identity, and the two greats of the generation lose their way and their composure. All the "big chiefs" like Rabin and Peres cared about were the elections around the corner, the coalition with the religious and ultra-Orthodox that they had dreamt would return them to power and the pleasures of compromise.

For three weeks, the entire national leadership of the party exerted heavy pressure on me, sent messengers, and expected me to take the chestnuts out of the fire for them by withdrawing my proposal and betraying my values. Some did it in candid conversations, in promises intended to be broken the minute they were given, and with smooth talk. Others spoke to me with direct and indirect threats, including the cold frowns of Rabin himself. They and their aides were not averse to any media manipulation possible. I stubbornly persisted, and the situation became a Catch-22: if the decision were overturned, they would lose the support of the young people who backed me, those who had had enough of the religious establishment, and of the emphatically secular element that traditionally supports the party. On the other hand, if the decision stood, they would have nearly no room for maneuvering with their religious coalition partners. They were caught between me and them. In the end, the party's institutions, its central committee and convention, convened and approved an embarrassing formulation in tortuous Shimon Peres style, whose essence was this gambit: even though the party convention made the famous decision three weeks ago regarding separation of religion and state, it actually didn't intend to separate religion and state, and so on and so forth. Both yes and no, and also maybe, both for and against the religious parties, and vice versa. I saw the sea of hands go up. The very same hands that supported me just a few weeks earlier removed me now from their agenda.

I stood in the hall choked with tears, small, pitiful, and humiliated. I had looked to the great Shimon Peres, and discovered, not for the last time, how callous his opportunism and hypocrisy could be. It was the lowest point of my political career. Until then, my actions in the political arena had been driven by values, principles, and beliefs. Every morning I got up for my public work with a clean and sincere heart. If this were to happen today, now that I'm experienced and scarred, I would react differently. I would get up and leave. But then I didn't have the resolve. I submitted to the harsh decree and to the cynicism of the decision. I said to myself, "That's how it is in politics. Sometimes you win, sometimes you lose." Or, "It's worth compromising because we still have many great tasks ahead: peace, justice, equality." I applied many mechanisms of self-deception so that I wouldn't do what might have been expected of me—to flee as far as possible. Not so much because of the substance of the issue or because of the public atmosphere that surrounded this small loss, but because with all the background noise and voices, I had stopped listening to myself. I accepted the quasi-democratic verdict and bowed my head.

It was the moment in which I told myself one of the two political lies that shaped my life. Separation of religion and state was not just another issue or compromise, one of many that any person is compelled to make in the course of his life, certainly if he is a political person who understands that politics entails constant compromise with existing possibilities. The minute I surrendered to Peres's machinations, I stopped being a man of substance and became a professional politician. I gave up on my mission for the sake of my career. I compromised on my internal identity in return for my external status. That was not how I understood matters then. It took me many more years to be able to look back without anger and understand that I had been wrong. If the captain of a ship is off by a millimeter in the vicinity of Malta and does not correct himself in time, he may ultimately reach Australia and not America. Those minutes, between the euphoria of pure achievement and the humiliation of odious compromise were my millimeter, my Malta. I got lost there, and I didn't find my true path again until I completely left the political track, freed myself from my previous bonds, and learned how to navigate anew and differently with my internal compass.

It was, however, precisely the hiding and disguise that made my public breakthroughs possible. During fifteen short years, from 1988 to 2003, the deeper I concealed my values and ideology, thoughts and understanding, the more I succeeded in climbing up the ladder. Member of Knesset, committee chairman, Jewish Agency chairman, Knesset speaker. And the horizon was still open and inviting. Sometimes when I analyze election results I sense that Israelis want to choose the politician who deludes them better than the others. The voter and the elected representative both know that it's a fraud. But for a moment, the moment of elections, there is hope, and for the sake of that, leaders who destroy hope are elected time and again. To tell the truth, it wasn't so hard to attain those positions. The secret was restraint, holding the stormy winds inside and appearing outwardly in the moderate garb that everyone loves so much, "because that's what everyone does."

CHAPTER SIX

DECLINE AND REDEMPTION (2001–2004)

N OT LONG AGO, IN 2014, I WAS RUNNING ALONG THE Yarkon River in Tel Aviv and tracking the signs announcing plans to rehabilitate the water source that not long ago was a symbol of the pollution of Israel's streams. Through beads of sweat and my rapid breathing I suddenly noticed not only the information, but the style of the language as well. The project's name was "Redemption of the Yarkon," no less. I stopped and laughed. In Judaism, there's no redemption without a messiah, so now there's probably someone who is the "messiah of the Yarkon." And he has a white donkey, on whose back he wanders along the Tel Aviv canal. (According to a Jewish tradition, the redeeming messiah will appear as a poor man riding a white donkey.) When I resumed running, the term "redemption" lodged in my head, and for many kilometers I reflected on this quintessentially Zionist word.

The early Zionists never bought land, or made real estate deals. They were busy with "land redemption." They never tried to refashion the Jewish body and soul here. They were far more comprehensive and ambitious than that. They were busy with "human redemption."

And redemption is a word so loaded with the baggage of the end of days, faith, and messianism, that it can't be assigned to the secular part of identity. From there my thoughts drifted to the Labor Party, which was the firstborn daughter of the Zionist movement. In fact, it's a party that developed in the womb of modern Jewish messianism, within the doctrine of human redemption and the redemption of land and ideology. It is not a secular movement in the Western sense of the term. It could be that my second self-deception stemmed from there, and from my mistaken understanding of the method of Israeli division between "religious" and "secular."

This lying to myself actually began the moment I joined the Labor Party. From many years observing Israeli, Jewish, and international public life, I had learned something very simple. In politics, in any politics, there are actually two basic strategies. One is "the strategy of the big ship," according to which if you can commandeer the big ship, you are king of the ocean. The second strategy—"the small boat"—is the complete opposite. According to this concept, the big ship is sometimes too big and almost always blind. It will always need the small boat, the pilot boat, to steer it away from icebergs, from hidden coral reefs lurking on its course, and to guide it safely to port, to the right pier and protected anchorage. Since I grew up in a political home that was always part of the fleet of big ships in Israel, I didn't devote any of my attention to clarifying my true internal character. I wasn't sufficiently aware that what was appropriate for Dad and his historic partnership in the team of big ships was really not appropriate for me. I wanted to achieve opposite goals, but with the same tools, and I didn't understand the internal contradiction. I never devoted time to thinking about who I was. A seaman on a giant ship or a sailor on a small boat? It turns out that at the start of my political path I got on the wrong vessel and told the second big lie to myself. I got on the sinking *Titanic* of the Labor Party; I didn't seek to find my natural place on the small boat piloting and navigating a course with much greater ethical precision.

From there it might have been possible to save the sinking flagship of Israeliness.

Today, I'm not an establishment person. On the contrary, I'm always comfortable with radical positions and feel at my best when examining unconventional ideas. I'm no longer addicted to the public's approval, and I'm prepared to be in strict and brutal personal and public isolation, as long as I am at peace with myself and with the truths that motivate me. Like many of my colleagues, it was easy for me on the political Ferris wheel, sometimes up, sometimes down, but always connected to the centers of power. Absorbing scathing criticism, but always having status. In our house we would say, "You can tell that guy has a thick skin." I had wrapped myself in a thick skin, not mine, until that thick skin became too heavy, and it was all over. For a few years, I kept walking in the air like a cartoon character, without noticing that the land under my feet was no longer there. Only with time—especially after my intense term as the Speaker of the Knesset, which ended with the failure of my party during the 2003 elections—and upon further reflection did I realize that I was living in a political system to which I didn't belong at all.

The Labor Party was once the biggest ship in the Israeli sea. It was the stable ship in which I and many others had wanted to sail to distant shores. And it too sank, reached its expiration date as far as I was concerned, and with the decades and decay we had become incompatible. And when I continued telling myself the allegory of the ships, it became painfully clear to me from my failures that I'm not only a sailor of small pilot ships; I want to always be at their prow. But alas, in the party I represented and where I was active most of my political life there was no advance guard, no power, and no decisive capability whatsoever. Actually, this whole bloc, in its current makeup, doesn't have it. A neutered giant devoid of ideas and positions, aside from the constant thirst for power wherever it may be. All that remains of that heavy and formidable ship is just its weight.

One of the deepest tragedies of the Jewish left in Israel is that it has become very conservative. Every one of the political organizations that today make up the left zealously protects something that was, anchored in the past, part real and part imagined, but most of it irrelevant. Many of these organizations want to preserve their privileges and attendant comforts as well-established Ashkenazic Jews, to fix the minimum that needs repair and not change a thing. Very few new ideas, movements, or fresh cultural content have come out of the Israeli left in recent generations. And even if they exist, they are far away, on the fringes. This is sad, especially in comparison with what is happening in Israel's right wing.

Gush Emunim was avant-garde compared to the founding generation of my father and his cohort of political operators. Gush Emunim (Bloc of the Faithful) was an Israeli messianic, right-wing activist movement committed to establishing Jewish settlements in the West Bank, the Gaza Strip, and the Golan Heights. Emerging from the conquests of the Six-Day War in 1967, it encouraged Jewish settlement of those lands based on the belief that, according to the Torah, God gave them to the Jewish people. It was a determined, ideological, and daring group that galvanized a substantial following behind it. One would have expected things to eventually calm down and settle into established patterns as the pendulum swung back to the other side of the political map. But the avant-garde phase didn't end, it continued in the same direction. Their children, the hilltop youth, are just as frightening. They are rebels who have come out against their parents, the political operators of Gush Emunim—those who just a generation ago were great innovators and have now become entrenched conservatives.

The politics of the right is paved and inlaid with avant-garde content that is extremist, outrageous, but innovative. And our left is old and tired. Not only in its sociological and demographic profiles, but mainly in its terminology. Time and again we repeat the mantra, "We founded the state," as if it were still a work in progress, though it is pushing seventy. There's nostalgia for the good old days, though I suspect that those days were never as wonderful as imagined by those who miss them. Very little is invested in disrupting the present and creating a different future with a completely different social and human agenda. The words are the same words, the arguments almost never change, and the yearning is for a return to "the good old Land of Israel." The Jewish left—which had shattered all conventions with its bold Zionist rebellion against mother Judaism in the diaspora, that didn't hesitate to come out against the wheeler-dealer culture of the *shtetl*, against the patronage of the lords and synagogue officers, that presented an alternative worldview of egalitarianism and socialism—has become the bastion of secular conservatism in Israeli society.

S O IT TURNED OUT THAT I HAD ERRED TWICE: I EMBARKED on the wrong vessel to cross the stormy political ocean, and among the big ships, I boarded one that wasn't fit for me at all—the Labor Party—the mother of all conservatives. It actually never was and will never be a substantive, real left. Because left is not just the rhetoric of a diplomatic settlement and an endless flirtation with the peace process in order to avoid paying the price of peace itself. "I prefer to compromise in words and not in acres," Shimon Peres once confided in me. And I'm not sure that the Nobel Peace Prize really changed his approach. A real left is a much more comprehensive conception. Real equality between all citizens, with no difference between men and women in any area; uncompromising struggle for secularization of public space and separation of religion from the state; constitutional, governmental, and moral equalization of all citizens, Jewish and Arab, in all spheres; a social and democratic effort to narrow gaps and fairly distribute public resources—virtually no one offers all this to the Israeli voter. It would be wrong to say that the left in Israel has vanished—it is simply yet to be born.

It is difficult for me to write and read these things. It is sad to think of what might have been. On that path, I reached the top of some of the loftiest hills. I had the privilege of standing in high places and seeing long distances. I can't complain about my "career," but I also can't ignore some of my blind spots back then, and some inappropriate compromises I made with myself, between my politician self and the part of me that is a believer, between my progressive self and the part allied with the conservatives. The narrow crack between these two worlds was revealed to me by coincidence.

In 2002, I was sitting at home, lost in thought after one of the worst defeats I had suffered in my life—the race for leadership of the Labor Party. I had won the internal elections, and then the corrupt establishments, led by the best of the thuggish party hacks, stole the victory from my voters and me. The millimeter of Malta had grown to a meter. Those were sad days. I knew that I had to decide about my future, but I couldn't identify the alternatives I had to choose from. I felt that something essential was changing in public life, that a deep corruption of democratic processes had been expressed in this ugly struggle. I already felt the earthquakes and saw cracks in structures that seemed eternally stable. Though I didn't know the precise nature of the ugliness descending upon us, I knew that it was coming and I knew that it was bad. The thoughts, the soul-searching, and the turning inward for renewal went on for many days. Outwardly everything went on normally. I smiled when necessary, stung and bit when I could—business as usual. But inside everything was at a boil.

"Dad, I know why you lost," my dear firstborn son said, suddenly slicing through my tangled threads of thought. We were both sitting at the kitchen table, eating breakfast and preparing for a day that had just begun. He was still sleepy, and I had been awake for a few hours after another restless night. He was staring at the cereal box, and I was browsing the morning paper.

"I didn't lose," I snapped at him without thinking.

"Who cares?" he replied, cutting through the curtains of words. "I know why."

"So why?"

"Because you didn't want it," he said and left the table.

For many days, I carried around that thought in my head. His arrow pierced the center of the target, right in my forehead. How could he say I didn't want it? I had invested so much time and energy, lost family time, and made personal concessions. I had poured so much into my career—is someone who doesn't want it ready to pay such a price? I asked myself the most banal of rhetorical questions and in the end, I honed my answer. I had wanted, but not that. I wanted something else. And he, who came from my heart, knew me from the inside better than myself. In retrospect, it was a terrible but also wonderful moment. My boy, "my strength and first fruit of my vigor," revealed to me the flagrant violation of my internal balance. For half of my life, until then, I had fled public service, refused it, and was hostile to it. In midlife I was swept into it out of a commitment to high and lofty values and aspirations that were entirely pure and worthy. And there I was at dawn next to my adolescent son, who told me with adolescent bluntness, "Dad, you're not what you wanted to be, what you could have been, what you should be."

T HIS THOUGHT BECAME A PART OF MY BODY. THERE wasn't a place where I didn't encounter it. Everything was accompanied by the question, Do I want it? Want it enough? Really want it? Is this what I want? Is this me at all? This is a profound question that forces you to jump high over the hurdle of desire, the immediate need for achievement. To transcend the childish inability of many of us, living in the consumer era of the modern world, to delay gratification. This is the real question that activates the internal compass, time and again. At first I thought of desire as part of the ego. Yes, I had wanted strength and power "in order to have an influence and bring change," I reassured myself. I'm no stranger to strength and I understand the importance of power. But very deep inside I wanted recognition and status. I wanted to show Mom—who never stopped telling me, "they won't let you"—how wrong she was. And besides, what political person doesn't need those two assets, recognition and status, as his constant companions? Slowly the meanings of this desire changed. From desire for self-gratification to another desire, more measured and much more reflective. The desire, and with it the readiness to live according to my beliefs as they are. Today I am what I am by virtue of what my eldest son, and later the rest of my children, brought out in me.

Obviously, this required me to examine deeply what those beliefs are. It's difficult to be inside a political system and live fully according to your convictions. For thinking people, for perfectionists, politics is a kind of jail. The constant compromise, the necessary caution, the endless tradeoffs, and living at the whim of others are prison bars that are difficult to breach. When you're inside, you're so accustomed to the schedule, way of life, the wardens, and the menu, that it's not clear to you at all that you're confined. I gained these first insights in the very early stages, but I didn't know how to decipher them.

Once, in the early 1990s, I spoke from the Knesset podium about the ideas of Yeshayahu Leibowitz. When I came down from the podium after my remarks, the plenum was almost empty except for a few of the plenum regulars. Who cares about the ideas of an annoying philosopher? One of the veteran parliament members from the Labor Party came over to me and said, "You spoke so well, well done, but what an extremist!" She was a case study of surviving in the system. A model parliamentarian, industrious and hardworking. A typical example of the perpetual Knesset member. Always in the exact middle of the center. "Not extreme right, and not extreme left." She symbolized responsible discretion and always managed to get elected time and again, though no one knew what her real views were, as if she didn't have any at all.

A decade later, I defended in the plenum an article I had published in the international press entitled "Zionism Is Dead." Knesset members from the right attacked me, and I teased them joyfully. How many times in life is the Knesset agenda devoted to a polemic against your values and ideology? And again, as was customary, I stepped down from the podium expecting feedback from my colleagues. And again, one of the Labor Party Knesset members, the heir of the previous one (who finally retired at an old age) and much blunter, warned me, "With opinions like those you won't be elected again to the Knesset." She gave me credit, and spoke with a kind of collegial responsibility as she understood it. She too had spent many years in public service and had reached high-level positions. And her opinions were also not exactly known. Because according to the rules of our politics, the less the voters know about your opinions, the greater the chances that many will vote for you.

The high point was inside me, in the plenum of the heart. Early one morning in 2004, like every morning, I sat alone in my corner at home and wrote. In those mornings, I tried to understand, for myself, what would be the quid pro quo for which Israel would be prepared to give up its denied atomic bombs. The bombs from Dimona, which became a highly important asset during the years of existential threat to Israel, and are becoming a growing burden in the Middle East and internationally before our very eyes. At dawn I thought and wrote, testing my limits. Later the sun shone and evicted me from my desk. I went to the Knesset—my place of work at the time. I was a member of the Knesset's constitutional committee, and with perfect timing the topic on the committee's agenda was "the terms of release of Mordechai Vanunu." Vanunu is a former nuclear technician and peace activist who was accused of exposing the details of Israel's nuclear weapons program to the British press in 1986 and was ultimately convicted and sentenced to eighteen years in prison. Near his release date in 2004, members of the security and intelligence establishment presented members of the committee with the terms under which "the atomic spy" would be released. It wasn't the first time, nor the last, when I found it hard to escape the feeling that these people don't really understand what law is, what punishment is, and what they can and cannot do. Apparently, a country without defined and recognized borders cultivates such people, without inhibitions or limits, and makes them responsible for guarding its non-borders. As they spoke about the draconian,

Soviet-like conditions they planned to impose on Vanunu as he returned to civilian life after serving his full sentence, I was stewing in
my thoughts.

The truth is, I had to admit to myself, Vanunu and I wanted the
same thing, at least in theory. A Middle East free of weapons of mass
destruction. I think about it as a fairly patriotic political intellectual,
and he was involved in real treason, for which he was convicted and
sent to prison. A genuine division on the surface—but at bottom, no
difference. Like in many cases in my life, the opposites meet at their
roots. Then came the operative thought: can I say this here, in the
committee room? Should I share my ruminations with my colleagues
and cause them to think differently? And the obvious answer was—no.
Don't you dare, I warned myself in silence. It was doubtful that I would
have been able to explain myself, doubtful if they would be able to understand me or the content of my remarks. One thing was clear—the
angry shouts would cut me off before I would be able to express the
logical sequence of my position. So, I kept quiet. Because in the open
prison that is called Israeli public politics there is no room for such
thoughts. And perhaps there is no room for free thinking at all. That
was the moment in which I effectively began making my way out of the
political system. I understood that I can't write, represent, and express
my convictions and still be a member of such a party and the kind of
parliament we have today. I wasn't yet familiar with the areas outside
formal politics. I felt that I didn't belong anymore, without knowing
where I would next find a better way to express myself and have an
influence.

And maybe it's deeper. Political life in Israel is one of the most intense in the world, both regarding the issues on one's agenda as a public
figure, and because of the complete lack of personal intimacy in the
Israeli public domain. The issues often touch upon life and death, war
and peace. And even if they don't, we make them that way with our
utterances: "I'm willing to kill myself for this"; "Death to the leftists";
"It is good to die for our country"; "You can't capture the mountain

without a grave on the slope"; and "A good Arab is a dead Arab." These are common expressions here, because death is a companion even in our verbal distraction. Not only wars but also traffic accidents, not only security but also cases of profound neglect, with the resulting constant Israeli wait for a tragedy.

Sometimes I can't help feeling that only when the most terrible thing happens do we experience momentary calm. Then comes the great despair that always accompanies such a human event, and with it the start of the countdowns and wait for the next shattering upheaval. There's not a moment to stop, think, ponder, plan. All of life is a long series of continuous tactics, and the accumulation of local tactics creates the illusion of strategy. But real planning, long-term sustainability, does not exist here at all, not even in the prime minister's office, as someone reported to me.

During all my years as a member of parliament (1988–2004), Ariel Sharon served in the Israeli parliament as well. During those years, I never said hello to him, and he never even so much as gave me a nod. I considered him a war criminal. He probably viewed me and my comrades as people who had mortally harmed his political career and maliciously sabotaged our national strategy, the new order he wanted to impose on the Middle East. In the midst of my term as Knesset speaker, in 2001, he was elected prime minister. "Avrum," my good friend Reuven Rivlin told me, "you can't be Speaker of the Knesset and not talk to the prime minister, you must meet him." After many years of political frost, we met. He was warm and friendly and made a great effort to open up to me, at least during the meeting. I asked him to tell me about his political outlook.

"I believe in the Lego system," he surprised me.

"Meaning?"

"I learn from my grandchildren; all their Lego pieces are collected in a big box. They're always missing some small piece, a *shmichik*, that can't be found. So, they dig and rummage and search, and this tiny piece defiantly remains hidden. Do you know what they do then? They throw all the Lego pieces in the air, everything scatters, and suddenly the piece is found. I believe in the politics of Lego. When everything is stuck, sometimes you have to throw everything up in the air and hope that the longed-for piece will be found."

In the war in Lebanon, I had been Sharon's shmichik. He threw me and my comrades up to the sky as he tried to construct an illusory tower in the image of his sick, megalomaniacal dreams. After eighteen years, that war was concluded with a unilateral Israeli withdrawal from Lebanon. We left behind us a trail of 1,200 Israelis killed, and 18,000 dead on the Arab sides that were involved—some of them innocent civilians. We had all become the price of the deception and thuggery. Human fragments scattered on the floor of history like so many game pieces in the hands of an evil player. And one more price in addition to all these—the young and promising agreement with Egypt was dealt a mortal blow and turned from warm potential into a cold peace.

Arik Sharon of the first war in Lebanon in the 1980s was the model of a total politician who did not take into any consideration other positions, criticism, or necessary public agreement. A complete contrast with the outlook of Levi Eshkol—the Israeli prime minister from 1963 to 1969, whom I loved and respected, who characterized his path this way: "I compromise and compromise and compromise, until my position is accepted."

I don't know if Sharon really changed over the years. I definitely went through a transformation. From a harsh and caustic protest leader, I grew much more moderate. I persuaded myself that in the Knesset—or, more precisely, in a society with such powerful currents as Israel—there's no place for absolute positions. So, I too became a good swimmer in the middle of the current. I was as official and representative as I could be, and I avoided as much as possible expressing my views accurately and in full. Until one day I read a quote from Malcolm Muggeridge: "Never forget that only dead fish swim with the stream." I had never felt so lifeless as I did in that moment.

WHEN THE WALLS COMPLETELY CLOSED IN ON ME, TO the point of suffocation, I embarked, in late 2001, on a personal journey on the Appalachian Trail, the over 2,000-mile-long hiking trail that requires half a year of constant walking to cross the United States from Georgia to Maine. I was swallowed up in it. I walked on foot with a backpack, sleeping bag, and a little food. Few people, with no Jews. Just me and Creation. After a few days, you completely lose your sense of direction. Kilometers upon kilometers of ferns, trees, and creeks. A "green desert" that very much dulls thought, blurs detail, and compels you to stick with generalizations and the big patches of color. When I came off the trail, after several weeks, only one statement resounded in me, an imprecise patch of understanding that with time became an insight: "Avrum, your rhythm is off." For many months, years, this statement still echoed inside me.

In the meantime, my term as Knesset speaker was up in 2003, and I returned to the back benches of the opposition, as effective, active, and loud as before. My status in public life had changed, but that flashing light refused to die out and fall silent. On one of the Sabbaths during my parliamentary term, I went out for a run as usual, but I couldn't control my thoughts or discipline my consciousness. The thoughts ran amok in my head, playing by their own rules. And all those thoughts had to say to me was, "The rhythm is really off! You don't want to run five or six kilometers anymore, you want to run marathons. You've had enough of the quick, confused, instant gratifications of rewarding politics. You want to work for the slow and distant bigger meaning: reorienting Israeli society and its communities. You don't want to express yourself anymore in a minute-long speech in the plenum or in a hundred-word press release. You want to write books that will contain your searches for your ideas and outlooks."

When I understood that, and the two lies I had told myself and my constituents, I couldn't stay there for even one more minute. I decided to live and express my internal self externally as well, and my career

came to a screeching, sudden halt. Barely a week later, those words—
"your rhythm is off"—took practical form and pierced the threshold
of my consciousness: I left the Knesset. Because the time had come. I
moved from the plenum and the committees to writing, reading, and
social activism.

PART II

LEARNING

CHAPTER SEVEN

RUNNING AND WRITING WITH A KIPPAH

OOKS HAVE BEEN MY COMPANIONS FOR AS LONG AS I
B can remember. Adventure books and biblical philosophy, theology
and politics. My library is an eclectic collection of thousands of books.
From the old Jewish texts through the classics of world and Hebrew
literature to the complex suspense thrillers of Jo Nesbø and John Le
Carré. Hidden among them are all kinds of finds from used bookstores.
Old articles by leaders of the Jewish community in pre-state Palestine,
whose leadership has long expired, works by long-forgotten writers,
original publications from the days that we were the people of the book
and read books, items found in trash cans before they were to be collected by the big green garbage truck.

My library is a constant free association. A kaleidoscope that always
surprises me anew. I had looked for Eli Amir on Iraqi Jewry and found
Yehoyada Amir on Franz Rosenzweig. Staring at the poetry shelf in
search of a nice passage from Wisława Szymborska, I was suddenly
greeted with open arms by Hannah Arendt with *The Jewish Writings*. So
it goes every day. In our home the difference between a young scholar
studying a Talmud problem and an uneducated person was diagnosed
thus: "The young scholar sits down to study. The uneducated person

comes for bargains," or *metzies,* as my father would say with his clever Yiddishist smile. In my library I am a wandering bargain-hunter, like the early risers who go down to the beach with metal detectors. I never despair of finding the treasure that may not be there at all, or that someone has lost and given up on, and was meant just for me. A find.

This is a characteristic I learned from my father's giant library. Our entire house was full of books. In every room, in every corner. He arranged them according to an order and logic clear only to him. In every book there were paper notes with associative remarks, lines marked with a thick pen, and pages folded like Jewish origami during reading on the Sabbath, when writing and marking were forbidden. With his photographic memory, Dad documented every page and every note. But that didn't help him in his constant arguments with Mom. She was a Hebron native and he was the formal *yeke,* or German immigrant, but when it came to putting things in order, cleaning, and being on time, she was the actual yeke of the family. "You have two options," she would always say, giving him an ultimatum, "arranging the books by size or by color."

"But Rivka," he would beg and stick the books where he wished. He would mix, and she would organize. And so it was their entire life together. From the day he died she didn't touch the library. She froze his logical disorder as it was. A monument that stayed that way until she died and the house was emptied of all their memories.

A few years ago, I received from my wife and children a wonderful gift for my birthday. A professional librarian arrived at the house without my knowledge and tried to arrange my library. She worked and labored, put up and took down, switched and placed, and ultimately gave up. My library remained in its perfect state, just the way I like it, half ordered and half jumbled. Over the years, it would become more jumbled, requiring the further intervention of a professional, and so on.

This life, which appears to be in disarray, among the shelves, suits me well. There are people who live "in between," willingly confined there, because that is the place where they don't have to do anything. Others on both sides decide everything for them. For many people being in the middle is parking in the world's most convenient parking lot, the place of rest for those without an opinion. I too am today in some kind of middle, but my "in between" is completely different. It is not a comfort zone, but a churning whirlpool, a constant struggle. I am between worlds, but outside them. Time and again I find myself challenging and being challenged by more than one world. I am addicted to this complexity. Sometimes I'm worn out and get tired, but mostly I argue and debate in all directions with the hope that these disagreements will produce totally new creations for me and my adversaries. This life, between worlds, did not begin in Dad's library. Because its core was in the "big room," the bourgeois living room, which we were forbidden from entering on Sabbaths when respected guests arrived, those who could not be invited for a cup of black coffee in the small kitchen. In honor of these people Mom would spread a nice hand-embroidered or lace tablecloth in the salon, and place on it a silver serving plate shaped like a trio of delicate cloverleafs. In one section were homemade sugar-coated peanuts, in the second a mix of almonds and raisins, just like in a sad Yiddish song, and in the third cookies that she called strudel, which were unique and tasty, the likes of which I have never tasted, though they had nothing in common with Viennese strudel.

This was the place of the adults, a temple inaccessible to children. That is why when guests came, we found shelter with friends and neighbors. We went to play outside. The outside of my childhood home was an entire world. The house still stands, elegant as always, and my beloved sister carries on the family tradition there. You enter through the heavy art-deco gate and climb the wide staircase. Before turning left, toward the once-filled goldfish pools, or right, to the small garden, you see an alcove and above it a stone inscription in Gothic letters: "Villa Lea, 1 May 1934." The story of the house was never hidden from us, though in those days it was an embarrassing tale.

It was built by a lawyer by the name of Nasib Abcarius Bey, the source of its popular name, Abcarius House. Abcarius Bey was a Christian lawyer, Greek Orthodox, a native of Egypt, who arrived here with the British occupation. He was one of the most successful and respected lawyers in the country, an energetic operator who concocted a few real estate deals between the Greek Orthodox church and the Zionist movement, deals that facilitated the establishment of the important neighborhoods of Jewish Jerusalem outside the Old City walls. During the years in which he lived in Jerusalem and came in contact with the Jews, he fell in love with a Jewish woman from the ultra-Orthodox Mea Shearim neighborhood, whose name was Lea Tennenbaum. The city was atwitter, but he was resolutely in love and built her a house, far from crowded Mea Shearim and its malicious gossip.

I think that it was the only non-Jewish home in the Rehavia quarter, the neighborhood of pioneers and intellectuals of the 1920s. All the homes in the neighborhood, except ours, were Jewish homes, unlike the houses across the street, in the neighboring Talbiyeh neighborhood, which almost all belonged to rich Arabs, mostly Christian. Our house was built from the start "in between," between the Jews of Rehavia and the Christians of Talbiyeh, between the Christian man and the Jewish woman. The home of a gentile who lived with a Jewish woman who chose him over a proper arranged marriage in the ultra-Orthodox collective where she was born. Later she pauperized him with her wastefulness, and he became impoverished less than two years after the house was dedicated. She left him for other, more financially established lovers and he was compelled to abandon the beautiful home he had built for the two of them. The house is built in the Bauhaus or international style, and as my childhood home, my *Kinderstube*, it was not just an architectural style. It was the human "in between" style in which I grew up, a Jerusalem Bauhaus child.

Villa Lea is not just a grand Jerusalem house; its human history is just as fascinating. When Haile Selassie, emperor of Ethiopia, was granted political asylum in Israel after Italy conquered parts of his country on the eve of World War II, he moved into Abcarius House. (Abcarius Bey did not live there anymore, and his house was transferred to the property administration of the British mandate government.) When we were little and we were told, "A king once lived here," we thought it was just a legend, like other fairy tales that parents tell their children. Only later did we learn that in this Jerusalem there are true fairy tales.

After the founding of Israel, the house and its courtyards were transferred to the property administration of the fledgling Israeli government, and the new elite of Jerusalem and Israel gathered there. Before us, Moshe Dayan lived on our same floor. Then the floor was divided, and we shared it with Chaim Herzog, then a senior officer and the son of the chief rabbi, before he became president, and with many more that came afterward. The first finance minister of Israel, Eliezer Kaplan, who died before I was born, lived above us. His scary widow continued living there with her childless daughter and son-in-law. On the top floor lived Avraham Kidron, who later served as the Israeli ambassador to several countries and as director-general of the foreign ministry. In the pre-state era, he was an investigator and judge in the scandalous treason trial—the Tobianski trial—which ended with the only death sentence pronounced in the country by Jewish judges and carried out (except for the sentencing of Adolf Eichmann, but that's a different story). A house that was totally establishment, secular people, soldiers, socialists, and us.

Until age six I didn't know the differences among them all. From my first to last day in the Israeli education system I was in an environment of religious boys. Today it seems to me that my parents wanted to encourage this duality. I encountered everything denied me in the religious education system at home and in the playground. I grew up in between. Between my parents and their social circles and the house and its other residents who were very different from us. Between the new Israeli street and my parents' library that held worlds now vanished.

F ROM THE DAY I LEARNED HOW TO READ AND WRITE, THE written word was always there at my side when I searched for my convictions. I read a great deal, but I didn't write enough. For many years I wondered, even angrily, about my late father. So talented and eloquent, full of knowledge and memories. "Dad, why don't you write?" I would ask him, and he, with his natural affability, would evade me time and again. I was mad at him, and it didn't occur to me to think: and why don't you write, Avrum? Only when I started writing myself and felt the scathing self-criticism of the end result did I understand him.

It's very difficult for a person who is a talented speaker—which my father was, an exciting speaker, a sharp debater, a gifted teacher, and a fascinating preacher—to change his mode of connection with the public from speech to writing. They are not the same. The speaker is in constant and immediate associative contact with his followers and listeners. He reacts to their body language, argues when necessary, and flatters when required. And most importantly—the words of the speaker go into thin air. They are almost never firmly fixed or embedded. They can be changed, denied, sidestepped, added to, or diluted. Which is not the case with the written word. The black on white, the documentation that can no longer be altered, always confronts you as a constant reminder that cannot be denied. A monument to your words, a commemoration of the truth that was yours at the moment it was written. Writing is a commitment. A speech, on the other hand, especially a political one, flirts and floats, but only seldom does it give a commitment from which there is no return. And Dad, who right up to the last minute of his ninety years was busy with survival, was not ready to commit to anything, not even in the face of the grim reaper or his life's memories.

The increased reservations about my political mission came with thoughts, doubts, and complex comprehensions about our modus vivendi. Far beyond the Israeli collective Zionist paradigm I was born into and function in. My thoughts led to the 2004 decision to break away from active political life. I understood that I wanted to bequeath these thoughts to my children. I will never have property and wealth for them. But I don't want to hoard my thoughts and values like a miser.

I write for my children so they will have starting points for life and the directions they choose, if they want them. My generous mother always encouraged us to take different things from her. Cake and leftovers from the Sabbath, an extra stainless steel pot that was on sale at the supermarket, a giant roll of plastic bags that she found as a "bargain." "Why do I need you to wait until I die to get these things? Take them now and be happy I'm alive," she would say with a joyful smile. And in that sense, I want to be like her, in generosity of thought and openness of writing.

W RITING AND RUNNING HAVE TAUGHT ME TO TOUCH MY soul and spirit and express them, because they provide paths that enable me to search for the deep roots of what interests me. One of my most important and deepest teachers of the soul of running is Nahshon Shohat, a fantastic runner, brilliant legal mind, and the best "running intellectual" I ever met, who tells me sometimes that I don't run to mark the attainment of a specific objective; I look for meanings in the running. That's why I called my running blog *A Man Runs Inside Himself*. Because that's where it begins and that's where it reaches, inside the self. I write for the same reason. In order to reach the chasms and sinkholes that have opened in my internal spaces and to fill them. To read a book and discover my thoughts, not those of others. And go on with them to the furthest places inside me. Since retiring I have published a few books, a great many articles, and endless words; I have run marathons, shorter races, and tens of thousands of kilometers; and through writing and running, I have reached truths that were hidden and imprisoned inside me without hope for rescue. Through hard physical and spiritual work, I developed the stubborn patience of a marathonic personality.

For me, running is returning to the most basic foundations of our existence, to the moment before things were spoiled. I look at my grandchildren learning to walk, and I am moved. I learn each hesitant step with them, the hand reaching for help; I accept with great love the smile that comes with great achievement; I embrace the fall and disappointment and do it over again. And now they're running and moving away from me. Where are they going? Like toddlers but with moments of grace, as adult runners connect to the simplicity and innocence of their early days. Paradoxically, the more the technology of the shoes, clothing, and gear improves, the more runners can reach their own (pretechnological) foundations. This is a sport of return to the natural, return to the self. Every small child and toddler knows how to run. First, they crawl, learn to walk, and immediately run. Later, with the careful consideration, social passivity, and other antiphysical patterns of the contemporary era, the modern individual becomes a cumbersome lump. Our parents' generation viewed a potbelly and slow walk as evidence of gravitas, respectability, seriousness, and personal abilities. We, on the other hand, invest in diets and body sculpting, much more than the entire Western world invests in eradicating hunger in developing countries.

During one of my campaigns for another respectable public position, one of my supporters in the Knesset plenum told me, "Avrum, you don't stand a chance."

"Why?" I wondered.

"Because you're too thin," he replied. "Israelis like their leaders fuller." When I looked at the rest of those present in the plenum, I had to agree. When the contest was over and I was elected to the post, it turned out that some of the members of the electing body were Jews from abroad, who preferred me to other candidates because "a slim man is disciplined and restrained." In time, I realized that I wanted to be opposite things at the same time: slim and unrestrained.

Very early in my life I was swept up in the fascinating vortex of relations between Israel and the Jewish diaspora. Every time I was attracted anew, like a butterfly to a warm and friendly fire, to the spiritual pluralism of American Jewry. I saw how the health trend was growing there. People exercising, eating right, and in their spare time running

and walking. I too tried to shake off my automatic aversion to sports imposed on me in the far and dark days at the yeshiva, an aversion that was
a combination of the values of the Torah world, which despises the Hel-
lenistic culture of the body, and the legacy of the army, which turned
every sports activity into torture and hazing. I began slowly and mod-
estly, and since then I run a lot. Most years, the hour of running was my
vital break. The only moments I had to myself, alone. Without phone
calls or tasks, without inquiries from the public or any disruptions.

Today I run for meditation. I run to the lost kilometers. To the sub-
lime peak of the run, which is like a moment of nirvana. A serenity of
being utterly clean. A reality in which the mind, thoughts, and obsessions vanish, and you run as if by suggestion. It happened to me for the
first time in the Tiberias Marathon in 2003. I meticulously tracked all
the data: pulse, breathing, drinking, the energy gels, and the kilometers
marked at the side of the road. I turned around at Ein Gev, ran another
kilometer, and suddenly I was in Tzemah. Wait a minute, how did I get
here? Where did the last kilometers go? I don't know. I wasn't there, I
was somewhere else. I was swallowed up in the infinity of the serenity,
and in the words of Rachel, the poetess of the Sea of Galilee and its
surroundings, it seemed as if I were absent. Since then I have tried to
re-create that feeling every time. There are practice sessions in which I
manage to erase a few hundred meters, sometimes even more, and the
more I get to the vanished kilometers, the better my run and the calmer
my life is. I still haven't found the formula and mechanisms to get there
of my own volition and in control. Sometimes it happens, and many
times it doesn't happen at all. Thoughts run in all directions. Indeed,
this is not foot running, not even cardio running. It is the running of
thoughts, or more precisely, the thoughts that you do not try to control
and take control of. The minute the head is freed and capable of soar-
ing, the body, as well, reaches the lost kilometers. The most beautiful,
meaningful, and calming kilometers of life. I know, I was there, after
Ein Gev on the way back to Tiberias. Those were the most enchanting

kilometers of my life. And when I returned from eternity, I had my first book in my head, the whole book: beginning, middle, and end.

T HE THOUGHTS WERE NESTING THERE FOR A WHILE. I heard the new rhetoric of Jewish and Muslim preachers getting louder and full of negativity; I listened to American politics and to the impact of Christian demagoguery on President George W. Bush. I find it difficult to distinguish among Jewish, Christian, and Muslim religious fundamentalism. And I realized that with the turn of the century, the incoming twenty-first century would be much more religious than the outgoing secular twentieth. All of these thoughts and voices around me found their way into my first book, *God Is Back*. It was written about the religious dimension of the twenty-first century. In it I described the central Israeli structure—the distorted relations between religion and state. I identified the erosion of Western secular conversation and the similar erosion that is happening in Israel. In the book's pages and chapters I tried to look at life through two lenses: through the Hubble Space Telescope I peered with curiosity at distant galaxies of the humanity of our time, and with the electron microscope I examined the minute details of the realities familiar to me that threaten us. That is our era: you can see the farthest and biggest, and at the same time see the near and small. I wrote about global manifestations of religious fundamentalism and shameful local expressions of Jewish paganism. With the telescope, I tried to decipher the tremendous religious forces that drove President Bush, and I examined what lies behind the people attacking abortion clinics and women seeking the right to choose and have control over their bodies. At the same time, I wanted, through writing, to examine my religious identity.

A few years before the highly anticipated Y2K, I began by looking for an answer to a very personal, really microscopic question posed to me by a boy settler. I was on a visit to the land of the settlements south of Hebron. It was Chanukah time, and the tour began in one of the kindergartens in the historic region. One of the toddlers, with long sidelocks and blue eyes, beautiful as a divine angel and wearing an oversized kippah, fixed me with a stare.

"Who are you?" he asked.

"My name is Avraham," I replied.

"And what are you doing here?" he asked.

"I came to visit you," I answered.

"Why?" he queried.

"What do you mean, why?" I said, almost insulted.

"You want peace with America and the Arabs. You are a Hellenizer! You eat pork at home? Why do you wear a kippah?" he lashed out at me.

At the time, I didn't answer him. And I had never answered myself. Now the time had come.

When I studied in elementary school I met an unusual person, a wonderful teacher named Meir Bakshi. Smart, sophisticated, and with a healthy sense of humor. He would call me up sometimes to the front of the class, take the kippah off my head, knock on my skull, and say with feigned satisfaction, "the Dome of the Rock." He was the best at such puns. Both a head hard as a rock and a holy place like the one liberated by the brave Israeli soldiers last year. There was no typical kippah then for schoolboys. Everyone brought what he had at home. The school kippah was not knitted. Every boy had a different kippah: made of felt or cloth, a "Jerusalem good boy" kippah or a black rabbi's kippah. The kippah was mandatory in school, but not really required at home or during play. Everyone did in his free time what was customary at home. I came to school every day with a big Swiss skullcap. My everyday kippah had decorations of white flowers, the edelweiss of the Alps, and my Sabbath and holiday kippahs also had a woven tail and a pastoral embroidery of Swiss cows. I have no idea why my parents decided that this was the appropriate look for me, their only son.

I can imagine myself then. A small Jerusalem boy with slanted bangs in the style of the sixties, wearing the giant skullcap of cow herders high up in the Alps. What were they thinking? I ask myself. The wonder increases even more when I think about my parents, who made every effort to avoid falling prey to the gossip around us. "What would they say?" was the motivating motto of our lives.

In Israel's early years—during the fifties and sixties—the weekly *HaOlam HaZeh* (a news magazine published in Israel between 1937 and 1993, famous for its highly unorthodox and irreverent style) was at the peak of its power. It was virtually the only voice in opposition to the chorus of the establishment and the national consensus. This daring and courageous paper combined brave and consistent exposure of the political reality that the establishment wanted to hide and cover up, along with pornographic nudity in the style of those modest days. The ideology of the paper was "without fear or favor." A black bar covered the eyes and private parts of the weekly beauties on the back cover, and naked and unrestrained politics filled its inside pages. A political person, like my father, could not function in the roiling Israeli arena without this uncensored information, without knowing what was actually going on in the real world, the one not reported in partisan publications and the slavish media. Which is why we would get *HaOlam HaZeh* every week.

My mother, on the other hand, could not live in this world with the knowledge that, God forbid, someone would know that something so abominable was entering our home. I was the point of contact between these colliding worlds. One of my official jobs at home was to take out the garbage. Every day, and sometimes twice a day, I was sent with the family refuse to the local garbage can. A ritual that repeated itself every day, except the day in which we threw out *HaOlam HaZeh* from the previous week. There was a set drill. I took the garbage and went downstairs. I knew exactly where Mom's sing-song voice would reach me, "Avraham." As an expert courier I would return, and Mom would open the garbage bag, look for the old copy of *HaOlam HaZeh* and make certain what she had already made sure of five times before at home—that the embarrassing back page was folded inside. "So that if God forbid someone pokes around the garbage of the Burg family . . . "

They were very modest people. Until their last days, the house contained the used furniture they had bought right after their wedding.

We never spent extravagantly on ostentatious events. On the contrary, my father was a minister in many of Israel's governments, and during most of my childhood years he was eligible for an official car and a driver provided by the government. The driver, Baruch Vessely, was a member of the household. A friend. His children were my friends. We grew up together, similar and equal and different in the same way all human beings are different from one another. One difference was visible. Every morning Baruch took his son to the school in which we studied, and I was forbidden to get into Dad's car, not even on rainy and snowy Jerusalem days, because of "what would they say?" That is why, when I think about the kippah they put on my head, I wonder where those fears had gone. Then additional questions come up: Why this kippah? And why a kippah at all?

The kippah is a symbol, and perhaps the institution, that has accompanied me more than anything else in my life. From the time of my childhood until today. Before I knew how to read and write. Before I led synagogue services for the first time. The kippah was always there. A kind of basic instinct. You don't go out of the house without a kippah. You don't walk out on the street without a kippah. I remember the first times that I ran without a kippah on the streets of Jerusalem. I didn't have too much hair left on my head by then, and there was nowhere to pin on the kippah, so I was compelled to run bareheaded. What a strange feeling. It would have been easier for me to run stark naked than to run without a kippah. Someone once taught me a joke, a *vitz* based on a Hebrew wordplay, according to which a kippah, unlike socks, shoes, and a belt, is worn by compulsion. I was never compelled to wear a kippah. It was simply there.

Since my parents never did anything without meaning it, I'm trying today, with the perspective of time, to understand their hidden intent, the distant message they sent me from my early days to these years of my maturity. The contours of the landscape are distant, blurred, the Israeli value system has changed unrecognizably, and their old world, the world of yesterday, which combined a strong diaspora consciousness with an almost sacred joy of independence, has been replaced with a tough local cynicism. The delicate complexity made up of equilibrium and balances has grown tired and worn, giving way to a totality of positions. "Keep it simple," we say in spoken Israeli and run into trouble time and again. Members of the complicated, complex-ridden generation are no more, and I have no one to ask.

Dad bought the kippahs in Switzerland, in Zurich. Always Zurich. The bourgeois, respectable, quiet, and orderly Swiss city became over the years a city of refuge for my parents. My father went abroad often. There was something in him that embodied both supply and demand. He knew how to speak in so many languages that instead of sending three emissaries to three different places, he alone would be dispatched. In the morning in English in London, in the afternoon in French in Paris or Brussels, and in the evening in German. And in between, informal communication in Yiddish or any other European language. He could talk about politics and policy, about the weekly Torah portion and general philosophy, about contemporary literature as well as "The Song of the Nibelungs," the thirteenth-century epic German poem. He had a cultural supply incomprehensible to today's Israeli, like myself, limited to our cultural confines in the here and now. But he also had demands. He wanted to travel, he loved it. Or to be more precise, he needed it. He had what to offer, and he asked for something in return. Every time he traveled somewhere in the world, he always asked to go through Zurich. To the Far East through Zurich, to the far West through Zurich. It was such a fixture in the family landscape that we never talked about it. Once, in his old age, I asked him, "Dad, what's the story with Zurich?"

"What do you mean?" he asked evasively, using his usual acrobatics with me to buy some time to compose an answer that wouldn't get him in too much trouble, refusing to commit even in his final moments.

"Why did you always travel or return through Zurich?"

He needed a long time to reply and in the end, he groaned and said limply, "I couldn't live without it." I waited. After a while he continued.

"I actually never took proper leave of Dresden. The beautiful city, the city of my happy childhood. I escaped it in a hurry. I left behind an elderly mother to die, and wonderful, precious memories. I was never allowed to mourn, to bid farewell and recover. Zurich is a bit like Dresden. A cultured European city. Not too big and not too provincial. With a train station—the Hauptbahnhof—a river, a main street, and shops that have always been there. A city where things change very slowly, if at all. In Zurich, I found consolation. In Zurich, I was always refilled."

Once we were together in his beloved Dresden. After the fall of the Berlin Wall the three of us traveled—Mom, Dad, and I. Three adults, experienced and astute, going back in time to one of the important points of departure of their lives. We toured the city and its restored landmarks, and in one place, a wonderfully aesthetic local pastry shop, Dad blurted, "Ah, just like Zurich."

When he confessed this non-Zionist deviation to me, I was reminded of a story from the family mythology. Thirty-five-year-old Dad brought twenty-three-year-old Mom to meet his German immigrant friends. Members of his group were regulars at one of the cafes on Ben-Yehuda Strasse in Tel Aviv, playing chess, chatting, saving Jews with mere speech, fighting the Germans or the British with words and theses, and establishing a state in their dreams. Probably all in high German mixed with heavily accented Hebrew. And suddenly someone else shows up and breaks into the circle rooted back in Germany, the painful, longed-for phantom. Dad introduced her to them, with her rabbinic and Hebron pedigree, and after she went on her way one of the friends asked him, "Was, Yosef, mit einer asiatischen Frau?" (What, Yosef, with an Asian woman?) I reminded him of the story and asked him if there was a connection. "Very much so," he replied. "It's not easy with you Asians, natives of the country. I need to occasionally go back and recharge, to go back and remember the forces that positively drew me to Zionism and the belief in the State of Israel."

After one of those many visits he returned with a gift for his boy, a large Swiss skullcap. It's not clear to me whether he gave me a present or built himself a monument on my head, so that every time he looked at me he saw the unseen. In Zurich, he had thought of me, and when he looked at me he thought of Zurich. As he gazed at what was above my line of sight, something apparently percolated from the Swiss cap he gave me into my consciousness.

W HAT IS THIS KIPPAH, ANYWAY? WHY DO SO MANY PEOPLE, like the boy settler, berate me in anger: "Take that kippah off already"? And why do so many sympathizers who identify with my words end up asking me, "So why is it that you wear a kippah? You're just like us"? Many years ago, when my eldest son was a mischievous boy in kindergarten, he crossed the line one day. I don't remember the precise incident, but we gave much thought to the correct educational way to deal with it. In the end, we told him, "Tomorrow you're not allowed to go to kindergarten with a kippah. A kippah is a symbol of good behavior, and you don't deserve it." His distress was touching, really heart-rending. He wept bitterly for a long, sad day. Until now, years later, when he no longer wears a kippah on a regular basis and is raising his children in his own wonderful way, that event is still mentioned in family conversations with a smile. Since then I have done a lot of thinking about the place of the kippah in our family and the place of the kippah on my head.

Group pictures of previous members of parliament hang on one of the walls in the Knesset corridors. During all my years in the Knesset I passed through those halls thousands of times. I never stopped for a minute to look at those pictures. The only time I did, I had one of the big surprises of my life. There was a picture of my father and teacher, who served here as a minister and member of the Knesset from its inception until his retirement in 1988. But alas, in every one of his pictures in the first five elected parliaments, he is photographed without a kippah. My father, the leader of religious Zionism, an Orthodox rabbi by training, who prayed three times a day, who never missed morning prayer or afternoon services, had his picture taken without a kippah? I went to the Government Press Office to look for the original print. The estimated date, according to the assessment there, was early December, 1951, when he had been a minister for a month and a half in the third Israeli government. I assume that a secretary received a request, a directive to tell the minister to go to the Government Press Office and have his picture taken, so that there would be an official photo of the Israeli health minister for anyone who might need it. What a picture! The one and only, in black and white, and still so colorful. A three-piece suit, the finest attire at the time. The dotted tie not quite centered, and the left collar flap of the white shirt a bit too prominent. Handsome, stylish glasses. He's so serious, in his early forties, younger than I am today, but when I look at him, he is so respectable and adult, an elderly Jew—he looks like he could be my father . . . I looked at what was left of his thinning hair, which quickly became his wonderful signature shiny bald pate, and indeed, there was no kippah. None. Simply none. I turned the picture over to the other side, and there was no kippah there either.

I immediately called Mom. I had to get to the bottom of this. And she said without hesitation, "Yes, it's possible. Then he was still German." A year and a half after the founding of the state, six years after the opening of the iron gate of Auschwitz, twelve years after he was ordained as a rabbi, my father, an Israeli minister under Ben-Gurion, remained a "German" for my mother. Her perception was that he did not become an "Israeli" until after the Six-Day War, because only from then did the kippah become a fixture on his wise head, in official pictures and in daily reality. Many pieces of the puzzle fell into place then. The more I think about it, the more I know: You were wrong, Mom. Dad's exposed bald pate in the official picture, like the heavy kippah he wore during the rest of his history, was the pure Israeliness that he wanted us all to inherit, and which changed before our eyes on his big head.

Many people approach me to this day and tell me that my father was their teacher at the Herzliya Gymnasium in Tel Aviv. Judging by their number, little Tel Aviv would have had at least ten million residents at the time. These people have a kind of pleasant glow on their faces. They talk about a beloved teacher, a teacher of life. About that period, Dad told me, with real admiration, that David Shimoni, the fiery national poet, was with him on the teaching staff of the gymnasium, and that "Shimoni taught literature bareheaded, and the Bible with a hat." Once he told Dad that at a fairly young age he had stopped putting on tefillin, but after the pogroms in Ukraine in 1920 he resumed wearing them. "He told me, 'I have complaints against the Almighty, and I can lodge them only when I put on tefillin. Otherwise I just complain . . .'" This made a strong impression on Dad. "This shows a depth of feeling and thought," he would say.

Today I ask myself if that same depth of feeling and thought can be attributed to Dad's admission: "I taught history bareheaded, which was not the case with Talmud." When he taught history, he taught it as an ordinary person, so he stood in class without a kippah and without any head covering. And when he taught Talmud, he wore a kippah and taught the essence of rabbinic Judaism in the heart of the secular stronghold of Tel Aviv as a Jew for all intents and purposes. It seems to me that many of his students then, elderly Israelis today, miss that duality, the value system that can take in such contradictory worlds, like modernity and roots, reconciling them in a harmony between ideological garb and external clothing.

My trajectory in life was the opposite of his, and our kippahs, along with our religious outlooks, are evidence of the reversal of directions. In the world he was born into there was a clear separation between the Jewish space and the general environment. I don't accept the thesis that the Jews of Germany walked without kippahs in order to avoid attracting attention. There was a much broader worldview at work here than just fear.

Anyone who was around my dad knew he was Jewish. In school, he didn't write and wasn't tested on the Sabbath, on the street it was known that his father was a wine merchant whose stock included strictly kosher wines brought from the new wineries of the settlements in Palestine, and at the university in Leipzig it was known that he was not only a doctoral student, but also a student in the rabbinical seminary. So, the more I think about it, the more I'm convinced that the separation was a separation in essence. There are areas that are Jewish realms of activity—tradition, religion, customs—above which the kippah is displayed. And there are areas and realms that are not Jewish, and they are bareheaded and have broad horizons. There is and must be a separation between general life that belongs to everyone and the unique life of those who choose it.

We—my wife, our children, and I—have lived more than half of our lives in a small community on the outskirts of Jerusalem. A community whose members come partly from religious homes and partly from secular homes, and there is no tension between us. An example of what Israel could have been had it really wanted to take a different path. Over the years, we established a very special synagogue for ourselves, a place of gathering and consideration for others. It doesn't have the classic separation between men and women, and is meant for women, men, and families. There is a mixed area for those who want it, like us. The service is also virtually completely egalitarian. Since this prayer group was founded I refuse to take part in any religious or cultural activity that is not completely egalitarian.

The Jews among my readers as well as travelers to and from Israel know the moment during the flight in which the observant but annoying people try to organize a *minyan,* ten Jewish prayers needed for the praying ritual. Whenever any of them approaches me on the plane and asks me to join, I ask with mock innocence, "Is this an egalitarian service?" When people try to compel me to complete a random male quorum for prayer, I point to the women around us and ask why they don't join the group. This revolution in the life of our community took several years and was not at all easy. There was anger and insults. Friendships were broken and new connections made. But in the end, things settled down and calm returned to our lives, or more precisely, to the lives of our friends. Because for me a much larger crisis erupted with the conclusion of the revolution that I'm so happy about. For a few years, I happily attended the common synagogue where I sat with my partner and children—boys and girls together—in the mixed area, satisfied with this rare and special arrangement. But once the physical impediments, the chauvinistic divisions between men and women, were removed in the synagogue we had established for ourselves, I took the time to study the texts of the prayer, and I was alarmed. Those same ancient prayers, wrapped in melodies and tunes that I love so much, are actually texts that I cannot accept under any circumstances.

Sacrifices? The Temple? The chosen people? A gentile faith that is "vanity and emptiness"? The revival of the dead? A God that determines our lives? The messiah? I don't believe in any of these things. On the contrary, I think that some of them are embarrassingly simplistic and primitive and some are alarmingly dangerous. The day I left politics I swore to myself never to live a life of lies again. I make every effort to reach my deepest truth and live by it as much as possible, whatever the price. That is why I have not gone to my community's synagogue for many years. I have difficulty with the beliefs and religious content, and I don't want to start another religious war with my friends and loved ones about the content of their Judaism.

I left the synagogue because I want entirely different content in my Judaism. Dad never gave up his place in the synagogue, especially because he wanted to preserve virtually every jot and tittle of what was and is no longer. From early childhood, I liked synagogue events very much. I liked the gathering, the early morning walk with Dad, a rare moment in our lives, until we met the other worshipers who latched on to him and separated us, as usual. My childhood was spent in two synagogues. One, known as Beit Hillel, was very close to home, attended by students and lecturers, and younger at heart. A lively mix of young and old, children and homeowners. We always sat on the right in the second row. On the left side in the first row sat Professor Akiva Ernst Simon, tall and impressive with his white mane. "He is a real yeke," we would say with genuine reverence. But despite the supreme compliment in the scale of family praise, neither he, his wife, nor their children were ever guests at our home, nor did we visit theirs, although we lived at opposite ends of the very same street. Something very cold and official stood between him and Dad.

With me, on the other hand, he was very friendly. He always smiled warmly at me, sometimes shook my hand with adult formality after the end of services. Every time I performed a role designated for children in the synagogue he spoke very highly of me. When I made a mistake in pronunciation or chanting a tune he came over to me quietly after prayers and asked with extreme politeness whether he could exchange a few words with me. He was sixty and I was six, but politeness was obligatory. When I agreed to talk with him, he commented very quietly about how a particular word should be pronounced or a particular tune I had sung off-key should be sung. It was between us, while between him and Dad something just didn't click. Hello, hello, a touch to the brim of the hat as they passed one another on the neighborhood streets, and that was it. They didn't even cross the street for some small talk. Occasionally something about him would be revealed, like his bravery and the German Iron Cross he was decorated with in the First World War. Like the "frightening" fact that he was a liberal, heaven forbid. And that he had said things that were "best not repeated." I didn't care then, nor was I sensitive in the least to these nuances. I didn't know that he was an important thinker, one of the pillars of German Jewry in the pre-war generation, whose ideas would eventually become part of the organizing ideas of my life.

Our second synagogue was Yeshurun, then the main Jerusalem synagogue. We went there on holidays, on Independence Day, and on special Sabbaths. Dad always had his regular place in the third seat in the first row on the left. "This is the first synagogue I attended on my first Sabbath ever in Jerusalem," he would repeatedly say with gratitude. On the wall next to us was a commemorative plaque for the Conservative movement, which founded the synagogue, but who knew the difference then between the roiling Jewish streams whose wellsprings were in German Jewry? That was where I was called up to the Torah on my bar mitzvah. It was there that I sat as a boy in the lap of Ruby Rivlin, who later became the Knesset speaker, succeeding me, and a beloved president of Israel. That is where presidents and dignitaries, official visitors and important figures came. Sitting in the rear section of the synagogue, always hunched and sullen, was Professor Yeshayahu Leibowitz, the most significant person in my life aside from my parents and family members. Dad knew him from there as well. But I don't recall any contact between them. Not even a nod of the head. By then Leibowitz was already a popular teacher. His lessons on Maimonides and the weekly Torah portion attracted throngs. But we never moved in his circles. I always recognized his gaunt and bony figure lurching forward with the old leather bag in his hand. I never said hello to him in the street, and he never showed that he recognized me.

After my military service, I worked in the College for Jewish Heritage and Leibowitz was one of the admired and important teachers there. In my first week of work, the principal sent me to "organize something" with Leibowitz. I called him, introduced myself only by my first name, and asked to meet him. "Happily, happily," he invited me with his raspy voice. I came to his house at 63 Ussishkin Street. We spoke for a long while about the planned seminar and its content. A room full of books, and this old and warm man showered me with his spiritual generosity, with more and more of the full galaxies of his knowledge and wisdom.

Every so often he would leap up from his seat, climb a wooden ladder, take down a remote book from one of the upper shelves, and order me to write down a citation. Then he would sit back down and continue lecturing me. Suddenly in the middle of it all, in our first meeting ever, when I knew who he was and didn't think he knew who I was, he blurted out, "You father was actually a smart man, I wonder why he went into politics."

That was the start of a great love that I felt for this wonderful man. The moral intellectual, who with his bare hands, with his rare courage, tried to save Israel from its two great ills: the malignant occupation and the incestuous corruption of religion and state.

I returned home and told Dad about the meeting with Leibowitz. "Ah, yes, he's very smart. We once had many debates in Berlin." At the time, I didn't understand the heavy baggage that separated them. I didn't know that Leibowitz had tried to be a politician and failed, I didn't know a thing about the debate that tore apart religious Zionism—between Ernst Simon and Leibowitz on one side and the big establishments of religious Zionism on the other. And Dad, who wasn't very good at making decisions, was torn between them and stuck in place.

In the Germany before they immigrated, in Zionist Berlin, they argued about the image of the State of Israel that they had dreamed so much of founding. In Israel's early days they continued their debates. A few years before I was born, Simon laid the foundations for the most scathing critique of the religious Zionism of my father and his colleagues. Then came Leibowitz, who improved on Simon's argument and confronted them with his penetrating philosophical truth. Without mercy or any fear. Simon wrote a weighty essay that wondered "whether we are still Jews." His premise was that historical Judaism was catholic, general and encompassing all areas of life. The invasion of secularism and Zionist nationalism into the realms of the old Judaism led to the loss of the historical monopoly of Judaism over the Jews. Suddenly we had new masters of the house: the Enlightenment and progressiveness and secular realms of life that were not at all religious. Following Simon, Leibowitz demanded separation of religion from the state in order to resolve the dilemma for himself and for us. Religion, according to their perception, does not extend to the whole of life. They recognized secularization and created different departments for different behaviors. There is a religious department and a general department, and they do not necessarily overlap.

I know all this in retrospect. The more I think about it, the more I understand why our families were not closer. "They're not like us, they're not *unsere menschen,* our people," was the immediate and harsh judgment rendered around the Sabbath table, and the case was closed forever. But apparently their seeds were sown inside me already in those distant early days. For many years people have been trying to catalog me. There's always someone shallow enough to ask me, "But what are you? Religious, Orthodox, Reform, Conservative?" Usually I refuse to cooperate with the desire of that person to make the definitions troubling him more convenient—let him make an effort, let him think. Aside from the fact that this is one of those invasive questions that immediately make me very harsh and unpleasant. But sometimes when the spirit moves me, I reply—and my facetious answer stems directly from Simon's dilemma—"I am a Protestant Jew."

I really don't believe in a central religious establishment responsible for belief and religious law. I am not prepared to accept and do not want these institutions to encompass the entirety of all aspects of my life. On the contrary, I'm ready to fight with everything I've got against the religious occupiers who are trying to annex all areas of existence with their quasi-Catholic aggression. They should get out of our pockets and out of women's uteruses, out of what we eat and out of our souls. I dream of a proper country and society, in which there is a clear separation between religion and state, as well as a commitment to equal citizenship for all citizens, regardless of their spiritual choices or tribal origin. I yearn for a spiritual and cultural life in which the current corrupt reality, where "religion is the mistress of politics," in Leibowitz's words, will have disappeared.

Dad wasn't capable of walking those paths with them. He wasn't capable and didn't want to. And from this stemmed his great anger with Leibowitz, who once told me, "A learned person who has no opinion is worse than a carcass." And I was very insulted on behalf of Dad, who was not explicitly mentioned by the philosopher who was so important to me at most stations of my life. That insult was magnified because I thought there was a grain of truth in his oblique criticism. But only a grain. Because deep down, Dad had faith, not blazing, not burning, not zealous, but very clear. Different than Leibowitz's in its content and style, but real faith. He believed with all his heart that the State of Israel is "the first flowering of our redemption." Once, during one of our arguments, I harshly denigrated the chief rabbinate and its rabbis, and he grew red with anger and told me, "But it's such an important institution, for that we established the state." And indeed, he had a secret dream of getting out of the religious ghetto he shared with his friends and expanding it to Israeli society in general.

Now that I am more moderate and not angry at all—when Dad is gone and I miss him so much—I know how wrong he was. How much most of Israeli society, following his wisdom and weakness, adheres to the past and fails to understand what is growing before its very eyes, afraid to decide. "Whoever makes a change loses," he would say, defending himself with an old Talmudic saying, and he was defeated. I, on the other hand, haven't the slightest doubt that the renewed Jewish meeting of religion and rule, faith and power, zealotry and nationalism, are leading us to perdition, to the destruction of the third Jewish sovereignty. That is why I, knowing them so well, their internal language and their real intentions, must confront them, offer a comprehensive alternative to them, and if there is no other choice, fight them with all my might.

My parents needed a very long time to find their exact place along these complicated continuums. By 1968, by the time Dad had finished being German in Mom's view, an existential decision much bigger than them was made in the Six-Day War. In that cursed war, Israel erased the borders surrounding us externally as well as all internal boundaries. Our reality became entirely limitless. There is no limit to our gall and occupation, no limits to anything. And even the few distinctions between religion and state have been totally erased. In 1948, my parents were active and enthusiastic partners in the establishment of a secular and socialist state. In the twenty-first century, my grandchildren were born into a completely different Israel: Orthodox, capitalistic to the point of brutality, and nationalistic to the point that it sometimes doesn't realize how chauvinistic it is. The Israel of my parents failed,

and my grandchildren are being born into it. And when all the borders
were erased, Dad also erased his borders between religion and state and
became a Jewish Catholic who would never again leave the house for
any purpose without a very big kippah, too big, on his head.

In the mid-2010s, I was supposed to appear on a television program. The researcher for the program questioned me at length about
my opinions and positions, about everything. I answered her at length,
patiently, and finally she said, "Can I ask you one more personal
question?"

I replied, "Of course."

"So, by what right do you wear a kippah?" she asked, her anger evident in her effort to control her voice.

Does that belong to you? Do you have entitlement to my appear-
ance? Or a monopoly over permission to wear a kippah? Or a religion-
ometer to accurately determine those who are qualified and those who
aren't? In the past I would have thrown all that in her face and not come
to the program, but the past has settled down.

"Can I ask you an intimate question?" I wondered.

"Uh . . . yes, please," she replied.

I asked. A very personal and intimate question. There was a long
silence on the other end of the line.

"See you Monday at the studio," she said and quietly hung up.

The next week I came to the studios and was interviewed. After the
program, I stood alone in a room and removed the makeup. "Can I
bother you for a minute?" a woman staff member asked me.

"Why not," I replied.

"I'm the researcher. I wanted to answer you," she said. "Yes. The
answer to your question is yes. But I understand. I'm sorry I asked, I
shouldn't have invaded your privacy and intimacy."

In the following year, I officiated at her wedding. A Jewish ceremony for all intents and purposes, without the coercive framework of
the chief rabbinate. It was worth restraining myself. And I still wear a
kippah.

It is difficult for me to take it off, but I think that I have no choice. The kippah on my head—I explain to those interested—is my antidote to the arrogance that has brought so much pain and suffering to humanity in recent generations. The kippah is my border. It reminds me how small and limited I am. That's a nice, original speech. A surprising argument that leaves others silent. But it is hollow. At best, I wear a kippah for others, because "it's important for us to know that there are also religious people like you." Though to tell the truth, the kippah on my head is just a remnant of the religious existence of my previous incarnation. Today I am not a religious person. I am secular, enthusiastically soaking up Jewish culture. I don't think that Judaism is a belief system or petty observance of commandments, and I'm not prepared to play this game anymore with these players. Judaism for me is a cultural civilization, of which religion is one element but not necessarily the most important component. And the religious element needs deep and comprehensive reform in concepts and texts, particularly a dramatic shift from the total "Catholicism" that today organizes all of Israeli life, to a much more Protestant concept in which there are clear divisions between religion and the state, between the general secular realm and private areas of identity and content. In the West I have many liberal partners, progressive and pluralistic—Jews and non-Jews. In Israel, I sometimes feel like there's no one to talk to about these things.

As time passes, I understand that the kippah on my head is a kind of illusion. As if I'm still somewhat connected to those worlds. But that's so untrue. I left political religious Zionism even before joining it. I turned my back on Dad's Catholicism and followed Leibowitz almost the whole way, except for his stubborn Orthodox dogmatism. I can't connect with my friends' traditionalism because of the troubling texts underpinning this tradition. And the kippah we all share, the knitted kippah that is there all the time, in every situation, on my head, is the last imagined link with the world of which I am no longer a part. Because the kippah, like so much traditional garb, is ultimately meant to set apart. To create distinctions between those who are "like us" and those who are not part of our solidarity. But I don't believe in this sweeping "us." My world is not divided into Jews and non-Jews. My division is completely different. I divide the world into good people and bad people. Whoever is good is my brother or sister, and I don't care what their faith is, their race, or cultural affiliation. And anyone who is bad is my enemy, even if he or she speaks Hebrew, wears a kippah, and observes the Sabbath. I have no automatic, racial patriotism that favors all Jews, even the worst of them, over the gentile, even if he is the finest human being. On the contrary. And because of that, I don't want anything that will differentiate me as a person from the community of the rest of my humanistic partners, regardless of their faith and culture.

When Judah Leib Gordon, one of the poets of the Enlightenment, wrote, "Be a man in the streets and a Jew at home," he coined the motto of the Enlightenment movement, which sought to bridge the Jewish and modern worlds. Dad was such a bridge, until the whole structure collapsed on him. A rabbi with a doctorate, a German-speaking immigrant and an Eastern European Jew, educated and traditional, both in high German and juicy Yiddish. For "Father Burg, Part One," one of the early years in which there was a clear separation between the holy and the profane, the movement of the kippah on and off his head was the sign of this precise internal and external division. Whatever was Jewish wore a covering, and whatever was general, civil, and belonging to humanity at large was bareheaded. This division between the man and the Jew was actually lost by Dad when he became "Father Burg, Part Two" and adopted the habit of wearing a kippah all the time. No wonder it happened to him after the Six-Day War. He was, after all, an official and practical part of the border nullifiers, and through that actually erased his own borders. I hope that by the time these lines are published I will have succeeded in becoming a divided man like his early version. Wearing a kippah as a Jew, and bareheaded in all other dimensions of my life.

It's not easy for me—it's like an amputation, or disconnecting a tube that has become part of me like a vein. And still, I want to go back to my father's first division. To the days when he was still an Israeli-German. To the worldview according to which everything Jewish is done with a kippah, and everything general is done without a kippah, and the separation between religion and the rest of life is clear and natural. Like in Zurich, like in Dresden. As it was when there was still hope here, so that there will be new hope.

T HE FIRST THING I DID WHEN I LEFT THE SAN FRANCISCO airport in the early 1980s was to take off my kippah and all other identifying paraphernalia. At the time, those were the security guidelines for Israelis traveling abroad. It was my first visit to the United States. I had been invited by the New Israel Fund, which was very, very new. It was run by Jonathan Jacoby, my guide to American Jewish life, who became one of my dearest, cherished friends. Johnny is one of the most accomplished strategists I have had the privilege of meeting. Virtually with his bare hands he established one of the most important organizations of politically progressive American Jewry, and he is the most sensitive and committed friend I have. I traveled with Johnny to his home. On the way, we stopped for a cup of coffee and a bite to eat. I took out my wallet and counted the cash I had. "Avrum, here it's all backwards," he told me, "Here you can walk around with any kippah you like, anywhere, anytime. No one will bother you. But don't take your money out of your wallet in public—you could get mugged."

The next day I was mugged.

The comfortable, familiar order of things was breached, and the foundations of new worlds were laid down inside me, worlds in which I will continue to move until my last day. Johnny took me to meet the man who would become one of my closest friends, a soul mate in word and deed. Brian Lurie was then the charismatic executive director of the San Francisco area Jewish Community Federation. I knew nothing, absolutely nothing, about American Jewry, its leaders, institutions, and organizations. "They're plastic Jews," someone back home had told me before I left. Until then, I had met very few American Jews; most were friends of my parents. Immigrants or refugees like them, Jews of the synagogue, Psalms, pastrami, lox and bagels, accented English and lively Yiddish. At the time, I had yet to meet a religious Jew who was not Orthodox. Reform and Conservative Jews were demons that one must be very wary of. That is why we would pass by the Reform synagogue on the way to elementary school with real physical fear. In the hierarchy of our lives they belonged somewhere in the infernal depths with Christian missionaries and the rest of our enemies who in every generation try to wipe us out.

We went into Brian's office, and everyone introduced themselves. "I'm a Reform rabbi by training," he began. I was so scared, really. If the chair and floor had answered my prayers I would have been swallowed up and disappeared at that very moment. Reform Jew. *Gevald.*

"What do you do here, in the community?" I wondered aloud with any remaining politeness I could muster. I was not familiar yet with the first principle of politics: don't ask a question unless you already know the answer.

"Lots of things," he answered. "But today is especially important for me. After my meeting with you I'm going to a meeting in which we will decide to increase by thirty percent our contributions to hospitals that treat AIDS patients."

"What is AIDS?" I asked. It was 1983. And while the earth had failed to swallow me up half an hour earlier, his eyes bore through me on the spot. Brian has those kind of eyes.

"It's acquired immune deficiency syndrome," he patiently explained. And I understood even less.

"But what is it?" I probed politely.

"It's a homosexual disease." That was the belief at the time, and that is how that terrible illness was branded.

"But there are no Jewish homosexuals, so why is the Jewish community contributing to it?" I heard my mother speak from my mouth.

And thus began a journey of faith, friendship, and partnership, which has included unique experiences, good deeds, and especially

a common study of human and Jewish fate, a journey that has been
going on now for more than thirty years. I learned from him about the
United States and its spiritual movements, about American Jews and
the trends among them. About philanthropy and fundraising. We don't
always agree, but I have always loved him unconditionally, and I learn
something new with our every encounter.

In 2008, I officiated at my daughter's wedding in our house, in an entirely Jewish and completely egalitarian wedding. Later, Brian married
her in San Francisco in a civil marriage, so we were partners in the same
chuppah—not only in the limited sense of the family celebration, but in
the wider sense of the struggle for a humane Judaism, different than the
one represented here in Israel by the repellent rabbinic establishments.

D AYS AND YEARS HAVE PASSED SINCE THEN, AND MY LIFE
no longer revolves solely around what happens to me. Change is
also reflected in the content of our children's conversations, including
during the familial Shabbat meals that we so cherish. When they were
little, we talked around the table about teachers and studies, games and
hobbies. As army service approached, militarism asserted itself on their
side, and on our side, there was sad concern for them. When they were
released from the army the conversation shifted from service to studies,
work, and their future. Then the room was filled with the happiest of
subjects—their weddings, the new families they were going to have.
Now there are lots of grandchildren, and the commotion starts anew.
Not all our children are married, and for some the conversation is very
practical while for others it remains theoretical. In these worlds of theory, we always tried to delicately sketch the outlines of the future bride
or groom. To assure them that we genuinely believe the broad human
message, according to which there is really only one test at home for
any who come in—that they be good people. What do I care whether
someone is Jewish if he is fundamentally bad or evil, racist or violent?
And what will stop me from loving my new daughter-in-law or son-
in-law if my children love them and they will bear my grandchildren?

In 2013, I was in a public debate in Netanya. The audience was very right wing, and the conversation was heated. The arguments continued long after the lights were turned off and the hall was closed. It was nearly midnight when I finally got to the parking lot, eager to get as far away from there as fast as possible.

In the darkened lot only my car remained; everyone had already gone home. Next to the car was a group of young people wearing the kippahs of the Chabad movement and wearing T-shirts of the extreme rightist Kahane Chai movement. Bad news. For a minute, I was afraid. My mailbox is full of threatening letters from their ilk, and it's clear to me that one day this violence will catch up with me. Was this the moment?

"Burg," one of them began, "he wants to ask you a question." He directed me to the one who looked like the biggest thug in the group. They all chuckled in expectation of the intellectual knockout punch that would soon be thrown at me, the hated leftist.

"Tell me, with all these views of yours, would you be ready for your daughter to marry an Arab?" I sounded my internal all clear and relaxed my tensed muscles; this wouldn't come to blows. Not tonight. I explained to them that in my view there was no difference between my sons and daughters. That it wasn't me who approves my children's marriage partners. That they had been educated to be independent, ethical people who make the decision about their lives themselves. "And most importantly, if my daughter will come home and tell me, 'Dad, I have two marriage proposals, which do you recommend? One man is a Jewish Kahanist, racist, studies with Arab-hating rabbis, a violent activist who participated in two lynchings of Arabs'—someone like you for example," I said, pointing at the questioner. None of them responded to my provocation, so I continued. "'And the second is an Arab doctor, active in human rights groups, a volunteer in the community clinic in the mixed city in which he lives, he has Jewish and Arab patients and he's a veteran peace activist,' whom do you think I would recommend to her?"

"He definitely answered you," said the one who started the conversation, and they quietly moved away. But the incident was not over. Out of the darkness came two young girls, bearing their identities on their skin, Ethiopians. They said that they were at the debate and wanted to ask me a question.

"Of course," I replied.

"Would you also not care if your son married an Ethiopian?" Unlike the baiting question of the group of youths, this was a painful question, full of tears.

"Yes, my dear girl, I don't care who they marry. Tall or short, black or white, I don't care what his or her faith is. I will have only one test for whomever they bring home. That they be good people."

"Non-Jews as well?"

"Of course! If they are good, what do I care what their faith is? And if they are bad, what good does it do me that they are Jewish?"

"And a homosexual?"

"Yes, even a homosexual or a lesbian. There is only one test for partnership and humanity."

One of them began to cry, and the second told me, "We've been in Israel for years. We've studied in religious institutions, and we always knew there was something else, but we didn't know how to say it. This evening you said it for us. Thank you so much. Drive carefully."

I've reached a point in life in which my family is the center from which other circles emanate. Imposed closed tribal and national frameworks repel me. I need human space without barriers. I want to define my own borders and connections. I don't feel genuine automatic membership in collectives only because of our common ethnic, genetic, or religious origin. I have too many relatives who are real moral enemies, and there are distant relatives I don't even know who are potentially very close to me. At the same time, pure, egoistic individualism repels me no less, and does not satisfy me at all. The family is therefore the framework in which I feel most comfortable.

Mostly it is filled with solidarity and brotherhood, but sometimes it generates quarrels and resentment. Despite everything, it is a microcosm of humanity in a size that I can grasp. Not billions or millions of partners with whom I have no real connection, and not myself alone.

From my extended family, I look at the world and try to understand the contexts of my relatives' lives and our future. Our family is old-fashioned in every respect. Most of the marriages are stable, the relationships are healthy, tensions are contained and not externalized, and all generations speak with one another. From my old-fashioned family I watch and even stare inappropriately at the new families. What happens to them interests me a great deal. Through the old families, I better understand the past and the old world, and through the new families I try to understand the renewed humanity and the future waiting for us all.

When I was a child, all children had a father and mother. The Sephardic children usually also had a grandfather and grandmother from both sides, and we, the Ashkenazic children, had almost none. The children of today are exposed to far greater complications. Many have more than two pairs of grandparents. Sometimes more than one mother or father, or less. Same-sex or single-parent families, divorced or separated parents, and so on. Biological children and test-tube children in the same class. I don't know what it does to the souls of these small children, but it certainly demands the ability to absorb far more complexity than we encountered at their age. The new structures of parenting, the complicated and separated families, the erased borders between generations of parents and children—all these raise the question anew for me, where is human society heading? I once knew the answer—what was, what will be, because the basic social core, the family, had remained as it was. Now I no longer know. I can't guess what future society will look like, because I don't entirely understand the modern family. I accept it as it is, and I am hopelessly curious about the new intimacy, which I am sometimes witness to, but don't understand—yet. How can someone from my background understand someone such as L., one of my new friends in the wide world?

L. is a friend I love very much. He is a Lutheran theologian who is gay, and who was born in Germany and lives in Holland in a happy family with his two male lovers. A standard family of three men. And they are not alone. A. is a single-parent mother who received a sperm donation from her former partner whom she divorced through the rabbinate according to religious law. K. and Y. are two test-tube babies whose marriage I officiated. And their family happiness is even richer and more complex.

In order to better understand the new realities, I've been watching established rabbinic Jewish weddings, and I don't like what I see. The bride and groom stand under the chuppah, like scarecrows in their own play. The rabbi mumbles some incomprehensible words that to many sound like a faint echo of ancient voodoo rituals. And the audience waits impatiently for the end of the forced ceremony in order to sit comfortably at a table, eat a good meal, chat with friends, and dance before the dawn of a new day of work.

Whoever takes a deeper look understands that this is a meeting of two terrible wrongs: the distorted perception of women by the rabbinic establishment and the coercive involvement by the authorities. The first in that marriage is an ancient ritual that is basically the husband's acquisition of sexual ownership of the woman from her father. Yes, it must be acknowledged that the roots of the ancient original Jewish wedding are planted, among other places, in the flowerbed of trafficking in women. The man purchases the woman with a ring that is "worth a penny" and becomes her "husband," that is, her owner. And she, on the "happiest day of her life," effectively becomes his property. And the second—as if the first were not enough—in that the Israeli wedding has three people under the chuppah: the bride, the groom, and the State of Israel. The state, the regulator, intrudes into the sexual relations and partnership of the two lovers and imposes on them very specific religious content, though that really should not be its role.

For many years, I wanted to offer couples a different kind of wedding. One that is entirely derived from tradition, but turns the damaged into the meaningful and the discriminatory into a declaration of love and a completely equal, committing partnership. In the wedding, humanity, and family that I believe in and am committed to, there is no trafficking of people. The weddings have to reflect and echo the values and commitments of the couple getting married. But so long as my children were not married, I couldn't come out with my plan. I knew what people would say: "Ah, you married your children by the book, and you're offering us a second-rate wedding." That is not my intention.

An egalitarian and respectful wedding, committed to human and universal values, is the deepest and most comprehensive expression I can give to up-to-date Jewish culture, combining what is good in tradition with what is wonderful in renewal. In every wedding I now conduct, all that is inappropriate is erased or changed: there is no ownership, no monetary marriage contract between the woman and her partner, there is no fictitious sadness over ruined Jerusalem, because the city spreads from Jericho to Netanya. All these ancient symbols are endowed by the bride and groom with new and egalitarian meanings, so this ceremony has real, actual significance.

With this commitment, we conducted the weddings of our children as ceremonies of union in which the man and woman are completely equal to one another. We stayed true as much as possible to the ancient texts and traditions of the wedding celebration, and in places where the meanings of the tradition could not be papered over, we exchanged his ownership of her to a partnership between them.

The weddings of our older children (in 2008 and 2009), which I was privileged to conduct with them and for them, exposed me to many other couples getting married. First, to the circle of our children's friends, and in recent years, to couples getting married from wider circles, much further away. I have several preconditions for every one of the couples that I marry. The first and main one is equality between bride and groom. As the weddings increased and I listened to the many messages that emerged, I became more aware that I was effectively involved in a battle that had been nearly decided. The recognition that every woman is equal before God has already penetrated so deep that it can't be rolled back. Along with my belief in equality for women, I also realized that if I am indeed committed to the principle of equality between all people, then every person has the right to have a family, to be happy, to raise children, and to pass on his or her legacy and beliefs through them. So why not have an LGBT wedding? That's what I explicitly tell my children: personal preferences are not important, what is important is a positive personality, no?

It didn't happen immediately. On the contrary. One day in the early nineties, when I was serving as chairman of the parliamentary education committee, a group of political activists came to see me. As soon as the routine opening remarks were made, I was sorry that I had agreed to meet them. "We are LGBT community activists, and we want . . . " I devoted the rest of the meeting to evasions, excuses, and obfuscation. "That's the last thing I need," I rationalized to myself. I was closer then to my mother, who didn't believe there was such a thing as a Jewish homosexual, than to Brian, who mobilized his community in San Francisco to help AIDS victims. At the end of the session with the activists, they asked if they could have their picture taken with me and issue a press release about the meeting. "It wouldn't be good for you . . . " I convinced them.

Today, gazing back from the keyboard over time, I think a great deal about my status and my positions in those days. Usually I was more thoughtful than I had been that day. Many people came to me to consult, to share, to take advantage of my experience or connections. It seems to me that all of the advice I gave then, or at least most of it, was good . . . for me. Like that empty statement to the LGBT activists. Today I am entirely the opposite. When I'm asked, I try to reply with the most accurate truth I see before me, even when it is entirely contrary to my interests.

A whole generation has passed since then, and when Gal and Moshe approached me and asked that I marry them, I agreed. I was grateful to them, because I felt that they were challenging my Jewish conventions and theirs. For many months, we studied—together and separately—Jewish sources on marriage and the wedding ceremony, sexuality and same-sex relationships. In the end, we developed a complete ceremony that integrated ancient Jewish content with their unique same-sex familial bond.

At their wedding, I felt that there were two other people standing with us under the chuppah, my late mother on the one side, and Brian on the other. In the moments of silence, always part of the intimacy of the chuppah, I imagined Brian whispering to her quietly, "Yes, Mrs. Burg, there are Jewish homosexuals." But while I didn't manage to imagine her response, I know there are questions that people like her, of her generation and upbringing, would never leave unanswered. Johnny's warning against being mugged in broad daylight was right on the mark, because in many respects, which have increased over the years, he and Brian mugged me in broad daylight, stealing the limited identity with which I had arrived in San Francisco. But in their spiritual generosity, unlike other thieves in my life, they granted me far better alternatives than those I came with to my first meeting with them.

Not long ago, an Arab partner and I interviewed a candidate for a job. She was a young Arab woman from a Muslim home and a lawyer by training. "Let's assume," my Palestinian Israeli colleague asked her, "that tomorrow you could choose the citizenship you want, Israeli or Palestinian. Which would you choose?" She thought for a moment and answered, "The one that I think will safeguard as many of my rights as possible as a secular woman with equal rights."

It will take more time before there is equal treatment in all aspects of our lives for women and every individual, like my daughters, the job candidate, and the brides I married. But this revolution can no longer be turned back. The issue has been decided, though victory has yet to be declared. In every place that I fearfully see and hear Jewish fundamentalists who devote themselves entirely to exclusion of women, homophobia, and xenophobia, I know that we are taking another step closer.

Because the more women are liberated, earning a living, important and equal, the more men's hegemony is threatened and hence their harsh and violent response. The recognition of the equal value of all people is penetrating deeply everywhere, and it is especially threatening to those of religious or traditional persuasions. And the more they are threatened, the more extreme and strident they become. That is why their extremist move to the dark side is evidence of the gains made by our brighter side. And because in recent years they have been very vociferous and aggressive, I know that they will be defeated.

I T TOOK ME MANY YEARS TO UNDERSTAND THAT THE place of women in society—any woman in society—is the litmus test for the degree of equality in that society. The boys-only schools in which I had studied, the male combat units in which I had served, and the long years in local political life in which there are few women—all these environments gave me plenty of opportunities to understand and express my commitment to the equality of women and their status, a commitment whose basis is so simple: a society in which women are discriminated against is a flawed society, and an egalitarian society— among all and for all, not only for women—is a proper society. That is how we raised our girls and boys together. We didn't want our boys callous and insensitive, and we didn't expect to have fragile and needy girls who have no active role in building the world.

During the nineties, in the years before my children's bar mitzvah and bat mitzvah celebrations, we sat down every Sabbath and studied together. Every child chose his or her topic, and from the broad and deep study, the speech on the festive day emerged. Not an incomprehensible and inexplicable speech like mine, dictated by father to son, but their own words, expressed as they wished. To this day, ideas are still sprouting from those seeds. Equality, freedom, justice, sensitivity, environment, vegetarianism, and a great deal of brotherhood. Roni wanted to learn about "the status of women in Judaism." At age eleven, when we started these studies, she was already a veteran of the feminist wars. In the religious public school where she studied, the principal wanted to forbid the girls from coming to school in pants. She confronted him, launched a school movement named "Modest in Pants," studied Jewish sources, prepared a sharply worded petition, got male and female students to sign, and had the decree rescinded.

Before her bat mitzvah, Roni expressed a desire to read her weekly portion from the Torah in synagogue. Together we studied the traditional melody and the Torah trope. At first it was a bit strange for me because I had never heard the Torah read and sung with a woman's voice. In my ancient, primitive consciousness, the Torah belonged to the male world, and its sounds were somewhere in the area of the bass and baritone. But with her help it became more natural. In alto or soprano, the Torah sounds so beautiful, new, fresh, and right. We studied every Sabbath, and each time I would witness her wonderful progress. As our studies progressed, the complexity of the topic deepened.

The bat mitzvah date drew near, and the question grew more urgent: how can we have a shared family prayer when my parents, especially my father, were never part of the religious egalitarian revolution? "I'll talk to Grandpa," the young revolutionary said with determination. After a week, she came back with an arrangement. On Independence Day of that year we celebrated with her—the whole family together—the day of her entrance into the circle of Jewish responsibility. She read from the Torah and Dad, for the first time in his life, joined a mixed, egalitarian service. She and I completed the journey, and my father, in his eighties, embarked on his own path.

My sisters and I turned out very differently from what we witnessed in our home. The division of labor among my parents was classic for that generation: Dad was the breadwinner, and Mom was the homemaker. He was outside, she was inside. He was the representative, and she was with the children and at parent meetings. It turns out that precisely there, at the place furthest from what I consider the proper model for relations between a couple, that the seeds of that model were sown in me.

I don't think that Dad knew how to do any of the household chores himself. At the end of the family Sabbath meal everyone would mobilize to clear off the table, clean and wash the dishes, take out the garbage, arrange everything again in the refrigerator, and set the table for Sabbath morning. We all worked, each with an assigned task. Mom cleaned the pots, my sisters shined the glasses—"don't forget to hold it up one last time to the light to make sure there are no stains"—and I cleared off the dishes, shook out the tablecloth—"outside please"—and threw out the garbage. Dad had one task: to remove the salt and the challah knife. He treated the chore with dead seriousness, walking slowly with the light load in his hands and loudly declaring, "Achtung, vorsicht." German words of deterrence and warning that he was familiar with, automatic language he retreated to when he encountered situations outside his control. And that was it. He did nothing else.

In her old age, Mom was once out of the house—abroad or in the hospital—I don't remember exactly. And my father, who was always cold, felt an even greater chill because of the absence of his love. With uncharacteristic determination, he went by himself to the biggest and most expensive electric appliance store in town and bought himself a heater, because he had no idea how to run the heating system at home. On the way back he stopped at the nearest grocery and bought a giant jar of coffee, a spoon, and a cup, because he simply did not know where all these were in his own home. Never, until that moment, did he ask himself how his coffee appeared in the morning, precisely when he wanted it, and how the cup refilled, seemingly by itself, next to him at his desk. That was how dependent he was on Mom's work at home. In short, a real man.

Whoever was familiar, even in the slightest, with their relationship discovered mutual admiration that did not fade with the years. She admired his wisdom, he her earthiness; she, his worldliness, he, the fact that she was a native; she, his sophistication, he, her common sense. If a jigsaw puzzle had been formed in their image, it would be impossible to know where he ended and where she began, and vice versa.

So, this feminism of mine was something new in my life, an egalitarian rebellion against all the inequality that my mother experienced.
All her life, I was saddened and almost angered by her refrain, "I gave
up my career as a teacher in order to raise you." Or, "I could have been
something else, but I promised Dad that I would support him and his
political activity." And the worst of her sayings: "All my life I've belonged to somebody. I was the daughter of . . . and the sister of . . . and
then the wife of . . . and now I'm the mother of . . . " And I always
wanted her by herself, not through the prisms of all the others who, I
believed, she thought defined her.

In short, from such a home—a mother who sacrificed herself and a
father who spent most of his hours and years outside, a home in which
he was the breadwinner and she the manager, in which he studied the
daily Talmud page every night, while she was in the kitchen, responsible for cooking and cleaning—from a home like that nothing could
grow that resembled the ideal of equality to which I am committed. No
wonder that I never attributed these foundations of my values to her,
or to them.

I learned my feminism from my partner, who is better than me at
everything, while developing our relationship as a couple at home
and the ways to raise our children. Later, when the fruits of our tree of
life began ripening, and our children became independent, I received
much more from them, especially from my daughters. For many years,
I thought I had not learned this from the home where my sisters and I
grew up, an old-fashioned home. I was wrong. Again, it turns out that
the ancient Jewish Aramaic saying, psychological before Freud, is practical and relevant to this day: "The lessons of childhood are not forgotten." I understood these roots of childhood only at the last minute, next
to my father's deathbed.

He wrote the first words of that saying on my wall a few years before
he passed away (in 1999, at the age of ninety-one). But I didn't really
notice their power. That happened in one of the rare times in our public lives when we were officially together on the same stage. He was in
his traditional role of presiding judge at the international youth Bible

quiz, and I, as chairman of the Jewish Agency, also had some official role there. I was asked, ex officio, to say words of welcome to the Jewish youngsters from abroad.

"What do you want to speak about?" Dad asked me a few days ahead of time.

"About the idea of equality in the Bible," I replied.

"In three minutes? You won't have the time."

"I'll have to try, Dad, I'll try."

On the appointed day, I ascended the big stage in Jerusalem. I began, as customary when my parents were present, by acknowledging them, and then continued:

> With your permission I would like to welcome you, the contestants, and pray for the Torah's triple blessing of love. The blessing contained in the commandment, "You shall Love the Lord your God," is entirely equivalent to the requirement to love my neighbor like myself, and there is no difference between them and the eternal requirement to love the stranger, the other among us, the one different from us. And remember this—all these equated loves, love of God and his worship, love of the neighbor and love of any person, even a stranger, is not applicable to men only. Because in the great revolution in Egypt, the one whose call, "Let my people go," still echoes to this day, Moses tells Pharaoh explicitly, "We shall go with our young and old, with our sons and daughters, because we must observe the Lord's festival." Moses represents there, before Pharaoh, an entirely different inner truth: in his view, worship of God is not only man's worship, but of believers from both genders, "our sons and daughters" together. If that is how it is between human beings and God—all the more so between people, and between Adam and Eve.

The whole message took no longer than three minutes. Very little—if any—applause came from the hall, which was packed with Bible buffs, most of them equality-challenged Orthodox Zionists. Of all the dignitaries on the stage, only Dad, who I could see from the corner of my eye, applauded. In the evening, I called him to see how he was doing and ask how his day had gone. "You indeed did not exceed three minutes," he answered, without elaborating. A warm German Jewish compliment. Who could ask for more?

A few minutes later he called me in the car. "Where are you?"

"I'm with the kids on the way home."

"Can you arrange for everyone to hear me?" he asked.

"Yes. I'll put on the speaker."

"I wanted you to know," he told me, "that you said very important things today. They didn't understand you, but I understand. In the revolution of equality for women, the Jewish people doubles itself in one stroke. Humanity doubles itself. And not just a doubling that duplicates the same thing, but something entirely different, much better. Like your mother, not like me," he added with affectionate cynicism. "The Jew discovered the one God. That is the main pillar of Jewish thought. But the Jew also discovered humanity. And humanity is the entire human race, including women. That is the real meaning of the revolution in Egypt. An end to slavery, an end to subjugation. That is the source of Maimonides's vision of the end of days, 'without subjugation by other authorities.'" With that, he ended his short phone lesson.

Two years passed, and his strength was sapped. We all sadly felt that these were the last days, and that his body would no longer renew itself. Dad, like the good, organized German Jew that he was, planned his funeral to the last detail. Who would come, who would escort his single sister from New York, what would be inscribed on the tombstone, and who would speak. Those moments were so special. Some so sad they would move us to tears, and some funny, because we always laughed at home. Delicately, suggestively, but right to the heart. During his preparations with us he said, "After my death I no longer owe anything to the chief rabbis, right? So maybe they don't have to speak at the funeral, right? Let them read a chapter of Psalms, that's enough for them."

That was the way my wise and gentle father transmitted his message. Truth hurt him, and honesty required him to acknowledge reality. His attempted revolution had failed—there is no official rabbinical authority in Israel, at least not one he needs to bow to, on his last day. Something happened to religious society in its meeting with modernism, freedoms, and democracy. So maybe saying Psalms will save it.

In his life, Dad knew these things and kept them inside, because he saw his role in life as a preserver and protector of past glory. A representative of the conservatives. Only before his death did he loosen up and reveal something to us of what he really felt. Next to his grave, when his body was lowered into the pit, another surprising and penetrating truth of his rose up to the heavens. It had started a few weeks earlier.

In the last weeks of my father's life, my sister and I gathered every day near his bed, fluffing up the pillows, asking how he was, shaving him, putting on his tefillin, wrapping him in his beloved prayer shawl, continuing to prepare for the inevitable. One day he said, "Let's talk about eulogies."

"You," he said with a smile always reserved for me, "you never listened anyway when I told you what to say, especially what not to say. I know that I can't tell you what to say. So at least say it well." Then he turned to my sister. They always had a deep understanding, tremendous appreciation, and a rare love reserved for the two smartest people in our family.

"You," he told her softly, not out of a desire to hurt her, God forbid, "you are a woman of action, not words like us. But I would like you to say a few words at my funeral."

"Of course, Dad, whatever you want," she said, kind as always.

"Do you have a paper and pen?"

"Yes."

"Then write please." And he dictated his request.

A few weeks later, he closed his eyes forever. His funeral took place at the plaza of the Yad Vashem Holocaust memorial, with which he was very involved to his last day. Throngs of people, thousands, gathered in the big plaza. National leaders, ministers, rabbis, and intellectuals, and with them thousands of the ordinary people he loved so much. And they, the masses, returned his love. He saved some during the Holocaust, he supported others with personal charity, the mother of one was his student in the Herzliya Gymnasium, and with others he had studied in the rabbinical seminary in Berlin before everything went up in smoke. Many took the podium to deliver eulogies. All men, including me, maneuvering between my role as eulogizer of my father and my role as a public figure. After the rabbis and politicians, my sister took the podium. A lone woman eulogizer among the men.

At first, she said what a daughter always says in these moments. Delicately, painfully, with the longing that had already permeated our lives, even though the deceased had yet to be brought to his final resting place. And then she raised her eyes, looked at the crowd, and took from her pocket the piece of paper on which she had written the things that Dad had dictated to her. The last earthly message with which he wanted to bid the world farewell: "When I sat next to his bed, Dad asked that I speak at his funeral, and expounded his view that the most important revolution of the last century, the greatest of revolutions, is the entry of women into the world of action and creation. This is a greater revolution than the French and Russian revolutions, because as a result the world gained full partners in action and creation. In every place that this revolution was accomplished, society gained another 100 percent of human beings who became partners in social life. Dad added that he feared that not all parts of our society are aware of the importance of this revolution."

Because this was the funeral of a beloved man, and because I was not only circumstantially saddened but deep in my heart as well, I couldn't break out two smiles that threatened to spread across my face. One smile at the sight of the astonished faces of the throngs of mourners, Jews who advocate the separation between women and men, the exclusion of women and male superiority, the very same Israelis who are still not aware of "the importance of this revolution." It turns out that we had grown up our entire lives in the shadow of a complete feminist, and we didn't know that he had led them in this spirit, and they also had not been aware of it.

His last words were the most courageous I had heard from him during my entire life. Words that made me want to smile the second smile that has not left my face since, the smile of liberation and disclosure. Many friends tell me that only after the death of their aged parents do they dare do and believe in things that they could not as long as their parents were alive, if only out of respect. In our home, there were no real limits on thoughts and words. And still, this new ideological freedom was the last and greatest natural gift that a father could give his son, leaving him alone in the commotion of life. From the brink of his grave, Dad challenged Orthodox thinking in our time and in the future. I remember well the thought that struck me through the pain of bereavement: this is Dad's legacy, this is his spiritual last will and testament, the will of equality and justice. There I must go.

VERY FEW TIMES, IF AT ALL, DID DAD TALK TO ME ABOUT God, about his belief in the Creator. This issue was a constant, a driving force that we almost never discussed, and we never doubted its existence. There was always water in the faucet, electricity in the sockets, Mom's frozen food in the freezer, Dad at the head of the table on one end, and Mom at the other end facing him, and God. We accepted them all automatically and did not spend time on them. The whole house focused on people, God's creations. Creation and creatures without a Creator, results without causes. That is why our door was always open, that is why the house was full of books packed with the views of wise men from all cultures and all generations, that is why there was not a speech in which Dad did not cite such a man, one of our sages, or one from another nation. Every day, Dad was a Jew among Jews, but sometimes his ideological and spiritual windows would open up, and through them he was revealed as a great universalist. And between the "Jew" and "universalist" he was not God's Jew.

I often thought that after the Holocaust he must have stopped talking to God and devoted all his energy to conversations with the creatures of that God who turned out to be false. Just like music. He had a very musical ear, and in his youth he knew how to play bourgeois and Jewish instruments, like piano and violin. But I never saw him really playing or singing. Some trauma at some point put a sudden and complete halt to that.

With the completion of my father's cycle of life it became clear to me beyond a shadow of a doubt that despite everything, my Judaism is like my parents' Judaism, and my feminism also comes from them. When people ask me, with a look of smug self-satisfaction on their faces, "And what would your father say about you?", and when their cowardly brothers lash out at me with anonymous trolling such as "You are a discredit to your parents," or "Your father is turning over in his grave," I tell them in my heart the story of Dad's funeral, and I know that the civilization that I believe in and am trying to develop is a Judaism of complete equality between people, whoever and wherever they are.

We will not shed blood; on the contrary, we must wage a constant, all-out war against any manifestation of subjugation, violence, occupation, or discrimination. With the power of my father's spirit in life, and in his will from the grave, we are mobilized for a still-unfinished struggle for equal status for women and others discriminated against by society. Dad was absolutely right in his very last words: "Not all parts of society are aware."

CHAPTER EIGHT

OF ISAAC AND ABRAHAM

M Y NAME IS AVRAHAM—ONE OF THE MOST ANCIENT
Jewish names. I never liked it. So old-fashioned, moldy with antiquity. But what choice did I have? I was named after my late grandfather who passed away in Germany in the dark days on the eve of World War II and was buried under a large granite tombstone in the Jewish cemetery in Dresden. For many years, when the Iron Curtain still separated East and West, guests would occasionally come to the house and bring us pictures of that cemetery. In the center of the picture there was always a shiny black tombstone, on which was inscribed: "Avraham Burg, of blessed memory." And the more he was of blessed memory, the more I had to be alive. I was the bearer of the dreams of previous generations and of the hopes that bubbled up from so much despair of my parents and their generation. I always wanted a much more Israeli name. A name of nature and landscape, of the Land of Israel and its memories, of beautiful and revived Hebrew. Once I wanted to be called David, a name of bravery. Another time Nimrod, like the statue of Yitzhak Danziger. I also thought Uri was a nice name. I started with Avraham, and became Avrum, the shtetl version, to my friends.

With the years and the accumulating names of my children and grandchildren, I think a lot about a person's name and the baggage it carries. Sometimes I try to find characteristics of people or wonder about their cultural and spiritual condition that stems from their name. I have no religious friends called Nimrod, nor observant friends named Hagar. These are revived names, names of the Zionist rebellion. There is no Jew today who answers to the name Ishmael, though the ancient Rabbi Ishmael should have been a model for contemporary Judaism, and not his rival, Rabbi Akiva. It seems to me that only a few ultra-Orthodox towns have streets named after him.

Rabbi Akiva was the most destructive and dangerous messianist up to the rabbis Kook, father and son, and their contemporary successors. His doctrine and students were directly responsible for the destruction and catastrophe of the second century. Grand self-destruction that was inflicted by them, not the Romans. The fact that the Bnei Akiva youth movement is named after him reflects the threat of destruction emanating from it no less than from the original Akiva.

Sometimes, in a person's name, in the algorithms of his identity, I manage to see the expectations of his parents, and his place. "Every person has a name," wrote the poet Zelda Schneurson Mishkovsky (1914–1984), and every name has far greater meaning than a calling card or information sticker or doorbell.

Over the years, it has become clear to me that there is a very strong relationship between my character and the essence of my ancient name. When I think about the name given to me by my parents, I try to be attentive to the voices of the official, established contemporary Judaism of Israel. It's very hard for me to connect with most of those voices, whether they come from the visible or hidden Judaism. "This Judaism, it's not mine," as one of my children told me in one of our many discussions on identity. At the same time, I miss the beautiful, honest, and pure elements of the core identity my parents brought me up on, though it wasn't mine at the time. Dad and Mom's Judaism was humanity at its best. A love of people woven with love of the hidden God. A fabric of faith with open and attentive positivity. An identity so different than the ocean of Jewish negativity through which my children have to swim on their way to their own identities. My name, that antiquated Avraham, is a lifeboat, or at least the straw on which I try to cross the ocean of our common identity.

Our patriarch Abraham, the father of the nation, was a man full of energy. In the eighth decade of his life, our eternal mythology tells us, he discovered God, converted men and supported his wife, who converted women, smashed the idols and beliefs of his father, rebelled against King Nimrod and his authority, and founded the new faith: monotheism. Without a doubt, an astonishing record. And at precisely the time when everyone else would have retired, withdrawn to his home, reveled in his achievements, followed the results and consequences of his life's work, and enjoyed the respect reserved for the few great men of the world. True of others, but not of Abraham. He founded the Go Forth doctrine, a worldview, a psychology of constant restlessness. The Abrahamite, a person walking in the footsteps of the founding father, will never bask in his previous achievements. From the moment they are achieved, he is already taking on the next mountain, the peaks that await, the challenges he has yet to meet. This Abrahamite is always a radical, a traveling revolutionary, spreading the seeds of his ideas wherever his spirit may carry them.

In contrast with the Abrahamic model is the Isaacian model. Most of my Israeli friends are Isaacs, bound up, victims of their mentality and fixed in their ways. We will never know why and what exactly happened there on the altar on Mount Moriah. In our historic memory two have remained, the father and son, who have taken a vow of eternal silence. All that we have left of those earth-shaking moments is the *akeda,* which literally means "binding." Abraham bound his son on the altar. Symbolically, Isaac remained much more tied. This is not the place to decipher the terrible meaning of the culture of human sacrifice that is at the basis of Judaism. We, the late readers of the ancient story, learn that the manifest pinnacle of Isaac's life is not the binding on Mount Moriah, but his immovability in the Land of Israel, always and unconditionally.

Isaac is the only one of the three patriarchs who never left this place. I have cousins like that—like him, they were born in the land of Canaan, they will die in it, and never leave its borders. Isaac is the archetype of all the bound-up Israelis. The further his father goes, in his wanderings and revolutions, the closer and more connected he is. Tilling the soil, planting, and harvesting. Digging wells and trying very hard to deepen his roots here, in the land cherished by his parents. Abraham is the river churning forward, and Isaac is the mountain always standing in place. The world apparently needs both—one to surge forward, the other to remain. One who will change what has decayed, and one who will preserve what deserves to be perpetuated. Perhaps that is why we are named after Jacob-Israel, who was a combination of the two. Native-born, but a wanderer; restless, but longing. In short, the original Israeli was . . . pretty Israeli.

I'm not an Isaac type, but a restless Abrahamic wanderer. Wandering in the fields of spirit and consciousness and refusing to be tied down. I see my Judaism as a continuing interface with other cultures, an equal human being, not chosen by God. In that sense, the name of the founding father, Abraham, carries a personal commitment for me. "And you shall no longer be called Abram, but your name shall be Abraham, for I make you the father of a multitude of nations" (Genesis 17:5). It would be highly presumptuous of me to make the empty claim that "I'm like that," but I aspire to be that way.

The Abrahamite sees himself as a parent—a father—not just to us, but to a multitude of nations, to all members of the human race who desire to be part of it. And without patronizing and condescension, and with no coercion and violence. The Isaacs, on the other hand, view their identity through national prisms and are constantly fearful for themselves, their fate, and the one place where they are rooted: here in this land and in the State of Israel. It's not that one concept is right and the other is wrong, kosher or unkosher. Both are legitimate; both have a basis in history, in the sources and in consciousness. It's a question of connection. The Israel of today, and most of the Israelis in it, connects much more to the Isaacian element in our past, and I think that Isaacian Israeliness is limited and is condemned, as it was in the past, to destroy itself. In my view, the time has come to go back another stage to Abrahamism, and thus to effectively move another step forward.

No wonder that I've lost so much of the popularity I enjoyed during all the years I followed the false consensus. To be an Isaac is to be a conservative, and to be an Abraham is to be avant-garde. And now I very much like my old name, and I'm committed to it. What I miss is the universal Jewish voice, not only calling for fighting and killing and being killed for nation and country, but a voice that defines Jews as "the nation of the world," part of a great universal responsibility for all of humanity wherever it may be. I feel that Israeliness alone is not enough for us and for me. We need more.

By "more" I mean this, for example: "The Jewish element had been largely dominant in the revolutions of thought and sensibility experienced by Western man over these last one hundred and twenty years. . . . Without Marx, Freud, or Kafka, without Schoenberg or Wittgenstein, the spirit of modernity, the reflexes of argument and uncertainty whereby we conduct our inner lives, would not be conceivable."*

This Abrahamic element is sorely lacking for me in Isaacian Israeliness. I hear the whole range of Israeli voices—from those fearful for the future of the place to those who are self-confident, without doubt or consideration—and I ask myself, Where are the Jewish voices that embody creative doubt and thoughtfulness? I see a lack of Israelis who are involved in the global conversation, not only in ours. The standard Israeli Isaacs that I know ask almost no questions. And whatever pondering they do is about us and our problems at home. I can barely remember any debates here on essential issues that go beyond us. It seems to me that out of the broad scope of Jewish culture, my parents could not have chosen a more appropriate name for me than the name of the first revolutionary, the original Jewish radical. Because my Abrahams

---

*Paul Mendes-Flohr, *Progress and Its Discontents* [in Hebrew] (Tel Aviv: Am Oved, 2013), 15.

are never satisfied with the answers they receive and achievements they have already attained.

In many respects, being an Abraham is being liberal, open, and attentive. He was determined to fight for justice, not only for his family, but for the people of wicked Sodom, even at the price of defying God (Genesis 18:25: "Far be it from you! Shall not the judge of all the earth deal justly?"). Could it be that the patriarch Abraham was a leftist? The first to have the land promised to him and the first to offer a partition plan to his cousin Lot? At least that's how I portray him to myself. All my adult life I identified as a leftist. That is how I perceived myself, that is how I educated my children. In politics, I was always a natural part of groups on the left, attending peace rallies, enlisting in political initiatives, representing these ideas on every possible Israeli stage at home and abroad. With time, it has become clear to me that I was a leftist Israeli-style, not someone who really fits the definition of "left."

THE LEFT-RIGHT DIVIDE IN ISRAEL RUNS SOLELY ALONG the political issue: the left is supposed to be for diplomatic agreements, while the right is opposed. We've almost entirely forgotten the other layers that make a person a member of a genuine leftist camp. The desire of most of the left for peace or a political settlement does not necessarily stem from conceptions of justice and morals. "I want peace so the Palestinians will get out of my face" is not the crude statement of a gruff man in the street, but the political strategy of many of my influential friends. The absence of concepts of equality and justice as the organizing ideas of the leftist political camp is one of the main reasons I feel that all these years I was a hollow leftist, and that I belong to a camp that is mostly ideologically empty.

The left in the world I have gotten to know in recent years stems from a full and complete worldview, whose most basic element is the uncompromising belief that all human beings were born equal and have to live their lives that way: in equality between men and women, the majority and the minority, members of different religions and faiths, and people of various sexual preferences. Everyone has the right to realize themselves and their abilities in full equality at the starting line, with no "buts." Together we are a political camp that is committed without compromise to secularizing public space, fair and just distribution of public resources, and complete constitutional protection of citizens and their rights. In our country the political issue, the conflict, the occupation, and the rest of the malignant diseases of modern Jewish nationalism have taken over our lives and eaten up almost all of the healthy cells. That's why peace in our country is talked about as an interest, not a value; that's why people want a political settlement, because "it's good for us," not because it's right or moral. The talk is about the costs of peace, not the rewards—about the risks, not the opportunities. The more these thoughts go through my head as I write, I sense that they were always there, but I didn't pay attention to them. And then I go back to the two moments of Yitzhak Rabin, the pinnacle of his life and the climax of his death.

When Rabin informed the public about the Oslo accords in 1993, I was overjoyed. I let go of all the anger—personal and political—that I felt toward him. I forgot that I called him repeatedly the "minister of war" during the first Palestinian uprising. I uprooted from my consciousness all his anti-democratic statements. It was part of the outburst of joy and euphoria that swept up many of us, that erased borders and resentments and turned the despair of previous years into a very great hope. In that wonderful wave, there was one sound that I found discordant. Rabin made every political and parliamentary effort to pass the Oslo accord in the Knesset with a "Jewish majority." But democracy belongs to all its citizens, and equality is an idea bandied about by everyone; the heads of the Labor Party poetically called it "the morals of the prophets," no? So where did all this equality go precisely at the moment of peacemaking? From where did this ethnicity come into our democratic life? I couldn't bear those statements, turning me into part of the mechanism of tribal Israeli democracy. Of course, I was for the agreements, but my eyes were downcast. Because I had been humiliated. I tried to think of parallels in other countries, about Churchill seeking to go to a world war, supported solely by a Christian majority in parliament. Or Truman seeking to end World War II without "the Jewish vote." But at the time, in all the exhilaration, there was no one to talk about it with. Not even with myself.

Two years passed, and Rabin was murdered. Like an efficient boomerang, his discriminatory statement came back and took over the public conversation in the days after his assassination. The headlines, the eulogizers, family members, and others who spoke publicly talked about "a Jew murdering a Jew." While they were mired deep in the Jewish swamp, to which Rabin in his weakness surrendered many times in his life, my cry was that "a human being had murdered a human being." My familiarity with Israeli democracy does not permit me to be party to the soppy cliché according to which "Israel is the only democracy in the Middle East." We are an open, impressive, and tolerant democracy, mainly for Jews. Especially those who, like me, were born to the pedigreed, lordly Ashkenazic Jewish class that can allow itself to defy any restriction. Unfortunately, our genuine democracy is much more limited. Israel is the only half-democracy in the Middle East. Not only because of the occupation and the structural discrimination against Palestinian Israelis, but also because of the large web of restrictions imposed on me as a Jew.

If I were active in politics today, I assume that I would be fighting with all my might for full equality as the defining value of our political camp, I would be seeking partners to establish a joint Jewish-Arab party, and I would make my support for any legislative initiative or political act conditional on canceling and erasing the term "Jewish majority." Today I frequently ask myself, if I had been living in the 1930s, would I have volunteered for the international brigade in Spain? And if I had been living as a non-Jew under Nazi occupation, would I have had the courage and emotional fortitude to be a Righteous Gentile and save persecuted Jews? I'm not sure. But at least I can make the effort. Sometimes I feel that here, in Israel and the Middle East at large, the borders between good and bad, between right and wrong, will be set for all of Western civilization. Just like then and there. And this time it is my responsibility, with no excuses.

CHAPTER NINE

A TALE OF TWO HEBRONS

H EBREW IS THE LANGUAGE IN WHICH I WHISPER SECRETS
to myself, dream my dreams, and cry out most bitterly. I know
how to laugh in many languages, but I don't know how to cry in any
other language. Hebrew, as a language and culture, is my homeland,
my mother tongue. The warmth of its mysteries, its layers of meaning,
are as familiar to me as the cracks in the sidewalks of my childhood,
and make me at once into a lover and a beloved. The biblical Hebron,
the maternal Hebron, and the eloquent Hebron Hebrew of my mother's home—these all swaddled me from birth. I speak English fluently
and I understand contemporary French pretty well, and I can make out
German and chitchat in Yiddish and exchange a few words in Arabic;
but none of these can compare to the language in which I was loved,
and in which I first fell in love.

With Hebrew comes also landscapes and memories, intimacy and
openness. I never referred to the landscapes of my homeland and my
childhood by anything but their Hebrew names. I know how to speak
two Hebrew languages: Jewish Hebrew and Israeli Hebrew. They use
the same words, but with different meanings. Ben-Gurion sent us to a
"state" school (i.e., a public one) because statehood was his organizing
principle. He regarded the state as the systematizing principle uniting

all the fragments of the Jewish people who had gathered here. Maybe unbeknownst to Ben-Gurion, we prayed in school for a kingdom of heaven, not for any human government. In the army, we each wore a vest in order to bury deep in its pockets the weapons of destruction that a soldier needed in order to carry out his sacred and profane missions. But only speakers of both Hebrew languages understood that the word the army used for vest, *ephod*, was one of the garments worn by the high priest in the Temple. So, what are we, soldiers or battle priests? Gershom Scholem, the great scholar of Kabbalah, said, "God will not remain mute in the language in which He has been entreated thousands of times to return to our lives." The return of Hebrew to our lives restored God along with it, but not necessarily in the best way.

At home, Mom would correct our Hebrew punctiliously. She was strict about errors both major and minor, and about pronunciation, consonants and vowels, rare words, and exceptions to the rule. She was in charge of the local language, the language of our identities, whereas Dad was responsible for all the rest of the languages in the world—for universalism. He spoke fluently and eloquently in all the Latinate and Germanic languages. He could chat in Spanish, discourse in French, converse in English, and dream in German. Dutch didn't grate on him, and he was at ease in Italian.

Occasionally he would stop and ask Mom, "How do you say . . . ?" They both knew that he knew the answer, but it was part of the show they loved to put on, and it served to strengthen the wonderful bond between them. And she knew French and English, and from Yiddish she could slide easily into German. She was a Jewish Palestinian and a seventh-generation native of Hebron, but the more the years passed after Dad's death, the stronger her German Jewish accent grew. In Hebrew, "homeland" is a feminine word that connotes the one that gives birth. Dad came from over there, from the Fatherland. And Mom came from Hebron, the city of the patriarchs.

Mom could chat in Arabic. She was welcomed in the most illustrious salons in the world, but she was also best friends with her cleaning

woman. She would scrub the house beforehand so the cleaner wouldn't
have too difficult a job. Until the day of her death Mom exchanged
dishes and recipes, showed up with gifts, and inquired after the welfare
of all her friends. She never forgot where she came from, but she also
never remained stuck there, in the past—she never just entrenched
herself there. Mother came from Hebron, but she never returned to
renew her life there or revive the past that had been massacred and
destroyed.

Still, while you could take Mom out of Hebron, you couldn't take
Hebron out of Mom, its character, stubborn as a rock. "We are never
broken" was the message she passed on to us at every opportunity.
Until her final days she lived at home, insisting on doing it all on her
own, fully functioning, not passively allowing time to take its toll. At
the end of one of her last Passover holidays when she was already in
her eighties, she nonetheless climbed the tall ladder, as she'd always
done, and hoisted into the *boydem*—the overhead storage space—all
the heavy boxes filled with kosher Passover dishes, putting them away
until next year. Suddenly the ladder gave way, and she and the cartons
tumbled to the ground. All the dishes broke, the cartons ripped, and
the glassware shattered to smithereens. Everything broke—except for
her. Her friends suffered from osteoporosis, broke their hips, and endured the other ills of old age. But not her. A few black-and-blue marks
here and there, some natural aches from the fall, but that was it. "These
bones are from Hebron." She laughed away her pain.

THE HEBRON OF TODAY IS A CURSED PLACE. MOM'S
Hebron was complex demographically, but from her perspective it
was blessedly so. Mom's ancestors arrived in the holy city at the beginning of the nineteenth century and joined the Sephardi community
that had lived there at least since the expulsion from Spain in 1492. My
mother's forbears came to the Land of Israel long before the Zionists,
as part of a religious and messianic awakening that spread across Jewish
Eastern Europe generations ahead of Herzl and the political Zionist

revival. Grandfather, according to Mom's descriptions, was half and half. In the old pictures that always hung in our home, he wore a fur hat known as a *shtreimel* and a Hasidic robe, and he had a manicured beard and curly sidelocks. He was a man of the Old World when it came to everything external, but he was a supportive and active Zionist in the early religious Zionist groups. His prayer melodies, which I learned from Mom, belong to those olden days. But at the same time, a photo of Herzl was proudly hung on the wall of the home of one of my Hebron uncles.

Mom, in contrast, was almost entirely modern. We didn't know much about her childhood. Perhaps because she didn't remember much, perhaps because she simply didn't want to open some of the boxes that were locked away in the basement of her memory. Sometimes she would tell us about the Arab goat owner, who would pass by every morning and sell them fresh goat's milk, and their Turkish landlady, who nursed Mom's sister after their mother died at a very young age. We owe our lives to that Turkish woman. She was Mom's last stop in Hebron, and her first stop on the way to the splendid life that she—Cinderella from Hebron—would go on to lead. Who was this woman who shaped my destiny more than anyone else? The landlady who didn't just save me—she also determined the course my life would take. It's a simple tale about a good neighbor, but it became a formative tale of human heroism that knows no bounds, and no borders.

My grandfather (1880–1937) was the chief rabbi and the leading functionary of the Ashkenazi Jewish community in Hebron. He raised Mom and her five brothers and sisters almost single-handedly, since Grandmother had died so young. They rented an apartment from a local landlord, a reputable Hebron Arab. At some point in his life the landlord traveled to Turkey and brought back a wife. She was beautiful, according to the aesthetic standards in Hebron at the time: white and fat. She bore him two children, Shaker and Yasser, and the parents took their names from their oldest son: Abu Shaker and Umm Shaker.

At some point in their childhood, during the 1920s, one of the boys fell sick with a burning fever. At the time, Hebron did not have access to modern medicine. Penicillin, the miracle drug, had not yet been invented. The doctors despaired of saving his life. "He won't last the night," they informed the distraught parents. Grandfather, their tenant, the optimistic holy man, sat by the bedside of the sick child all night long, praying. When morning came, the boy's fever went down, and he returned to himself. The parents, Umm and Abu Shaker, were convinced that it was the rabbi's prayers that were responsible for their son's recovery. And they never forgot it. He saved their oldest son's life, and they went on to save everything for us.

In 1929, when Mom was eight years old, the ground in Hebron shook beneath her. "What do you remember from those days?" I asked her nearly eight decades later. "Practically nothing," she admitted. "I think most of my memories are stories they told me about those days, and I adopted them as my own, as if they'd come from inside me." It was a Sabbath day in the summer. On the weekend of August 23, 1929, the family had gathered together in Hebron to celebrate some festive occasion, but the air in the Land of Israel was already saturated with other emotions. The tension between Jews and Arabs was at its peak. They didn't know it, but that's when the Israeli-Palestinian conflict essentially broke out.

The British government, which had received the land as a mandate, did not do enough—it did nothing to calm tempers. In Hebron and in a few other mixed cities that year, it all came to a head in terrible savagery. Jews and Arabs, innocent and guilty, were murdered by the hundreds. Over the course of that Sabbath scores of Hebron Jews were cruelly massacred. When the riots began, the Jews of the neighborhood congregated in two houses: in the home of my uncle, Eliezer Dan Slonim, the one with the photo of Herzl on his wall, and in the home of my grandfather, Rabbi Yaakov Yosef Moshe Slonim, my mother's father and her only living parent. Eliezer Dan was young and well respected. He was the head of the local bank branch, he had a licensed gun, and he had made inroads in the British government and in the Palestinian leadership alike. On the afternoon of Friday, August 23, 1929, he was still running around the city, trying to calm tempers. He managed to save several potential victims from a cruel lynching, and he reached a few provisional agreements with the British and with some of the Arab leaders. The Jews had faith in him. "We'll go to his house, they won't dare to touch him," they said; nearly all of them were butchered in his home.

Sixty-five members of the Jewish settlement were murdered in an act of unprecedented evil over the course of two atrocious hours in the city of the patriarchs. More than a fourth of them were killed in my uncle's home. There were almost no survivors, except for my cousin Shlomo, who was all of two years old and suffered a blow to his head. Amidst the corpses and the wounded, and amidst the rivers of blood that flowed through the streets, the slaughterers mistook him for dead, and he was saved.

In the meantime, on the other side of the neighborhood, the rest of the Jews congregated in Grandfather's house. "He is a holy man, God will protect us in his home," they told one another, as Jews in every generation had told themselves. They prayed, they cowered, and they hid. Earlier, Grandfather went out bravely into the streets of the city and tried to negotiate with the representatives of the British government and police to protect his flock. But in vain. He suffered murderous blows from the enraged mobs. They struck him on the head with a thick rope tied with a heavy knot at one end, nearly killing him.

My aunt Malka, then a young girl of fourteen, left the house and snatched him from their hands before he lost consciousness. Thanks to her heroism, he merely lost his vision in one eye, but he survived. While the rioters were raging in the streets and screaming "Itbakh al yahud!" (Slaughter the Jews) and "Falastin lana w'al yahud kilabuna!" (Palestine is ours and the Jews are our dogs), the old Turkish woman sent one of her sons, Shaker, to fetch his father from the vineyards. It was the peak of the harvest season in Hebron, which is famous for its spectacular vineyards and grapes. At the height of the season, the vintners, just as in biblical times, would not come home every day. They slept in stone guardhouses and in vine-thatched huts so as to take full advantage of each workday—from first until last light. "Go get your father," she ordered him. "They're killing our Jews."

The events of those next dramatic moments were told to us again and again by Mom and Aunt Malka—Treyna, as they called her then, in Yiddish. Here is how my aunt put it:

A short while after my wounded father and I returned home and locked ourselves inside, our neighbor Abu Shaker suddenly appeared, riding his white horse. He tied up his horse and sat down on the stairs leading to our house, looked around, and surveyed the scene. Then he knocked on the door and said, "Don't open! I just wanted you to know that I'm here. I won't let them touch you! Don't open the door! Close all the windows and shutters! May God be with you!"

We sat there silently, holed up in the house, and he, Abu Shaker, reported to us on everything that was happening. "Those goons are killing the Jews," he said in a choked voice. "And there's no one to come to their aid. The police are with the rioters. The British police are accompanying the murderers to the homes of the Jews and waiting outside while they commit acts of murder, and then accompanying them onwards. God will punish them for this!" he said, and we knew in our hearts that our own end was nigh. We didn't believe that he, a lone old man, would manage to stop the inflamed, bloodthirsty masses who were drowning Hebron in rivers of Jewish blood.

The Arab said nothing about what had happened in my brother's house, just one hundred fifty meters away. He kept silent. He did not want to upset us. We heard the terrible screams of the murderers and the death groans of their victims. We didn't know that at that time my brother, his wife, and his

four-year-old son Aaron were still alive. My father stood up and
prayed. He cried out to God. We prepared to die. I remember
that I asked forgiveness for all my sins. It's so hard to describe
it. You're penned in your home, and you're convinced that
death is near, yet you can't describe to yourself what it looks
like, how it will come, where you'll be stabbed. . . . The whole
house was beset by a deathly fear, with only Father's lips moving
soundlessly.

The rioters came. We heard them raging murderously. We
heard them thirsty for blood and burning with fury. We also
heard Abu Shaker's voice: "Get out of here! You can't enter here!
Here you can't kill!" They pushed him aside. He was old, maybe
seventy-five, but he was strong. He fought back. He prostrated
himself over the entrance, by the door. He screamed at them,
"Over my dead body!" One of the rioters waved his knife over
Abu Shaker's legs and yelled, "I'm going to kill you. Traitor!"
Abu Shaker was not afraid. "Kill me! Kill me! The rabbi's family
is inside, and they're my family too. Kill me! I won't budge."
The knife was lowered. Abu Shaker's leg was ripped open. His
blood flowed. He didn't groan or yell, he just said, "Cut me! I
won't budge!" The rioters consulted with one another in a brief
moment of quiet. Then we heard them disperse. We knew we
had been saved. I wanted to bring our savior inside, to bandage
his wounds, to thank him. He refused. He said, "Maybe others
will come, my job is not yet over."

From the perspective of Zionist, Israeli, and Palestinian history, the
Hebron massacre was a formative moment. It marked the end of good
relations between neighbors, between peoples, between members of
different faiths. That was where the violent path we have all walked
down was first laid and paved. It is part of everyone's historical memory, but for me it has deep personal resonance.

My own mother was there, in that inferno, and her soul was miraculously saved by those incredible people, those righteous gentiles, an

Arab from Hebron and his wife, who never lost sight of their humanity. Since then, since that very moment, my family has been divided in
two. Half of them will never trust an Arab. There are members of my
family from my mother's side who count themselves among the most
right-wing, extremist, and fanatical of the settlers and their supporters.
The other half of us will always be seeking out Abu Shaker, that lone
righteous man, kind-hearted and courageous, with whom we can start
the dialogue anew, restart a better life and seek to set it all right. He,
as he put it, is "my family." And in many senses, he is more my family,
more part of the human family, than many of my own blood relatives,
who are my ideological enemies.

It's very hard, in hindsight, to distinguish between the official,
mythic memories that were immortalized in the pre-State annals, and
my mother's own personal memories. Even so, one of her recollections
always struck me as her own authentic memory, and not as something
she was told. "My brother lived at the entrance to the city," she told me
hundreds of times, "and we lived at the top of the hill, separated by an
empty field. From the window of our house we could see the steps to
my brother's house. On the ground floor of his building was the school
where I studied. On that terrible day, I looked out and saw feathers
fluttering over the stairs of his house. I thought it was snow. That it
was as beautiful as snow." Alas, my sad mother, alas, little Rivka'leh.
You were only a bit older than my grandchildren are today. And I so
much want to reach out and hug you again. Just one more time. A big,
loving, protective hug. Because on that day, on that terrible day, they
didn't take mercy on anything, not even on duvets. They slashed them
with fierce fury as if they were human throats. Mom, now I understand.
Only you could see the feathers that flew out of the slaughtered blan-
kets and mistake them for snow. Only thus did you manage to trans-
form that moment of utmost human degradation into the beginning
of our lives. They murdered, massacred, and raped almost everything
in sight—but they did not manage to annihilate your optimism. That
perspective, the perspective of a good girl who believes each morning
anew that her life is pure snow, opened you up to possibility. To be

larger than life. It is the optimism that kept you sane and balanced, joyous and so maternal.

A T THE END OF THE *SHIVA* FOR DAD, MOM AND I SAT IN her small kitchen. "Write, Avraham, write," she told me. "Write Dad's life story. You're the only one of us who can."

"But everyone knows everything about him, he's a public figure," I said, trying to understand.

"That was not what I meant," she explained in her stilted Hebrew. "Write about his world that is no more. Who he really was. The good man I loved," she said, her voice choking up. "Write about Velvey, you understand."

I think she wanted me to communicate to the future generations of our family the sources of our optimism and joie de vivre, which came not only from her, but also from him. Because on Dad's side as well there was someone that was always happy, and never surrendered to depression: Onkel Velvey. Zeev in Hebrew, "Zef" in German Jewish pronunciation, was Dad's cousin. He was part of a tight circle of cousins that grew up together in Dresden, Germany. Velvey was one of the youngest, and Dad the oldest, something like a firstborn son. On November 8, 1938, Dad was in Berlin, and very active in saving Jews from the clutches of the Gestapo. Young Velvey, just fourteen, studied at a yeshiva in Frankfurt. Today, when I think about him, my heart goes out to him, this little boy. A very lonely boy. His mother died of the same cancer that has devoured so many women in our family. His oldest brother had fled already to Palestine, and his father and younger brother had been expelled just a few months earlier to Poland. At noon Velvey left the yeshiva to go somewhere, and when he returned it was all in flames. He called Dad in Berlin from a pay phone.

"Yossel," the fourteen-year-old asked the twenty-nine-year-old. "What should I do?"

"Where are you?" Dad asked.

"On the street."

"Walk down the street. There's a Jewish orphanage there. By the time you get there, I will have spoken with the director, and he'll take care of everything. Don't worry."

That was the start of a long journey that ended with the rescue of another Jewish boy, who became an Israeli. Dad loved Velvey very much, like a brother, more than other surviving members of his family. Velvey was the happiest man of my childhood. Always smiling, always full of vitality. Totally different than Mom's melancholy sisters from Hebron. A man with good hands, whom nothing could stop.

I remember the triumphant smile on Dad's face when he told me once about the exploits of "our Velvey." He traveled to New York and got stuck in a traffic jam in one of the city streets. All the drivers beeped and got upset, except Velvey, who had seen more upsetting things in his life. He got out of his cab, which was driven by the restless Uncle Fischel, a Holocaust survivor and a lovable bundle of nerves ever since, and went to the front of the jam. A huge garbage truck had broken down and was blocking traffic. My uncle climbed up on the truck, opened the hood, and with a few coins from his pocket and some wire he found by the side of the road got the engine running again. This handiness and initiative, the ability to never lose hope, complemented Dad's inherent optimism. And when they saw one another they knew better than anyone else what was left buried there, under the ruins of their beloved Dresden. They knew what was etched forever deep in their hearts, and knew how to support one another like restrained German Jews—wordlessly.

Velvey and Mom were the two pillars that supported many of the structures of Dad's life. Through the tears that accompanied the writing of these pages, I couldn't escape a thought that troubled me. It will never be possible to know what really, deeply changed in their characters because of those traumas of childhood and youth. What orphanhood, bereavement, fears, and sadness did to their young souls, still being formed. Still, could it be that these two, Mom and Uncle Velvey, were good, happy, optimistic people despite it all, because in the one and only defining moment not all was bad? Because they had something or someone good to rely on? Mom had Abu Shaker and Velvey had Dad. Mom has a memory of pure snow out the window, and a humane orphanage was there for Velvey at the end of the street. I'm not an expert on traumas and post-traumatic stress disorder, but they have been around me most of my life, and I have seen that there is a slim but significant difference between those who have managed to latch on to something good in the worst moment of all, and those whom good had evaded, and since then they have no rest or happiness.

Days and years have gone by, and Shlomo, Velvey's son, is one of the closest and dearest people to me. "That's my cousin," I say about him. He is wise and generous, successful and cautious. And when I left political life for my other life, he spread his wings over me and became my guardian angel. Shlomo never judges me. He's just there with me and for me, like Dad and Velvey were there for each other. Always.

The optimism emerging from the destruction continues to shape our lives. We've seen wars and experienced the loss of friends, we've gone through the tragedies and comedies of our generation. Both of us will never let the anger at the missed opportunities stop us from trying to fix things. There's always some wire with which we can restart the truck of life. Both of us and our families love life and are optimistic and trusting. We know deep in our hearts that our parents needed their entire lives to overcome those distant traumas, and that it will likely take much more time for the local collectives to overcome the various painful memories that plague them. And us? Our job is to try very hard to provide that good moment for someone else in bad times. Humanity's love of life will do the rest.

HEBRON CONTINUED TO EXERT ITS HOLD ON OUR FAMILY. I can still remember my first visit there immediately after the Six-Day War. We all drove there—Dad, Mom, my sisters, Aunt Malka, and my little brother—to meet with the family who had saved us. To see the Tomb of the Patriarchs and to search for the place where the house stood until it was destroyed. For us, the stories about Hebron were always in the air. The steadfastness, the firmness, the connection to the place, our patriotism, as well as the sayings and melodies that came from there. Hebron was a sort of status symbol—anyone who came from there was part of the local aristocracy, one of those who was here before everyone else, the *Mayflower* of the nascent State of Israel.

My mother generously shared with us her memories of the Hebron of her childhood, but she knew to draw a clear line between her Hebron and the fanatical Hebron of today's settlers. The massacre committed by Baruch Goldstein in 1994 horrified and shook her to the core. Goldstein (born 1956) was an American Israeli physician, religious extremist, and a cold-blooded mass murderer who perpetrated the Tomb of the Patriarchs massacre in Hebron, killing 29 Palestinian Muslim worshipers and wounding another 125. He was beaten to death by survivors of the massacre. It subverted the foundations of my mother's existence, not just because it was such an inhumane act, a crime against innocents. "Now, because of him, the massacre in Hebron no longer belongs to us," she said. That criminal Goldstein profaned the murder of those she loved, reduced the Jewish massacre in Hebron to a quid pro quo.

A few years before her death, my mother was interviewed on one of the TV channels that caters to religious viewers. She spoke of her childhood in Jerusalem. "But Mrs. Burg," said the young interviewer, a right-wing religious woman, "why don't you return to live in Hebron?" Mom cut her off before she veered into forbidden territory. "Hebron is trauma. My childhood began in Jerusalem." And I understood then how she felt all those years. Hebron was trauma, and Dad and we were a new beginning.

After many years, in the late sixties, Umm Shaker came to our home. She was already very old. Aunt Malka found her in Hebron, and Dad pulled strings in order to arrange everything. It was a day I'll never forget. There in our living room sat the woman I had heard so much about. That Turkish woman, who had sent her husband to the frontier of humanity, where he was wounded by the rioters' knives but refused to relent. The woman who had saved my mother, and the woman to whom I owed my life. What a woman. It's no wonder that she was the only person in the world that Mom allowed to sit cross-legged and to rest her bare feet, just like that, on the great living room couch. Because what was forbidden to little Israeli boys was just fine for the old Turkish woman from Hebron. When she sat with her legs crossed in our German Israeli living room, it was a natural conjoining of East and West. In some sense that old woman from Hebron was like my mother's second mother. Her first mother gave birth to her and died, leaving no memory of her. But her second mother, who saved her life, was in our very home. Dad met her. I saw her, and Mom suspended all the rules for her. Yes, for a moment I had a Palestinian grandmother. Many of my peers, Israelis of various backgrounds and ethnicities, true German Jews and many others too, never had a grandmother like that, not even for a moment.

CHAPTER TEN

THE NEW MEANING
OF HEBRON

U MM SHAKER DIED A LONG TIME AGO, MOM ISN'T HERE
anymore, and the memories are becoming more distant. Other
traumas are plaguing the country instead. And I, the first generation
after Mom's snow, trying to be the last generation of feathers from the
slaughter, wanted to return one more time to Hebron. To feel what I
would feel.

My first meaningful visit to Hebron was during my military service,
a few years after the Six-Day War. I was a young paratroop officer and I
was stationed there with my comrades in order to keep the peace. The
Six-Day War had liberated our ancestral lands and led to the occupation of Palestinian land. We came to the city after police duty in Nablus
and Ramallah.

"We've transferred you to Hebron, the most difficult city in the West
Bank, because of your reputation. Bringing red berets into Hebron is
a message, since the days of the British mandate," we were told in a
briefing. Our good reputation also included our capacity for evil. We
manned checkpoints and forced work-weary drivers to unload giant
trucks loaded with crates of merchandise, ostensibly to make sure that
explosives and other weapons weren't hidden there, but in practice to

prove to them and us who was boss, and who wielded power and authority. Such unloading took hours, and meanwhile all city traffic was stopped. What a perfect mess. We zealously chased after rioters. We made our presence known and intimidated frightened residents in the cities where we were posted. This was the good reputation we brought to Hebron.

I don't recall a feeling of return to my family roots, any sense of closing the circle in Mom's city. It was just another mission. It was important for me to be a good commander, an exemplary role model, to follow orders to the best of my ability, and to be an outstanding soldier, in the spirit of the paratroopers. One day at dawn I took my soldiers on patrol in one of the prettiest riverbeds in the Hebron hills. A route through an ancient landscape of biblical farming terraces, grapevines and vineyard paths, farming huts made of stones, and mud channels carrying the water running from small mountain springs. I had planned the route the previous evening on a topographical map. On the map there are no people, no human realities, and no encounters. The map is indifferent; it only documents. The narrow donkey path wound along the edges of the farming terraces, trying to take up as little as possible of the precious land in the rocky Hebron hills. We walked in a row, keeping a distance from one another, wearing rubber-soled paratrooper boots, carrying packs full of gear and ammunition, rifles at the ready with the safety catch on. Sometimes we walked on the path, and sometimes we cut straight across the fields, packing down soil that had been turned over, inadvertently changing the course of water streams, breaking carefully tended vine branches, repeatedly disturbing the romantic calm of that hidden valley.

Suddenly the owner of the field reared into view before me, the commander leading the troops. A short, burly, and strong Hebron farmer, an older man. He had an expression of terrible pain on his face, a look of uncontrollable rage. He charged at me and my men hysterically. We were armed with the best modern weapons, and he wielded a pickaxe. One against many. My men loaded their guns, aimed, and opened their safety catches. I yelled at him in my best occupation Hebrew. He didn't understand a word and shouted back in his village Arabic, and I understood it all. He couldn't comprehend why anyone had the right to cut through his fields, destroy his work, and damage his ancient vineyard inherited from his forefathers. I understood his outcry, his pain and anger. He continued yelling and going amok, and we had to pin him down. Ten twenty-year-olds against someone who could have been our father or grandfather.

This was a minor incident that probably none of those involved remember, aside from me. Before and after it there were plenty of other occupation stories that were more terrible, brutal, and shameful. But those particular shouts were directed at me personally, and that is why they still ring deafeningly in my ears, from the inside. It wasn't a political shouting match, but it was the protest of the biblical Navot, the owner of the vineyard, against the indifferent oppression of the soldiers of Ah'av—us—just trying to carry out a routine order in the best way possible. I could hear a version of the biblical prophet's condemnation, "Have you conquered and also inherited?" and I was so ashamed. From these very vineyards Abu Shaker returned home and saved Mom and Grandfather and the rest of their household in 1929.

Decades later, I consider my military service in the city as a moment of great personal importance. My internal language changed then for many years to come. The minute I got tough with that Hebron farmer, hardening my heart as an oppressor, my Israeli nationalism jumped to a new level and over time nearly choked any other spirit in me. Something in me died then, and did not come back to life during my years of public service. I didn't know then that I had become an occupier, I just wanted to secure the route, to make sure all was well. And coincidentally I became something else entirely. In those vineyards, I learned the first lessons of Israeli nationalism.

Today I understand my friends, Israeli Jews, who are so fearful of thoughts that are not nationalistic. Because for them, like it was for me in the vineyards of Hebron in the seventies, it's all related. We only know one definition of our common fate, of shared nationalism and fraternity—a total, exclusive definition—either nationalist or traitor, without any nuances in between. Religion, language, authority, power, sovereignty, the land, and a new culture were all melted down, and they fused in me—in us—to create something unparalleled in my parents' generation. If you take out one brick, the whole structure will collapse. It's hard for us as people of this place, children of modern Jewish nationalism, to imagine Judaism without religion or Hebrew, a community without a state or a state without all the biblical territories, patriotism without Greater Israel, survival and existence without a huge preponderance of military might. And in general, few of us are aware of our political history. It is doubtful whether in 10 percent of the thousands of years of Jewish existence we lived in a reality of full sovereignty. All the other Jewish periods were different: a scattered diaspora, communities, autonomy, and more. Every time we tried to get the chariot of sovereignty moving again, self-destructive mechanisms were also triggered, and we were again banished to the diaspora and scattered again, without authority or sovereignty.

Most of our achievements as a people, as a culture, and as individuals are linked to the depths of non-sovereign existence. The era before Zionist nationalism contained many elements that could potentially succeed the current absolute nationalism. Separating the Israeli amalgam into distinct elements—language, culture, religion, heritage, tradition, place, and sovereignty—which don't necessarily overlap, can provide more channels of identity and identification than the binary option: all or nothing. My Israeli challenge is to do all I can so that the self-destructive mechanism does not go into action again. As opposed to the Israeli in me, the Jew in me must always be prepared for the next state of existence. These two—the Israeli and the Jewish—are constantly moving in me like restless twins in the womb of a suffering pregnant woman, with neither having the upper hand.

WHILE WRITING THIS BOOK I FELT THAT I HAD TO GO TO Hebron again, to clarify a few things for myself. It didn't happen immediately, nor easily. It began with my son, Dan. During his army service in 2003, he was posted in Hebron. He knows every nook and cranny there, every street, and he's familiar with nearly every Jewish rioter among the settlers. We talked several times about his service there. For him it was a long and unpleasant experience. An endless confrontation between his personal value system and the world of the Israel Defense Forces.

We, the Israelis, like the adage that "the IDF is the most moral army in the world." I very much hope that's true, though it isn't at all clear to me who has checked, what the criteria were, and who was in the control group. Besides the fact that the army is just a political tool, and a tool is not supposed to have a conscience, especially when the policy and the politicians directing the army are devoid of morality. In any case, what he saw and experienced there hurt him very much, scarred his heart, and was completely immoral. The terrible tension between his value system and what he was compelled to do was too much to bear. He had grown up, like his brothers and sisters, to be a humanist who loves people, all people, but the orders that molded his most significant encounter with the state as a citizen were patently immoral. Like breaking into a house in the dead of night and taking away a father or his son in front of the wife and children; manning checkpoints and letting Jews through while Palestinians are delayed and harassed; guarding illegal, remote Jewish settlements; enforcing racist separation on the streets of Hebron so a handful of Israeli zealots can carry on with their lives normally in the heart of throngs of Palestinians for whom normal life has been denied for years.

He served in a combat unit, sharing heavy responsibility for good and bad, including the injustices committed by the army. An infantry soldier, like I was at his age, a pawn on a board much bigger than us all. Military service was not good for him. With his heightened sensitivity, he couldn't bridge the gap between military rhetoric and his natural humanistic values. He was discharged from the army with great unease in his heart, a heavy load. He traveled far away, eastward. The simplicity of the Indian subcontinent suited him well, a life very close to its existential foundations. He returned more open, with greater coping skills, and very attuned to his inner truth, though the burden of the previous years and experiences was still evident. His sadness was wrapped in a great silence.

On his own initiative, Dan contacted Breaking the Silence—an organization of army veterans that collects testimonies from soldiers who have served in the territories since the outbreak of the second Palestinian intifada. Through the testimonies, the group tries to raise consciousness about the daily reality in the territories in order to create a public conversation about the moral price of ruling a civilian population. Many of the soldiers returning to civilian life, like my Dan, are frustrated and pained by the gap between the reality they encountered in the territories and the indifference and silence about it in Israeli society. Together they break the conspiracy of silence and make the voices of the soldiers heard, doing everything they can to get Israeli society to recognize the monstrous reality we have created with our own hands. Their activities include trips to Hebron and other cities in the West Bank.

In 2012, I went back to Hebron with Breaking the Silence and with my son in order to meet his memories. He went back to the places where he served as a soldier, and I returned to the deep and painful sources of my family and where I too had served.

After this first loaded and liberating visit, in which we both faced our private military and historic demons, I visited this tortured city many more times. One such visit, with a friend and partner to values and peace—Gertraud, the secretary general of the Bruno Kreisky Forum for International Dialogue in Vienna. I wanted to share with her my family's "killing zone," which became the launching pad for my aspirations for peace.

We started the visit at the Tomb of the Patriarchs. I hadn't been there in many years. I climbed the stairs slowly, remembering Mom's excitement when we visited right after the Six-Day War. Until the capture of the city by Israeli forces in 1967, Jews were not allowed into the sacred tomb complex. They were permitted only up to the seventh step, no more. I remember her tense, emotional expression when she put her foot on the eighth step, the ninth, and all the rest. I hadn't been very excited at the time. What did I know at age twelve about the weight of history? They were just steps, right?

Now, after decades in which I hadn't been to the place, not since my army service, I went up again to the Tomb of the Patriarchs. I wanted to see the place of my boy's testimony and pain, and I found myself bearing the full weight borne by my mother. Gertraud and I went slowly up the stairs, talking about history and archeology, local politics, and prospects for peace. In front of us an elderly man walked with difficulty, slower than us, supported on two sides by two strapping young men wearing kippahs. We passed him and kept going. I heard a weak call from behind me: "Avraham, Avraham." Few people call me by that name. Mom and Dad did, and a few family members, that's it. I didn't turn around immediately, I didn't understand that the call was directed at me. And again: "Avraham, Avraham." This time I turned around. I needed a minute to absorb what I was seeing. The slow and fragile old man whom we had just passed was none other than my cousin Shlomo. The two-year-old saved from the Hebron massacre, the orphaned son of the late Eliezer Dan, the last surviving family member from those distant days. We had lost touch. He's closer in age to Mom than to us. They grew up together, a fraternity of orphans, in the home of my other aunt, who adopted and raised them like a young mother.

"Shlomo," I said with excitement, "what are you doing here?"

"And what are you doing here?" he replied with a smile, answering with a question, in Jewish fashion.

I explained to him that I was there with a guest, that I had come to show her the city and its complex history and politics.

"And I'm here," he replied, no longer smiling, "because today is the memorial day of the massacre. The *yahrtzeit*. So, I came to pray a bit for their souls, to read Psalms, and say the *Kaddish* prayer in their memory."

Because I follow the Gregorian calendar, and I'm not always aware of the traditional Hebrew date, I didn't know that this particular day was so symbolic. After we parted, we continued our tour of the city. We saw the security apartheid, discriminating racially between Jews and Arabs, approached destroyed Arab shops, and crossed neglected alleys and checkpoints meant to harass the local population. Hebron today is an unpleasant place, a pure distillation of everything that is wrong with the Israeli occupation.

At the end of the day, with the last rays of the setting sun, we climbed up one of the hills in the city, Tel Rumeida, an ancient mound that has become another provocative Jewish neighborhood. Its residents are extremist and violent settlers, and it is entirely surrounded by soldiers, fortified positions, and sophisticated warning systems for protection. At the edge of the neighborhood, among some ancient olive trees that have survived the evil hands of the Jewish zealots, stands Issa's home. Issa is a young Palestinian activist who believes in nonviolence and civil disobedience. He invited us to eat dinner with him and his friends, an *iftar* meal, breaking the day-long fast during the holy month of Ramadan.

What a strange moment it was, in the most fortified neighborhood in the Middle East. Soldiers patrolling, security cameras swiveling constantly. Jews who had come to the city for the memorial day peered into Issa's private yard, as if it were a cage in a zoo. And inside, Issa sat with his friends, Gertraud, Yehuda, the director of Breaking the Silence, and me. An impossible mix. And the conversation flowed, dealing with everything, life and hope, prospects for nonviolent civil disobedience, the occupation's harassment of masses of Hebron residents trying to maintain their daily routines.

Out of the settling darkness that enveloped us, two more people arrived: Abu Shaker's grandchildren, whom I had asked Issa to invite and introduce me to for the first time in my life. God, what a day. I had come for the politics, I met my distant surviving cousin, and now here they were with me. We ate local hummus, fresh vegetables, and hot pita bread from the oven in the yard as we talked about our common past. Suddenly everything fell into place. Their stories about those distant days were like a mirror image of our stories. About Shaker, who always suffered from bad lungs, about their grandmother, who nursed little Treyna, Aunt Malka. About the grandfather who was in the vineyards during the massacre, about hiding the rabbi and his children in the house, about our visit in 1967.

On a clear Hebron night, all Mom's repeated stories became proven facts. But to one of their questions I didn't have an answer. "Why didn't you call earlier? Why did you come only now? Where were you all these years?" Why indeed. I was at fault. I'm the occupier, I'm the strong one. I should have looked after them during the many years that I could, and I had failed.

CHAPTER ELEVEN

FROM LOCAL TO GLOBAL IDENTITY

U NTIL RATHER LATE IN LIFE I NEVER THOUGHT THAT FOR an Israeli born in Israel there could be any other model of Jewish identity aside from an Israeli one: dogmatic, absolute, and homogeneous. This identity, which seemed so attractive during a certain period of my life, became complicated and embarrassing during other periods. It was very well-suited to the Orthodox lifestyle into which I was born. There is only one truth, and all secondary principles are derived from and subsumed within it.

My mother, for example, didn't really care if her granddaughters married men who were professionals, what they looked like, or what opinions they held. The only question she ever asked was "Does he put on tefillin?" She didn't have comparable questions for her grandsons' brides, because her Orthodox Judaism did not regard women as having any significant binding religious identity in their own right. In the Orthodox world I formerly inhabited there could be no Orthodox Jew who had more than one pair of tefillin, more than one truth, more than one definition, one question, or one answer. Our Orthodoxy was not limited to the religious realm alone; it was an organized worldview that extended out to everything else.

My total Israeli Orthodoxy limited my own truth, as well as my Jewish and universal truths, to a very local worldview. The Israeli truth took captives, and the Jewish truth was held prisoner. But no longer. "My soul still longs for freedom," as the poet Shaul Tchernichovsky wrote. I wish to bring this freedom of the soul from every end of the earth to all my relatives, to an Israeli reality that is so tortured and complicated.

My daughter Avital and her partner Yonatan have lived in New York for several years now. She is completely secular, and she has nothing but disdain and scorn for all the religious institutions and rituals in Israel. "We," she and her partner announced, "will never get married. We love each other, and we don't need any institution to authorize us to build a family or to bring children into the world." I appreciate their purely principled stance, and I agree with them. And so, it's hard to describe my shock when I learned that they had begun attending synagogue and participating in various communal activities in New York.

"Why, Avital?" I asked her, perplexed.

"Because here no one is judging me," she responded. "Here it's just fun. No one remarks on when I show up, or why I wasn't there last week. No one cares if I walk to synagogue or take the subway. No one dares to stick their nose into my spiritual affairs. No one measures the length of my skirt and my sleeves. Here I'm free." I understood, and I was even a bit jealous.

In New York, where she discovered an alternative to the Israeli way of life, I discovered running. I spent a lot of time outdoors. I loved that blend of the city and the greenery within it and around it, and I was inspired by the multitude of runners who fill the parks and gardens. I started running myself, perhaps to feel part of this phenomenon. I came back to Israel from one trip with leggings—tight running pants to avoid chafing, the latest thing in athletic technology. One of the local papers published a paparazzi photo of me, with the caption, "Avrum Burg was seen running vigorously around the Knesset in tight leggings. What, him too?" In the United States, running was a sign of a healthy lifestyle, but here, in lower Jerusalem, running in leggings awakens all the homosexual demons from their slumber.

As the years went on and I took on various public roles, I again and again encountered these deep gulfs in the spiritual make-up of Jewish life. In the West, if you declare, "I believe in democracy, I'm bound by the Constitution, I fight for the legal equality of all citizens—men and women, believers and atheists—I support the separation of religion and state and advocate for an equitable distribution of common resources," you are essentially a run-of-the-mill democrat. If you make those same statements in Israel, affirming those very same values, you are a traitor, an unpatriotic fifth column, and the rest of those derogatory terms. In Israel, they never informed me that there could be any kind of Jewish soul other than ours. But there, in the Jewish community in North America, I learned a completely new Jewish vocabulary.

J EWS AND WORDS WERE BORN TOGETHER LIKE CONJOINED twins. But sometimes they are conjoined in uncomfortable places. I've sat in many meetings about ways of improving the relationship between Israel and the diaspora. Each time a zealous Hebraist took his turn to speak—and there was always someone—he would put forth the same proposal, dressed up exactly the same way: "We need every Jew in the diaspora to learn a hundred words in Hebrew, because Hebrew is what we all have in common."

At first, I listened raptly. After all, words are the foundation of human civilization. And there's no reason for the Hebrew language not to be the foundation for a renewed Jewish civilization. Back then I had still not mastered any language; I knew how to communicate and express myself, but not how to listen. And even when I listened, it was just for my own needs, not to really pay attention to the voice of the other. So, I didn't understand that these Hebraists too were trying to impose their Israeli sensibilities and were not prepared to listen to the different sensibilities of millions of Jews who are not Israeli and often not Zionist. Their identity is diasporic and not necessarily Zionist. Their Judaism is comprehensive, but not bound to this place. It is fully independent and liberated, though not sovereign and ruling. During my first years in public life I could not conceive of a worldview that was not Israeli, or a Jewish tradition that was not sovereign, but rather diasporic, full, interesting, deep, tolerant, pluralistic, and almost entirely unapologetically so. I've since learned a thing or two.

Beginning in 1982, my adult life unfolded on the flight paths between Israel and America. The scope of America captivated me. I acquired many key life skills there. My English is very American. In America, they are fully accepting of those with imperfect language and communication skills. You don't need to know the complete writings of Mark Twain in order to participate in the American conversation. It is enough just to watch television and read newspapers and contemporary literature in order to engage with them.

It was in America that I taught myself public speaking—how to stand before an audience. And here I must make an important distinction: I learned there how to open my mouth and declaim, but not how to open my ears and listen.

Every time I traveled to North America, I made every effort to be there on a Sunday. I was addicted to the evangelical channels, to the orations of charismatic preachers who saturated the American media. I sat for hours glued to the screen, hypnotized. I tried to learn from them how to stand before a crowd of thousands of impassioned believers in stadiums, rousing them with talk of miracles and ancient texts, like the ecstatic communion of the preacher with his disciples. Their ministers' words, however, seemed as trite and simplistic as the hollow words of Torah taught by many rabbis in Israel.

On the other hand, the blend of mass fervor and individual charisma, of television and stardom, was staggeringly new for me. Instead of a television in the closet—like my yeshiva rabbi had—here was someone just like him, appearing on television himself. I'm embarrassed to say that it was there that I learned how to be a modern Israeli politician, speaking in a way that could not be more different than the sterile sermons of the study hall and casuistry of my teachers and parents' home. To this day, whenever I stand before an audience, I often suddenly find myself using techniques I learned there—energetic movement across the stage, dramatic pauses, raising the voice and whispering, moments of humor to break up the monotony, and excited flourishes to rouse the crowd.

There was one televangelist in particular whose techniques were spellbinding—Jimmy Swaggart. When he sensed that his audience was not 100 percent with him, because he had either aimed too high with his fervor or exaggerated his dramatic flourish, he would stop for a moment, as if he couldn't think of the next word. He'd ask the thousands of people out there, "Wait, how do you say that again?" and the whole audience would join in to help out its floundering icon. The term "transitional word" took on an entirely different meaning with him. It linked him with his followers, powerfully and intimately, like my parents, who would ask each other the same question: "Wait, how do you say that again?" And then Swaggart would go back to raging and roiling.

It was a magnificent technique, intended not just to bind the audience to him, but also to slow himself down from time to time, to adjust his pace, to breathe, to swallow, to reflect on his next words, which would in any case roll off his tongue like an avalanche. And his manipulative question, "How do you say that again?" sensitized me to the gulf between Israeli Hebrew and Jewish Hebrew. Each time I asked an American Jewish audience, "How do you say that again?" I was surprised once again by the breadth of their vocabulary. They knew Hebrew words that very few in my Israeli community would ever dare to use. The zealous Hebraists in Jerusalem wanted—and perhaps still want—every Jew living abroad to know a hundred words like "table," "chair," "hot dog," "bus," "government," "nation," "boy," "girl," and "soldiers." But the Americans knew words from my mother's Hebrew, Hebrew words derived from Yiddish. Words like: "repairing the world," "righteousness," "charity," "loving-kindness," and "justice." Our Hebrew is practical, useful, applied. Their Hebrew, which came straight from

Jewish tradition, was a language of values, morals, and Jewishness. Many of our words are very new; many of their words are very old. And one's vocabulary is a testament to one's mental state.

It seems that these two vocabularies also reflect the different values, conceptions, and worldviews of these two nonidentical twin communities. I flitted between Israel and America hundreds of times. I was in Afula and then New Jersey, Sderot and then El Paso. Back and forth. I felt fortunate, because I lived at once in both universes, in Israel and in the diaspora. Here and there. Seventy-eight percent of world Jewry lives in Israel and the United States, and I, lucky guy, got to live in both. I learned to distinguish between our existential definitions and theirs. The Jewish identity of American Jews revolves around the religious axis. If they are somewhat nationalist, it is a very different nationalism from that of their Israeli sister. Public space, communal life, and the Jewish sphere of private life are largely defined by religious concepts, holidays, customs, and traditions: the huge Chanukah menorah in the main square of the big city, or the Passover Seder in the White House. Shabbat is a weekly opportunity to engage with friends and community, and bar and bat mitzvah celebrations are often the first occasion for real engagement with one's Jewish identity. Israeli Judaism, in contrast, revolves much more around national definitions. The State, an entity that did not exist just a few generations ago, defines, binds, and rallies the Jewish populace in Israel.

After many years of constant back-and-forth between here and there, I arrived at an impasse. My identity is not defined by the totality of Israel nationalism, but I've also learned that the pluralistic, innovative Jewish identity of North American Jews is not enough to fill the void inside me. My late sister was a linguist. Once she taught me that biblical Hebrew has a vocabulary of about eight thousand words. In the Mishnaic period, that number doubled, and in the Middle Ages another five thousand words were added to the mix. There are about twenty-five thousand words that have shaped some of the greatest works of human culture. But in modern Hebrew there are two hundred thousand words, and contemporary English has nearly a million. In this gulf between Hebrew and the languages of the New World, I lack a new language with terms, concepts, and an internal grammar, which Hebrew today, and its speakers, cannot provide.

REMEMBER VERY CLEARLY THE MOMENT IN THE EARLY 2000s that my national language fell apart. I was sitting in a Jerusalem café with Barbara. I had known her for a long time, always exchanging hellos, but not more than that. Her partner, Phil Pinchas, was for many years the leader of the Conservative Jewish, or Masorti, community in Israel. My children had been members of its youth movement, Noam. I always considered him to be a kind of spiritual pioneer, who had the courage to confront, sometimes almost alone, the powerful establishments of religious conservatism in Israel, with which I had been personally familiar. I sat opposite her, a short woman who spoke fluent scholarly Hebrew with an American accent, and suddenly I felt a powerful current flowing from her toward me.

She told me about a project she had started in Sweden called Paideia, a one-year program of Judaic studies for young Jews from across Europe. Among other things, she said, "European Jewry was always a body of ideas." From then on I wasn't listening to her anymore. I said yes to all her requests, and was transported by her words to the highest heavens.

I understood. To be precise, I began to understand. Barbara didn't know that with her powerful words she had opened one of the doors that had been locked for me all my life. I knew that there was a Jewish world much broader than what I was familiar with. I sensed it, but my consciousness refused to acknowledge it. The heart conceals from the mouth, in the words of an Aramaic saying. Until Barbara came and uncovered what was obscured and hidden. For many months I listened and tried to understand my feelings. I listened to the students of Paideia in Stockholm. Young Europeans, looking no different from my children here and my friends and their children in North America,

along the universal range between jeans and H&M fashion. Up until
the moment when the conversation with them began and the substantive differences emerged almost immediately, they were European intellectuals. Some of them Jews, for whom it's natural to come and study
the Jewish texts and sages, and some not. Their coming to Paideia was
understandable given their geographic and spiritual circumstances.

Like the lawyer, a secular Muslim, a Shiite from Azerbaijan who
worked for NATO, who realized that she didn't sufficiently understand
the West and came to study Judaism for that purpose. Or another person of part-Jewish descent who came to study Judaism in order to know
and better understand. And a third, a Catholic woman who was studying Yiddish poetry because she wanted to restore Yiddish to its grand
and missing place in the fabric of cultural life of contemporary Poland.
Every one of them had new ideas, daring and inspiring, regarding European life. Just a few hundred graduates who carried on their young
shoulders more than a third of the renewal initiatives of the Jewish communities in Europe. They are living a heritage of ideas, of multiplicity,
and not reduction. Of constant expansion made possible, after years of
sadness and pain, by the reunion of eastern and western Europe.

The young people in Stockholm, Jews and non-Jews together, are
not only breaking through the European walls that were once there. In
their small cultural patch, they are reviving, almost from scratch, parts
of European Jewry that were destroyed, along with their conversation
with the non-Jewish environment. A Judaism of ideas as an experimen-
tal model that can be much broader and larger. They are growing a
third Jewish identity, neither Israeli nor American, but European. For
them it is natural and normal, for me it is new and exciting.

E UROPE WAS ONCE IMPORTANT FOR THE ENTIRE WORLD.
Today it is somewhere on the sidelines. Its tourist sites are still
breathtakingly beautiful, its cuisines admired, and its landscapes well
kept, but still, something is missing. It isn't as important as it was in the
past and it does not lead the world. The West talks a great deal about its

decline, about the rise of other forces in the East and the Far East that will replace it in coming human history. Every time I go into a bookstore in the United States, I'm amazed by the huge abundance of writing and thought about the end of the West, the collapse of the United States and Europe, or just musings about the end of civilization as we know it. But for me, Europe is still an attractive and interesting place with a great deal of potential. Because new opportunities can spring from the place where all was broken. It is a continent composed of societies and communities that have known how to reinvent themselves time and again, reborn for the future. Maybe I'm a hopeless romantic, but I see what doesn't exist. At the same time, the Europeans themselves, especially those who are pessimistic and melancholy, can't see what outsiders like me see.

"Fifty-two percent of the students in Amsterdam schools are not originally Dutch," a Dutch friend of mine said, struggling to come up with clean language for what she saw as a faulty reality, using a politically correct euphemism.

"Which means?" I asked.

"Which means that in a few more years more than fifty percent of the residents of Amsterdam will be Muslim. We've already lost Rotterdam," she blurted. Unlike her right-wing, Islamophobic partner, she traditionally voted for the social-democratic party. She was thinking about Amsterdam, which for many years was called the "city of freedom," and I was thinking about the demography of Jerusalem, "the holy city," and I wondered if it too was lost.

"Malmö has long been part of the Middle East," a Swedish travel agent warned. "And Israel is no longer Europe," I responded.

"The Germans control Europe again, nothing has changed. We just wasted two world wars," claimed a French intellectual in a research institute where I am a fellow.

"No one has the courage to stand up to Russia, it is waiting for our downfall," was the gist of a discussion there about the future of relations between the new Europe and the new Russia.

There are Europeans who see their own half-empty glass better than anyone else, and sometimes when the atmosphere is conducive to it, and I feel that people are listening, I tell them an anecdote from my parliamentary past.

One day, in the nineties, when I was still a member of the Knesset, I learned an important lesson. There were only a few Knesset members in the plenum. Charlie Bitton, a very kind person, though a very angry Knesset member from the Black Panthers, a social protest movement of Sephardic Jews, lashed out at the finance minister, who stood at the podium. Bitton was dark-skinned, short, and energetic, and the minister was fat, light-complexioned, and almost indifferent. The day's topic was yet another boring deliberation about the government's budget. The minister—from my party—was very satisfied with his budget proposal, but Bitton, the social activist who knew poverty and human needs, was not at all.

"Charlie, why don't you see the glass is half full?" I shouted at him, in a support for "my" government policy.

He turned to me, his eyes blazing with anger. "Burg, you Ashkenazi shit, have you ever tried drinking from the empty half of the glass?"

It was so biting and painful a retort that I shut up, silent and embarrassed. In the struggle between my smugness and his suffering I realized that he was right and I was wrong. I respected him then and have liked him since. For his directness, dedication, and courage to go against the flow of where he had come from. As a lesson, I tell my European friends and partners, "You are in such a unique position in history, you are not the Bittons of the world, so why are you so depressed? You have the most wonderful empty half of the glass. Drink from it." Yes, there are difficulties in your (our) European utopia; racism has not yet fully surrendered, ultranationalism is shocking the foundations of continental solidarity, new hatreds (xenophobia, Islamophobia, and more) join the bad old ones (like anti-Semitism). But still it is such an amazing achievement. The blood-soaked continent has once again renewed itself almost to the level of the biblical prophecy of Isaiah (2:4): "And they shall beat their swords into plowshares, and their spears into pruninghooks; nation shall not lift up sword against nation, neither shall they learn war anymore." So be careful but happy, pay attention, and celebrate it.

M ANY YEARS AGO, ON THE EVE OF ROSH HASHANAH, I sat in my car stuck in a typical Jerusalem traffic jam. The air conditioning in the car didn't work, and the open windows let in only heat and exhaust from neighboring cars. In the car with me were my father and Itay, my firstborn son. The radio report said that the jam was caused by a suspicious object downtown. "You and your Arabs," my adolescent son snapped at me, the child who knows better than any of them how to cut with laser-like accuracy to the core of my soul. As I was thinking about my answer, my elderly father took the reins of the conversation from the back seat.

"Yingele," he said with the nickname reserved for me when I was a child. "Everything going on between us and the Arabs is nothing compared to what happened between us and the Germans, and lo and behold, we're riding in a German car." It was a battered Volkswagen station wagon. "And with the new Germany we have wonderful relations. The Germans did much more to us than the Palestinians ever will, or than we will do to them. Don't be angry with me, but in your lifetime, there will be peace between you and them."

Dad meant it when he said "between you and them," excluding himself. Until his last day, he was at least half European, contrary to us Asians. His European half saw much larger pictures than just the Holocaust, Jews, and Germans. He had just returned from his first visit to East Germany, to Dresden, his beloved and sad native city. He had seen and understood where it was all going. "The new Europe is a prophetic story," he would tell me repeatedly, sharing his comprehensive historical perspective. "Who would have believed that Europe, the most violent continent, in whose fields everyone shed everyone's blood for a thousand years, would one day lay down its swords and become the ultimate continent of peace?"

I thought about him not long ago when I was driving on the highway in Austria and saw a giant billboard encouraging young people to join the Austrian army. What? Austria has an army? It turns out that in western Europe there are at least twenty-seven armies, with twenty-seven chiefs of staff and an identical number of air forces, headquarters, and nattily attired military bands. What do they need them for? It turns out that young people are joining the armies of Europe in order to serve in peacekeeping forces, on missions of rescue, mediation, and separation of forces in the most violent conflict zones in the world. The ways of the world are strange. Until recently, Austrian troops were divided between Israel and Syria. I would have never known about it were it not for a newspaper article that dealt with the difficulties faced by the Austrian logistics units. They were having trouble transporting the traditional portions of pork and Christmas trees to their brave soldiers because of the opposition of Jewish rabbis on one side and Muslim imams on the other. It was as if the messiah had come: Austrian soldiers bodily separating Jews from their enemies.

M Y FIRST MEANINGFUL PUBLIC MEETING WITH EUROPE went badly awry. I was the chairman of the Jewish Agency and the World Zionist Organization from 1995 to 1999. With two close friends, the late Edgar Bronfman, president of the World Jewish Congress, and his secretary-general, the wonderful and fascinating Israel Singer, we declared war on the Swiss banks who had hidden in their safes dormant accounts and concealed treasures of European Jews from the Holocaust period. For months, we clashed with them in all the international media. We mercilessly hammered away at them with the demagogic rhetoric of those who know that the other side cannot respond. The Swiss bankers made every possible mistake. They denied, lied, contradicted themselves, and could not understand where this Jewish avalanche had come from. It was the mid-nineties; the Soviets and Communists were no longer the international bad guys. Fundamentalist Islam had still not made its presence felt in the international arena. The media gleefully pursued the story we had provided about the Swiss bad guys.

I liked this struggle. I took part in meetings in Zurich, where I was accompanied by local bodyguards. The newspaper headlines called me "an enemy of the Swiss public," and the threatening letters kept coming. I discovered the international political stage and I thought it was right for me. This contest was also rooted in my own desire to understand the Holocaust and deal with it. All I knew was that this was the opportunity of my generation, and maybe the last chance to get a measure of accountability for the survivors and the victims. I had two motivations: the first, to right past injustices despite the time that had passed; the second, to uncover all the information about the economic aspect of the Holocaust. How did the Jews live? What did the grocer in Chenstokhov do with the money he had saved? Who were the beneficiaries of Grandfather and Grandmother's old insurance policies? What happened to the wedding presents of couples who never raised a family? And where were my grandmother's earrings?

At some point, at the height of this tremendous struggle, everything went wrong and I retreated. What had been a demand for justice and uncovering the whole truth ended up with me and my colleagues haggling over money. And this realm of Jews and money was precisely everyone's comfort zone. The bankers understood money, greedy lawyers in the United States filed astronomic class-action lawsuits, Jewish organizations drew up generous budgets, and the anti-Semites enjoyed seeing us fall in line with their stereotype. Without saying a word to anyone I stopped coming to the meetings. I distanced myself. I didn't have the resolve to come out publicly against my colleagues, but I felt bad inside. Jews and money is a Shakespearean play. It might have fit the diaspora mentality, but not my Israeli perception of the new Jewish identity. It would be almost another decade before I returned to Europe.

THE EUROPE I'M NOW GETTING TO KNOW OFFERS A wonderful model of kaleidoscopic identity. A new patriotism that doesn't need bloodshed and militaristic violence to preserve and express its patriotism. A Europe struggling to find and preserve all its identities and communities, together with those of its recently arrived new immigrants. The United States of America is an empire that erases identities. True, everyone there is proud of his or her particular roots, but the collective citizenry does not allow or tolerate any nationalism other than the American one.

This America always reminds me of the ancient kingdom of Judea. At its core was the hegemonic tribe of Judah, which swallowed its neighbors and turned the sons of Shimon, along with the Canaanites and the Philistines, into Jews. Today this tribe of Judah lives across the Atlantic Ocean. The kingdom of Judea of North America assimilates everything. In contrast to the United States, the changing and renewed Europe seems to me very similar to the ancient kingdom of Israel, a society of differences. An alliance of the rest of the Israelite tribes that was the bitter rival of Judea. It was not given an adequate place of honor in our collective memory, perhaps because the history we are familiar with was written by the historians of the kingdom of Judea, which outlasted it. But precisely that kingdom can be the ideological basis for a federation of the different. The kingdom of Israel of Europe is a federation with many expressions, pluralistic and varied in its culture and content, mainly because of the experience of its people, who are going through a wonderful metamorphosis. Once when I would think about Europe, it was always two-dimensional: Dad and the gentiles, Israel and the Holocaust. Today it is entirely different.

"Look at this room, look around you," the late Zygmunt Bauman, one of the great sociologists of our generation, told me. We were in

Vienna, at the Bruno Kreisky Forum for International Dialogue, the year was 2012, before Brexit and the refugees, prior to Trump's era. "What do you see?"

I saw Rob, whose parents are from Jamaica and today is from London; Zia the Englishman, from a Muslim Bangladeshi family, and today his identity is much more augmented; Sayida the German judge whose parents are from Turkey; Andre the Jew from Morocco; Julia from Poland; Ivan the Bulgarian; Gertraud, from the Bruno Kreisky Forum; and the German-born Lars, now living in Amsterdam.

"You understand," he said, referring me to a quote from his latest book, "this is Europe! Abundant variety is the most precious treasure that Europe has succeeded in saving from the great conflagrations of the past, and offers it to the world today." Then he expanded on the subject in a lecture, quoting the German philosopher Hans-Georg Gadamer: "To live with the other, to live as the other's other, that is the basic human task—on both the lowest and loftiest levels. That is perhaps the unique advantage of Europe, which was able and must learn the art of living with others."*

This could be so fitting for our varied society in Israel, and we can be part of this mosaic. But Israel, unfortunately, has only an American strategy. We have no European strategy, though we need it more than ever. And we don't leave openings for European influences. We're attentive to the best of American junk—from food and music to politics and arms, never to the Constitution and civil rights. With Europe, it is even worse; we have nothing to do with the social, cultural, and moral processes at work there. It would be appropriate for us if only because Europe is an accessible tourist destination for the average Israeli, and for Israeli statesmen of recent generations a generous source of guilt feelings, credit on which they can draw for any negative action,

---

*See Zygmunt Bauman, *Culture in a Liquid Modern World* [in Hebrew] (Tel Aviv: Hakibbutz Hameuchad, 2013). Originally published in English (Cambridge, UK: Polity, 2011).

injustice, or mistake by Israel, and have European officials sign off on it. Otherwise, from the Israeli political perspective, Europe is a nuisance that Israel would do best to ignore. I have no doubt that Europe has the rare ability for renewal and reinvention. It has done it so many times in the past, and its renewal mechanisms are working now again with full force.

Who would have believed me if I had said during the Spanish Inquisition that one day all of Europe would be a secular continent? I would have likely ended my life on the torture rack somewhere in the dungeons of Madrid. And if I had whispered to Martin Luther that one day there would be on his land a secular sect far bigger than the Catholic sect or its Protestant offspring—one that is completely indifferent to religious differences—I have no doubt what his reaction would have been. And when the Turks were at the gates of Vienna, it is doubtful if anyone imagined that one day there would be a discussion about including Turkey in the European Union, not to mention the millions of Muslim migrants that are changing its social fabric beyond recognition. Who believed 150 years ago that Europe would be the world's continent of peace? Nobody! Germany and France leading together? Impossible! A small, neutral, peaceable Austria? An Italy that was not militaristic? Peace-loving Nordic peoples? Naïve nonsense. And still, the facts speak for themselves. It's not easy; new encounters produce discord and dangers. And still, it is happening.

And indeed, something almost biblical is happening to the old continent. European history is replete with all manner of horrors, bloodshed, persecution, and hatred. And now, as if magically transformed, Europe is a continent of peace. Only a few people, such as Stefan Zweig and his colleagues, thought seventy years ago that it was possible and desirable, and that Europe's politics would look like this. Open borders, a genuine effort to include the other, with all the difficulties and problems, a real commitment to end wars, expand democracy and the discourse on rights, combine a growing economy with social justice, and make peace wherever possible. For Europeans, these are often pressing challenges. But to me and others looking from the outside, it looks like the realization of the ancient prophecy of turning swords into plowshares, and spears into pruning hooks.

In 1989, I watched the fall of the Berlin Wall, like the rest of the world, on television. It was strange to see history in your bedroom, like a passive voyeur, like Dad eighty years ago from the window of his room in Dresden. I didn't think at the time that this wall would open many private boxes that were hidden somewhere inside me without my knowing they were there. I was born in a divided city with a wall running through it, Jerusalem. I came of age when it was divided without a wall, and it remains that way, painfully for me. A wall, I learned in Jerusalem, is not only a structure of concrete and cement. It is first and foremost a state of mind. A wall between people whose foundations are a separation between souls and consciousness. This is the polarized message that keeps coming from "the united city," from the "eternal capital" of Israeli transience. It seems that the tangible Berlin Wall fell only after the walls in the consciousness of the adversaries collapsed. With an elegant European delay of forty-five years, World War II ended. The time of disconnection ended, and the time of connection began.

European individuals toppled barriers well before their political leaders. Gertraud, my friend and colleague, who makes possible most of the European projects I'm involved in, was born in Austria. At a very young age she abandoned the good old but oppressive Austrian world order and moved to Paris. Later she married the Italian Gian Battista and raised his children. He lived in Monaco, she in Vienna again, and the two of them together in Sardinia. She speaks German, Italian, French, and English fluently, and when I met her, she was busy studying Hebrew. She moves easily between eastern and western Europe, between the north and south, between the Middle East and Europe, and especially between the Austrian and Jewish past. She is the most wall-free person I know.

I got to know my friend Ivan through her. He was born in Sofia, but every time I look for him he is in another city somewhere in the world.

He is a fascinating partner to many discussions and thoughts, and very wise in the ways of political history and political science. He has a penetrating worldview and a rare ability to connect deep historical currents with the latest headlines, and to explain almost everything that is incomprehensible in our contemporary life. He is a Bulgarian whose children study in Vienna and who is a member of some very prestigious American research institutes. "How do systems collapse, how do empires end, how does a culture vanish? I know. I was born there," he says of himself and the European environments in which he lives.

Martin is the president of the European Parliament, born in Germany, a socialist. He is fluent in English, German, and French. He is proficient not only in the political register of those languages, but in the cultural, literary, and spiritual depth of every one of them. He understands the Middle East better than many, knows the inner recesses of Turkey, and is familiar with every nuance of European politics. He is attentive to everyone, but also expressive. He may become the leader of all of Europe one day.

Danny Cohn-Bendit is Jewish. His parents escaped from Germany to France during World War II and returned when it was over. Danny grew up in Germany, and in the mid-sixties arrived in France to study. He was the leader most identified with the student unrest in Paris in 1968. He later returned to Germany, always active and involved. An intellectual and an activist. In Germany, he became the deputy mayor of Frankfurt. At the end of the nineties, he returned to European politics, this time from the French side, as the candidate of the French Green Party to the European Parliament.

These are all my friends. Unlike me, whose identity is only Israeli, their identities are complex from birth, layered and sophisticated. They broke down the walls of Europe long before masses of Berliners took hammers and pickaxes in hand and smashed the concrete wall. All these were what my father was and could have been were it not for that cursed war and this country, afflicted by the war's malignant metastases. Maybe I'm wrong, and he would not have managed to break down his own walls. Maybe his great spiritual affinity with Jewish Eastern Europe and its shtetl romanticism would have bested him. But we—his children and grandchildren—could have been . . . actually, I can't bear the thought. It's too difficult and frightening.

And still, "Europe is a body of ideas." It gave birth to movements of religious reformation, psychology, and the sciences, unique aesthetics, ideologies and philosophies, churches and beliefs, Zionism and Jewish Orthodoxy, and ultra-Orthodoxy. Not necessarily religious, not essentially nationalist. But generating ideas and trends. Part of it expelled Dad and me before I was born, and part of it made room even for people like me. It was a place of paradoxes, from which humanity's worst ideas emerged, along with some of the worst ideas of contemporary Judaism. But the seeds of equality were also sown in it, the sanctity of the different, human liberties, and everything that is sacred to me. And in the midst of all these, the Jews of central and western Europe were like the fermenting yeast causing the dough to rise. In recent times Europe has also been the most fascinating laboratory I know for searching for the place of the "other." Again, at the forefront of Western and global innovation.

After many years, actually most of my life, in which I was just a total Israeli, I find myself more similar to my parents. Today I have a dual identity. I'm a European Israeli. My partner immigrated to Israel from France as a child. Her parents live in Jerusalem and physically live the existential duality. All their children, grandchildren, and great-grandchildren are Israeli. All their hopes and frustrations are channeled to this place. Their home is the most Israeli place possible, and at the same time an island of European French refinement with all its manners and culture in the heart of a hidden Jerusalem garden. They have a dual identity and culture. French Israelis, simultaneously Jewish and European. Traditional people in their personal life, committed to a public sphere that sanctifies the secularism of the state, the famous French *laïcité*. I learned from them the essence of the French conception of secularism, freedom of religion and freedom from religion.

Religion has no foothold in the institutions of the state, and the state is not involved in what goes on in the religious sphere. At the time of writing, this concept has no Hebrew entry in Wikipedia, the online encyclopedia, and I wonder if it is a coincidence that there is one in Turkish and even in Esperanto, but not in Hebrew.

When I left the Knesset in 2004, I knew that I wanted to embark on a journey to my roots, in the internal direction of Europe. I could have gotten a German passport as my father's son, maintaining his citizenship that had been cut off by the sundering violence of the previous century, and I could have requested French citizenship by virtue of my marriage to a French citizen. I devoted much thought to the subject. Doubling my identity, and the point of entry to that status, preoccupied me. In the end, I realized that there were no gates more symbolic than the French and German ones. I come from Israel, one of the most emphatic nation-states in the world. The old Germany presented the world with a concept of a nation based on a shared blood bond. France, which had its own set of problems, presented the model of a nation based on shared culture and civic values. On the one hand, I'm fascinated by and very much like what is happening today in the new Germany. In every World Cup, I root for the German soccer team. It's enough for me to see Germany's national team, composed of so many players of different origins cooperating under the same flag—Poles, Turks, North Africans, all of them German—to remind me that people, collectively and privately, are always open to change. I am a big believer in partnerships of ideas, alliances of values, and I have no commitment to genetic tribalism, not even to the Israeli blood-bonded nation emerging around me. The new Germany today is very far from those blood-based concepts. On the other hand, the symbolism of the past stopped me. From that point, the decision was simple.

I applied for French citizenship in addition to my Israeli citizenship. Like my partner and children. Like many of my friends. Considerable public fury, scathing criticism, and bitter cynicism have been directed at me since. As if people were doubting my patriotic allegiance. Because I'm no longer a public figure, I don't really care about the criticism, which is superficial and hollow anyway. Few people really take the trouble to listen to the reasons. Most prefer to hurl "your French passport" at me in order to avoid dealing with my Israeli criticism. I don't really need another passport. I returned my diplomatic passport, for which I have lifetime eligibility as a former Knesset speaker, to the authorities, and I never asked to have it renewed. Both because I was never elected to be a "former" and because I want to have freedom of opinion and expression, including harsh criticism of the country, its behavior, and its leaders. For that reason, I can't travel the world with a representative passport without representing Israel. I have paid my public dues to society and I don't want to continue being a representative stuffed animal, as some would like me to be. From the start, I wanted a European passport to get to places I can't reach with my Israeli passport. I've already been to Yemen to help the small Jewish community that remains there, I've explored whether I could get to Syria, and Tehran is also a goal on my map. I've been in all sorts of places, and I want to reach others, to speak with the local people and build human bridges to places where political ties and the Israeli passport still cannot reach. Along with the storm of controversy, I discovered more layers I hadn't thought of originally regarding the places I aspire to reach. They are not only physical and political places, but mainly ideological spaces found beyond today's Israeli conceptual world.

A S ISRAELI JEWS, WE HAVE AN AGGRESSIVE AND INSENSITIVE basic assumption that all Jews in the world are committed to dual allegiance: to their countries of citizenship—the United States, Britain, France, and the rest of the world—and to another country, Israel. At times, we exploit this duality with brutal cynicism, as was the case with Jonathan Pollard and with Ben Zygier, "Prisoner X." Zygier was an Australian Israeli citizen, a veteran of the Israel Defense Forces, and allegedly also a Mossad agent. He died in custody in 2010, apparently by hanging himself in a suicide-proof maximum-security cell. While he was imprisoned, he was referred to as Prisoner X, Mr. X, or Mister X.

I have nothing but contempt for this cynicism. I adamantly oppose this emotional manipulation and don't want to be part of it. Pollard is the best-known but definitely not the only person whom various Israeli agencies have used against his or her countries, regardless of the high prices for them personally or even of endangering the well-being of their entire Jewish communities. I want to offer an alternative. For me, being part of the "nation of the world" is to have dual responsibility, which is the complete opposite of the conventional divided and dual allegiance. The meaning of dual responsibility is simple: I do my best on behalf of members of my Israeli community, and at the same time I am committed to a better world according to my values. That is why anywhere and in any way that I can fight those who ruin the world, I am committed to this dual responsibility.

Europe is not just a geographic place; it is also a value system that I am trying to expand so that it envelops our lives and the lives of the Palestinians. I watch with great sadness the pessimism that drives the wheels of our region. Even the greatest believers in peace between us and the Palestinians find it hard to form images of a sustainable future for the State of Israel and the State of Palestine together. It seems that psychologically the terrestrial space between the Jordan River and the Mediterranean Sea is too small to contain such giant and hurt egos like those of the Israeli and Palestinian collectives. Peoples like ours need wide open spaces after the end of the wars and traumas. And still, I truly believe that our iconic conflict, between Israelis and Palestinians, can become an iconic solution, one that will be an inspiration to peoples in conflict and areas still driven by hatred and distrust.

I know that the reality I'm dreaming about is no more than a utopia at this stage in our history. For every one of us bearing the burden of being Israeli—earning a livelihood, wars, fears, and pressures—it is no more than a vision. "Maybe," I tell people in the heat of debate, "but it is my north star. It can't always be reached, but you can always navigate toward it. What's your star?"

Sometimes I tell them about the once-in-a-lifetime event in which science met the faith of my childhood. On every first Saturday night of the new Hebrew month we would go out to the synagogue courtyard right after services, crane our necks, and try to see the thin crescent of the new moon. We would say the prayer of the new moon as we faced it, dancing a bit and reciting, "Just as I dance before you and cannot touch you, so will my enemies be unable to touch me." Like other prayers, this was another protective layer of the constantly fearful Jew. When I was fourteen, Apollo 11 landed on the moon, and my father went through a minor theological crisis. "I don't know," he wondered aloud at the Sabbath table, "whether now that man has touched the moon, the prayer for the new moon should be changed, or whether our enemies will now be able to harm us."

That landing on the moon, which seemed impossible, which changed the world and caused my father to ponder a taboo—a tiny religious reform—is for me a source of inspiration. In almost every matter I deal with, I begin with the basic question, who is "the man on the moon" of this issue? What is the most far-fetched vision I can think of, and what are the paths leading to it? I have no doubt that I will live to see the day in which Israeli-Palestinian peace, based on principles of freedom, human dignity, equality, justice, and democracy, will be possible and self-evident. We will touch the moon, and the persecution will stop. I'm convinced that between the Jordan River and the sea every person must have the same rights. Such full equality between Israelis and Palestinians will be a source of peace that will radiate positively across the Mediterranean region, to southern Europe and to Muslim North African lands.

IN MANY RESPECTS, ISRAEL IS A MICROCOSM OF THE WEST. What takes place here frenetically occurs in the West at a more measured pace. War, terrorism, a weakening of liberal values, strange political leaders, xeno- and Islamophobias, and setbacks to democracy as well as hesitant peace, and the dynamics of history. Our world is shrinking into social network ghettos, and a media-driven politics focused on presidential tweets is undermining idea-based discourse. The roots of our contemporary reality, however, are much deeper and older. One of the most significant starting points of our time is World War I; that conflict, a century ago, gave birth to the world order that we now are leaving. The demise of the Ottoman Empire happened then, the new Soviet empire was born, and in the West, the stars and stripes of the United States began to light up the sky as it joined—and increasingly shaped—the new world order. The process was completed by the end of World War II, with the defeated nations, Germany, Italy, and Japan, enthusiastically embracing capitalism.

For Israel, the Six-Day War was somewhat akin to what World War II was for the West: the instant removal of a prolonged siege. The six days of the amazing military victory changed the face of Israel. The war redefined the strong and the weak and changed the face of the Middle East beyond recognition. David became Goliath, the heads of the previous Goliaths of the region were severed, and the Palestinian nation became the sole entity confronting Israel.

It is said that wars are won by the human spirit. But not everything that emanates from the human spirit is necessarily positive. What are the elements in the victory of the West at the end of World War II and that of Israel in 1967 that carried within them the seeds of failure? Why did the tremendous victory of those six days turn into an endless seventh day of nightmares? And why is the West failing in its attempts to reap the fruits of its victory in the complex realities of the Middle East, Eastern Europe, and the Far East?

Two powerful forces faced each other in World War II. In the end, the allies, with their greater resources and more advanced technology, triumphed. Germany was left isolated. Its reservoir of human resources had dwindled and it could not sustain its efficient fighting machine. Japan suffered defeat through cataclysmic nuclear technology dropped from the sky. Looking back after many years, it seems to me that their victories frightened the victors. The vanquished nations were forced to dismantle the totalitarian regimes with which they had threatened the world. Today Germany has no military ambitions and little desire to be involved in international conflicts. It would seem that Italy, pleasant, aesthetic, and tolerant, had never really belonged in the Nazi-Fascist valley of death. On the other hand, the victors sank into an orgy of soul searching, including a reckoning with the ability of humanity to wipe itself out.

The Soviet Union reached the conclusion that military superiority was the supreme national goal whose attainment would defend it from outside threats. The Russians vowed that no one would lay siege to Moscow and Leningrad again. No one would be able to destroy the collective soul in favor of material pleasures resulting from exploitation, discrimination, and inequality. Violence and deterrence became the defenders of human values in the new revolutionary society. The Soviet Union invested heavily in conflict, and in the end drowned under the burden of preserving a wall of isolation between itself and the surrounding world. Soviet citizens became weary of sacrificing their well-being for the good of the state's values, which offered nothing in terms of personal freedom.

The United States of America, by contrast, saw the allied victory as that of humanity triumphing over madness. In the euphoria of victory, America took the human spirit to absurd ends. Competitiveness at any cost. Individualism was the medicine that would ward off any symptoms of national collectivism, Nazism, fascism, or communism. The spirit of individualism and competitiveness brought America to a terrible indifference toward the perceived losers. Winner takes all. The arrogance of the lone wolf, concerned only with its prey, hiding under a generous smile and deep pockets of foreign aid. Today's presidents Putin and Trump are the quintessence of both civilizations; the Russian one, brutal and heartless, and the American one, aggressive and merciless.

Professor Eliezer Schweid, one of the most important and influential Jewish philosophers of the twentieth century, sadly summarized:

> Only the achievements whose effectiveness was proven in the cruelest wars have stood the test: science, technology, the efficient administrator. The natural conclusion was then to develop them at an accelerated pace in order to make the most of what they had to offer to satisfy universal human needs. The principle of free market competition between the individuals in every group and between groups in every nation was seen as the most efficient principle of economic success: It suits the selfish traits of human beings.... Liberal selfish-individualism took the place of an awareness of overall responsibility for a fair distribution of resources.*

From a distance, American society, especially Trump's America, seems to zealously sanctify these values, which conceal the seeds of its destruction. His America First policy, and a selective concern for world peace, are based on the dark legacy of Charles Lindbergh's America First. This America came to the conclusion that tough, rigid competitiveness in every arena is a worthy goal. Sophisticated technology can bestow personal and economic well-being, not just military superiority. However, the World War II victory exposed the weakness of American society: the widening economic gap between the nation's haves and its have-nots.

And this, exactly, is what the Six-Day War did to Israel. The overwhelming victory mercilessly revealed deep scars on the nation's soul. The first and foremost—the gathering around the tribal campfire and erecting an iron curtain of military might between us and the

---

*Translation mine; compare with Eliezer Schweid, *The Philosophy of the Bible as Foundation of Jewish Culture*, trans. Leonard Levin (Brighton, MA: Academic Studies Press, 2008), 23.

surrounding Arab environment, a curtain that prevented us from even noticing the rare times when an Arab hand was held out to us in peace. Power became the god harnessed to the great redemptive plan. A frightening synthesis was created between national militancy and zealous messianism to produce an extreme image of modern Israel. The distances between various strata of the population widened, so much so that the cohesiveness of Israeli society was threatened. The contention that the investment in the settlements robbed Israel of precious resources is misleading. The settlers coalesced quickly, with military efficiency, and managed to place themselves at the center of politics, ideology, and the economy. Jewish national fundamentalism moved from the periphery to the political mainstream around the same time that the Tea Party and Christian fundamentalists became more and more prominent and successful in North America.

All of a sudden, for me and for those like me, the situation no longer is an open, pluralistic United States on one side and a diminishing liberal Israel on the other. Today's partition lines are between those of us who are devoted to liberal values and those who embrace authoritarianism. Some of us on both sides of the ocean versus some of them, also on both sides of the same ocean. Equality and rights in Israel, the US, Europe, and elsewhere against those who fear openness, abhor equality for all, and believe in any form of racial, religious, cultural, or political superiority.

The future of liberal democracy is not local, here or there, but global. Democracy is ill and urgently requires demo-therapy. Trump, Putin, Netanyahu, Erdoğan, and their like are inspiring and empowering each other. And so should we. We must move from indigenous politics to global democracy, to a worldwide front of liberal values as a sand wall against the ocean of conservative hostility and intimidation.

CHAPTER TWELVE

OF TRAUMA
AND RECOVERY

THE CONVERSATION ABOUT EQUALITY DIRECTLY AFFECTS both sides of the Palestinian reality. It affects my Palestinian friends who have lived in the refugee camps in the occupied territories and other Arab countries since the 1948 war. And it affects my close Israeli partners, who are part of the tens of thousands of Palestinians who did not escape their homes in 1948 and eventually became Israeli citizens, and whose hardships, caused by the establishment of the state, are ignored. Every time conversations and debates reach the Palestinian refugees, the trauma contest begins. The Palestinian tells the Israeli, "You know, when you established your state in 1948, you created with your own hands the Palestinian national tragedy. Why do we have to pay the price for that?" And the Jew replies, "Some tragedy! Wait until you hear about the Holocaust. Ours is bigger."

A bitter contest in which nobody wins, and that can't be resolved. These are the psycho-politics that prevent any political solution.

As long as we don't learn to relate to the pain and trauma of the other, to respect them, and especially to make them present in our lives, it won't end. I am writing these pages in Jerusalem, in the library of the Van Leer Jerusalem Institute. One day, my partner at the table,

Professor Christoph Schmidt, left me a draft of a fascinating paper he was working on, in which he wrote, "Berlin owes its drawing power also to the fact that it has turned the confrontation with German guilt . . . into part of the architecture of the entire city. There is no street, house entrance, museum, or television program that does not mention these crimes. Berlin tells the story of the victims through monuments, signs and memorial stones. These symbols are the characteristics of a deep and profound moral confrontation, a symbol of the changed course of an entire city, of the whole nation. Berlin is Nineveh, the city that renounced the paths of evil."

This connection between the city and its past, between the trauma and the recovery, between the crimes and the rehabilitation, is what underpins the successful unification of the city and what draws tens of thousands of Israelis yearning for such a change of consciousness here among us.

The current question is, can the underpinning of hatred and anger built by us and the Palestinians be removed? The answer is yes, of course.

A few years ago, I wanted to translate into Hebrew an exchange of letters from the early thirties (during the lull between the wars) between Sigmund Freud and Albert Einstein on the question, "Is there a way to free humanity from the scourge of war?" After reading and studying the original text, I learned that it had already been translated. So, although I abandoned the project, my consciousness profited greatly. To one of the questions Einstein asks Freud directly—"Is there any chance to guide the development of human beings so that they will be more resistant to the psychoses of hate and extermination?"—Freud's answer was very clear: "Yes!" According to Freud, conflicts of interest, in the human as well as animal realms, are decided by force. In the past, the stronger person could choose between the complete elimination of his adversary and repressing him and subjugating him to his needs.*

---

*See "Why War?" in Sigmund Freud, *Collected Papers*, Vol. 5, ed. James Strachey (New York: Basic Books, 1959).

Force was decisive between the strong and the weak. That was the original situation, but it changed when government authority shifted from force to rights. My thoughts moved from those two Jews to the Jews among whom I live, and to an essential internal contradiction that we find convenient to ignore: the Israeli government system—democratic—is based on rights, but our relations with the Palestinians are based on variations of force, without a shred of recognition of their natural and inalienable rights, as individuals and as a collective. In the gap between the Israel of rights and the Israel of domination lie many of the evils of our reality. What, then, is the basic right that unites so many Palestinians in the West Bank and Gaza against us? It is difficult to discuss today, but a few years after the state was founded, Moshe Dayan examined it for a moment with a penetrating one-eyed clarity of vision unequaled before or since.

At the end of April 1956—when Israel was only eight years old—Ro'i Rotberg, a soldier from Kibbutz Nahal Oz, was murdered by infiltrators from Gaza. At his grave, he was eulogized by Moshe Dayan, then the admired army chief of staff, the man of political activism. Cold and calculating, but also courageous and poetic. It was a strategic eulogy, full of internal contradictions and riveting truths. He said, as I remember it:

> Yesterday morning Ro'i was murdered. The quiet of a spring morning blinded him, and he didn't see those lying in ambush in the furrow of the field. Let us not level accusations today at the murderers. How can we complain about their seething hatred of us? For eight years they have been in the refugee camps of Gaza, and before their very eyes we have been transforming the land and the villages where they and their forefathers lived into our own. We should not seek Ro'i's blood from the Arabs in Gaza, but from ourselves. We will reckon with ourselves today. Let us not flinch from seeing the hatred that accompanies and fills the lives of hundreds of thousands of Arabs who live around

us and are waiting for the moment in which they can shed our blood.*

Dayan knew better than many others that the "infiltrators" were mostly refugees from the villages where they were born and from which they were expelled. That they returned at night to their abandoned or stolen homes. Poor, uprooted, angry, and homesick. A son of this land, he understood their seething hatred and the brutality of their acts. He was also like that, a farmer who was brutal. As a celebrated military leader, he drew with his words the real map of hostility.

Today, if we really want to deal with the challenges of Gaza and the entire Palestinian issue, we must go back to the map of Moshe Dayan and "reckon with ourselves today." Why should we, in his words, decry the murderers and "complain about their seething hatred of us?" The time has come to turn inward and ask bravely, as he did: What have we done to dampen the burning hatred? Israel—the people and the state—was established on the ruins of many villages and communities that were here before us. The refugees, who were expelled and fled, were erased from consciousness, and the campaign of silence waged from above (by David Ben-Gurion), filtered down, to the last talkback on the Internet, sweeping us all up. But the hatred of the injured refuses to die. It is handed down through the generations. Not only because it has no solution, but because it grants no recognition. The Jewish Israelis still stubbornly refuse to recognize the Palestinian tragedy and the suffering caused by the establishment of the State of Israel.

WANT TO SEE A REALITY HERE IN WHICH THERE ARE NO wars, so I have to go back to the fundamentals. To the actual reasons why the hostility refuses to dissipate. The locations of many of the

---

*The eulogy became one of the most influential and collectively well-remembered speeches in Israeli history; it is reproduced in translation in many sources.

Israeli communities around Gaza were once someone's home and village. And that is true across Israel, as evidenced by the abandoned cactus rows and the memories of people who are still alive. The Gaza Strip is a strip of refugees. Half the population there (and perhaps more) is of refugee origin. That is the real fuel for the Qassam rockets fired at southern Israel. Only a brave Israeli reckoning with the pain of the Palestinians carries the potential of a change in direction and fundamental treatment of the causes of the war, not only its deteriorating symptoms.

In that fascinating exchange between the two great minds of that earlier generation, the father of psychology explains to the genius of physics that human beings have two types of urges: "Urges to exist and unite, and urges that seek death and destruction." If it were possible to put Israeliness on Freud's couch, he would have talked to us about his most complex and fundamental insight: "It is impossible to erase the aggressive tendencies of human beings. The way to weaken the destructive and aggressive urge is by strengthening the urge for emotional affinity and love."*

In real life, it means a strategic political decision of the highest order to weaken the lust for destruction by strengthening emotional connections. Instead of leaving the complicated issue of the refugees for the end of the negotiations, it must be immediately brought to the fore. An alternative Israeli policy based on rights and not force should be formulated. We must break down the barrier between our feelings toward ourselves and the callousness about the suffering of others. It must be a policy of "refugees first," with or without political negotiations, and even without an agreement on political borders (artificial lines on maps can wait, but people's feelings cannot anymore).

And there are just two principles needed to embark on this difficult path. First, it is impossible and forbidden to correct previous injustices by creating new ones. And second, there must be public Israeli recognition of the plight of the refugees and readiness to act. Understanding

---

*Translation mine; compare with Freud, "Why War?," *Collected Papers*.

that the birth of the refugee issue is bound up with the birth of Israel, with a real expression of willingness to deal with it together and suggest real solutions, will generate a totally different energy here. I truly believe that only a piercing look—like Dayan's at the time—at the bases of the past, and acts of atonement, unification, and building in the present, will make it possible to genuinely create a vision of the future for both Israelis and Palestinians, without wars.

THERE ARE MANY WAYS TO MAKE HISTORY FELT IN contemporary life. Some are completely symbolic, like the memorial "stumbling blocks" (*stolpersteine*) embedded in the sidewalks of many German cities, designed and installed by the artist Gunter Demnig. A quiet, unobtrusive, penetrating statement, commemorating near the entrances of homes those who left them and did not return. Parts of the old route of the Berlin Wall have not been erased from the city streets. In Warsaw, there are small signs in several languages commemorating what happened in each place. Not large and alienating monuments. On the contrary: a silent presence that is part of daily life for every pedestrian or bystander. In Israel, a place addicted to history and archeology, it would be very easy to do. Nothing would happen to anyone if history did not start in 1948, but with what was here earlier. Aside from the sense of partnership and respect for the place of Palestinian Israeli citizens, no harm would be done if we marked in every place all of Israeli history, both Palestinian and Jewish.

I don't believe that all the wheels of history can be turned back. But wherever possible, why not do it? The condition of the Palestinian refugees became one of Israel's strongest propaganda claims almost from its first day. "Look at the difference," the Israeli propagandists argued, "while we have absorbed a million of our refugees from Arab states, housed and rehabilitated them for the greater glory of Israel, they, the Arabs, have not lifted a finger for their refugees. To this day, they live in wretched camps, perpetual clients of the United Nations Relief and Works Agency (UNRWA). Constantly increasing, miserable and neglected." On the face of it, a powerful argument, but at bottom one of the hollowest of claims. Because Jewish Israel did nothing for the Palestinian refugees inside it. It's important to remember: according to Zionist rhetoric, immigrants are not refugees, by definition. Immigration to Israel is a positive ideological decision, and refugee status is a negative result of expulsion, flight, and defeat. In contrast with the Zionist immigrants, Palestinian Israelis are for all intents and purposes our refugees.

In Israel in 2017, there are more than a quarter of a million people who are refugees of 1948 and their descendants. Not somewhere in miserable camps on the outskirts of Beirut. Not in Jordan, the West Bank, or the Gaza Strip, but here between and among us. At the end of the 1948 War of Independence there were 160,000 Palestinians left in Israel whom the cleansing policy of the time did not succeed in driving away. Among them were about 40,000 internally displaced people who were expelled from their communities and compelled to live "temporarily" in villages and neighboring communities inside the borders of the nascent State of Israel.

Although Israel prides itself on its absorption of immigrants, it has not only done nothing for the displaced, but endless verdicts, along with public and governmental committees, have done their best to repeatedly violate simple government promises made to the residents when they left. Pledges that they would be able to return to their lands after the fighting subsided. Cemeteries were desecrated, holy places became warehouses and animal sheds, whole villages were wiped off their cultivated soil, and one people's place of mourning became the other's vacation spot, with more to come. That is the behavior of a callous country and society, denying the history of part of their citizens, and actually their own history.

It can be different. Israel can make a huge gesture to itself, to its citizens, and to the entire region if it makes the issue of those internal Palestinian refugees its top priority. It will be an appropriate model for the correct implementation of the right of return anywhere it is possible and practical. It wouldn't change the demographic balance sanctified by the Israeli "establishments of fear" because it is an internal Israeli matter. They are already Israeli citizens (though refugees in their own state) and do not change the infamous demographic equilibrium, which counts heads and not ideas or values.

After making room here for a variety of Jewish ethnic groups, the time has come to make room for the remaining fifth of the country's citizens. For those Palestinians who live in the occupied territories, the solution to their misery will be part of a larger peace agreement.

I have participated in many conversations, conferences, seminars, and peace discussions, and I'm still an integral part of the "peace industry." We're all friends, we all know each other's shticks, and still the conversations reach the same dead end. The content mostly revolves around the same axes. Dozens of years of the same arguments, the same questions and answers. Neither side, right nor left, Israel nor Palestine, changes its positions. When that frustrating point is reached, and it is always reached, I can't help being transported by my thoughts to an odd riddle typically featured in the weekend newspapers: a brain teaser in which you're supposed to create a bunch of geometric forms out of a very few matches or toothpicks. The solution is sometimes creative, standing a match up, breaking out of the two-dimensional plane to create another level and dimension, and then it all makes sense. I think the same will ultimately apply to the Middle East conundrum. Is it solvable? In the two-dimensional world—us or them, two states or nothing—the chances, unfortunately, tend toward nil. In a multi-dimensional reality, the chances increase greatly.

ONE OF THE WEAKNESSES OF MOST OF THESE INTERnational peace efforts is their temporariness. A few days, usually abroad, and everyone goes back home, without follow-up, without time for maturation.

But in 2011 and 2012, when I was privileged to work in Vienna with a group of Israeli Jews and Palestinians from Israel and the diaspora, things were different. The location was almost magical, the home of former Austrian chancellor Bruno Kreisky, where an institute named after him operates with the aim of creating and promoting international dialogue, in keeping with his legacy. With typical Austrian patience, with a perspective more historical than contemporary, Gertraud, my friend and the *chefin* (the boss) of the place, caused us to meet, converse, listen, express, argue, respect, and ultimately to formulate agreements that surprised us all.

Time played its role. The meetings, the personal relationships that formed, the understanding of the other—so close in physical reality but so distant in politics and consciousness—helped us sharpen our sensitivity and develop a concept of an agreement based on sharing and openness rather than separation and distancing. Only there, far from the region and its cacophony and close to my neighbor from across the hill near my house, I understood the absurdity of all the peace plans I had been part of and supported. All of them, from first to last, were based on the assumption of separation. A separation stemming from a sad strategy: Israel, even the Israel of the peace camp, does not dare think seriously about real integration in the Middle East. Many of us prefer a high Crusader wall separating us from the broader Middle East to a single moment of integration.

Many Israelis are convinced that Israel is the only guarantee for the future existence of the Jewish people. Some believe that force of arms will protect us from disasters, and many are convinced that we here in Israel are immune to the assimilation and mixed marriages eating away at western Jewry. Are marriages outside the circles of Jewish faith and genetics really such a great tragedy? I'm not convinced of that. But I'm pretty much alone in this position. The majority thinks differently. Very few people have ever thought about the question of what purpose is served by the continuation of the Jewish people, and why survive. What is it to be a Jew? They make do with Jewish numbers and demography. How many, and who is marrying whom, and who, God forbid, married a gentile man or woman. I sense that deep and dark concern everywhere.

When the Israeli-Jordanian peace agreement was signed in 1994, one of the weekend papers published an article about a couple, an Israeli and a Jordanian, a nice love story. But the squawks of those reacting in radio broadcasts and from parliament members who quickly submitted motions to the agenda told a different story. The story of purity of Jewish blood. There are many organizations busy "saving" daughters of Israel from falling in love with Arabs and pairing off with them. Many religious rulings against Arab employees in supermarkets where Jewish women shop are part of the landscape in the "Jewish state." An Israeli journalist (and he's not the only one) wrote about illegal African migrants sleeping with "our girls" and thereby threatening Israeli culture. This motto recurs everywhere: "our girls." As one of the greatest racist rabbis of our generation said, "I myself saw Arab students who came to Safed, and after two days here, they had already started flirting with the girls at the seminary. Modest girls who came to study in a religious atmosphere were compelled to turn around and flee."*

Never, in all my years as a peace activist, had I given genuine thought to a different option than the principle of separation. Only there, in distant Vienna, was I able to see the defining mistake I had committed along with my colleagues. All the meetings were in the same room, in the home of the Jewish chancellor, who many considered to have been the best prime minister of post-war Austria. It was a spacious glass-walled room that faced a spacious green garden. A great silence enveloped the place, and all the participants in the room were framed by a different aesthetic than the rough background of the Middle East. No barbed wire fences and separation barriers, no ugly concrete wall, and no rifles and gunsights through which I am compelled to see my neighbor, both near and far. These new and impressive friends, the atmosphere, the depth and thoroughness, the framework and the aesthetic all gave me a sense of opportunity. Here I was in a laboratory of ideas

---

*Sari Makover-Belikov, "Rabbi Eliyahu: 'Jews Should Not Flee from Arabs'" [in Hebrew], *NRG*, online, November 19, 2010.

and thoughts. Not a sweaty Levantine workshop with preconceived outcomes, but a real place for thought. And out of this political laboratory a totally new conception of the chance for a solution slowly took shape in me.

Another plane is needed, like the upright match in the riddle that today is outside the realms of imagination of the existing players, of the two communities so hostile to each other. Because the conversation about a state is actually a one-level conversation—the national level and nothing else. A national home for the Jewish people, a national home for the Palestinian collective—and that's it. Anything less than a state—identity, character, the citizens, and communities—are almost entirely outside the conversation, and anything beyond the state structure goes virtually undiscussed. The result is that many people on all sides feel just like me, that no matter what type of settlement is achieved someday, it won't solve the real problems. Even if a Palestinian nation-state is established alongside Israel tomorrow morning, it will be at best an inadequate interim settlement. Because those who want all of the territory—on our side or theirs—will never be content with half the land, and will continue to undermine the foundations of the partition settlement. Those who want partition actually want to push across the border the basic problems in our lives that have existed since the establishment of Israel, and more acutely since 1967: the traumas, the refugees, the domineering, and the occupation. Their counterparts on the Palestinian side want separation to avoid dealing with the Israeli challenge so present in their lives.

Almost daily I find myself in conversation or debate about the subject. And nearly every time the conversation ends with a shrug of the shoulders and the remark, "That's the way it is, there's nothing to be done." Like predetermined fate, like death or a car accident. Not only is the vocabulary lacking for such a creation, the feelings are also very opposed. If a settlement emerges from such negotiations, it will be forced and permeated with great suspicion and hostility. Many Palestinians are convinced that all Israelis are either settlers or soldiers—if only because that is the only side of us they are exposed to. Most of us, on the other hand, are convinced that "they"—all of them—are among the worst anti-Semites and that every Palestinian is a suicidal terrorist. The sour attitudes of Israeli prime ministers and ministers, like the suspicion of the Palestinian leadership, do not promise real change. In short, it doesn't look particularly encouraging.

Can a different future be molded from all these materials? Is it possible to have a structure encompassing a greater range of issues, that will extend from the individual and personal, Israeli or Palestinian, to the superstructure that organizes the lives of all of us? The working assumption is that none of the parties involved is about to disappear in the foreseeable future. The Israeli and Palestinian fates are so completely intertwined that even complete disregard cannot make anything disappear. Illnesses that go untreated on one side metastasize to the other, and there is no wall in the world that can stop them. Because of all this, it is vital today more than ever to build a new political and ideological structure. In order to give a positive answer to these questions we have to abandon the one-dimensional, one-floor concept, and add depth and height to it. The time has come for thinking about a three-story house.

The first level will be the infrastructure floor. The moral basis on which the whole future political structure will rest: every person between the Jordan River and the sea is entitled to the same rights, individual, political, economic, and social, including the rights to protection and security; to fair treatment and freedom of movement; to property ownership; to sue in court; to vote and be elected. It doesn't matter which country's citizenship you have—Israeli or Palestinian— you are committed to the same constitutional and ethical framework, and you are entitled to the same basic freedoms without any discrimination based on sex, race, ethnic origin, religious belief, or national affiliation. That is the civic infrastructure that comes before any conversation about nationhood or statehood.

The intermediate level above it will be divided between the two residents. Separation and agreed logical partitions between the two collectives in the form of two sovereign states. In each one, separately, the aspirations and values of the Israelis and Palestinians will be expressed. Everyone in their place, and every side in its way and according to its traditions. Each of the states on the intermediate level will conduct its own foreign, interior, defense, and economic policies.

But it can't end there. The historical hostility and violent friction of the past between the two sides could erupt again at any moment. That is why constant coordination is vital. For that the third level will be built, the superstructure shared by the states themselves. A confederation of Israel and Palestine that will function internally as well as externally. Internally, the confederative government will have authorities delegated to it from the two independent partners—Israel and Palestine. The confederation will be responsible, among other things, for the constitutional system between the Jordan River and the sea. There will never be calm and reconciliation if a common moral language is not created here. A murderer on one side must be a murderer on the other. Enough of the intolerable gap, in which an act is perceived as a horrendous crime on one side and the highest expression of patriotism on the other. Although each state will collect its own taxes with the agreement of its citizens and operate its own educational systems and cultural institutions as it sees fit, the infrastructures of both must be coordinated.

The third floor, designated for coordination, will ensure that the water resources in the mountains will be shared with residents of the coastal plain, that the rivers are clean along their entire length, and that the road signs are in the languages of all drivers in the region. There does not need to be a difference between streets and roads in Nablus and Netanya, just as there are no such differences between New York and California and between Italy and Austria, despite the differences between them. There will be positive and vital cooperation on the superstructure level to enforce shared constitutional principles, regulating judicial and civil matters and coordinating policy on issues of asylum, immigration, and the return of Jews and Palestinians to their national homelands. Externally, for the world beyond the historic space between the Jordan River and the sea, the Israeli-Palestinian confederation will be the interface that other national entities will be invited to join. Those who accept the commitments stemming from the ethical, democratic, and constitutional principles of the first floor will be able to join the new regional union.

The proposed structure seeks to provide other answers to most—not all—of the issues on the agenda. Whoever wants one state will find a partial answer in the confederative structure. Advocates of two states will get them in the intermediate level. And whoever is committed to individual rights will be pleased with their expression in the binding constitutional infrastructure.

"All is well and good, Mr. Burg," the cynics will say, "but security, what about security? An Arab chief of staff, an Arab defense minister? Not on your life. Are you crazy?" To the cynics I say cynically, "And you agree to all the rest?" When we achieve all the rest, it will be much easier to deal with security issues. To those thinking more deeply I pose the question: Did anyone ever believe in open borders between Germany and France? In peace between Spain and Holland? In reconciliation between Russia and Germany? When the environmental conditions change, the threats also change and so do security perceptions. And to the rest I say frankly: We—the Israelis—are so strong that we can allow ourselves to abandon the strategy of anxieties and traumas and shift to a concept of trust. If I am wrong, our situation would not have gotten worse, and we can always declare another war, no? And if I am right, then the current security obsession will change unrecognizably. Just as it changed toward Iraq that has disappeared, toward Syria that is being torn apart, and toward weakening Egypt, so will it change dramatically when confronted with an Israeli-Palestinian partnership totally different from anything we have known.

With such a peace, Israel and Palestine can and must be part of the united states of Europe in general, and of the European-Mediterranean region in particular. We will all be citizens of a human sphere much greater than the limited borders of our pain-filled and mournful homelands between the Jordan River and the Mediterranean Sea. This is the vision of the Mediterranean confederation, and it is possible and right for us. It is no less right and essential for Europe, coping with tremendous challenges of integrating minority communities and cultures. For the Romans, the Mediterranean was *Mare Nostrum*, "our sea," our common and shared space. Now, the shores of the same old sea can become the confederation of integration. I have been privileged to be such a citizen even before the full realization of the dream. I return gently, quietly, humbly, to what was violently stolen from my father in the days of World War II. I feel the power of the renewed connections, the interface still hurts me sometimes, but in fascinating, coping Europe, I also feel at home.

W HEN I COMPARE THIS TO THE POINTS OF DISCONNECTION of my Jewish friends from their roots in Islamic countries, I can't help but weep for the existential change wrought on historic Jewry by that great war and the subsequent establishment of the state. The Israeli sociologist Yehouda Shenhav defines himself as an Arab Jew. "If there is a Christian Arab and a Muslim Arab, then there was and there should also be a Jewish Arab," he passionately asserted to me in conversation. André Azoulay, an advisor to the king of Morocco, presents himself, with his plethora of heritages, as a Berber, Arab, Moroccan, and Jew. True, one must not forget for a moment the hardships that afflicted the generations of our parents in all of the Jewish diasporas, but by the same token it cannot be forgotten what could have developed here had history flowed a bit differently, with fewer ethnic divisions and more common spaces. I feel comfortable in today's Europe. In fascinating Turkey, which alternately opens and closes. I like Egypt, and take advantage of every opportunity to be in Ramallah and Jericho. The complexity, tensions, compromises, and cultures fuel my curiosity over and over again. I believe that the comfort of multiple identities and affiliations can and must be part of our Mediterranean existence. Yes, it could very well be that at the end of this process, after all the pains and prices, one of my grandchildren will come home and say to his parents, "Dad, Mom, meet Sawsan, my girlfriend. We are going to get married." Maybe it will be easy for them because they are tolerant, as we raised them, and maybe it will be difficult because their primary Israeliness had hardened them considerably, and the public Judaism they are familiar with will still handcuff their consciousness. It will likely be a great challenge for them, as well as for the parents of Sawsan. But that is a much healthier challenge than the challenges of war and hostility that we received from our parents and bequeathed to our children. A price worth paying. And I? I would be very happy to meet her parents, be present at the couple's wedding, maybe even marry them, and kiss our common great-grandchildren. And hope.

CHAPTER THIRTEEN

THE HOLOCAUST
IS OVER

O NE OF THE MOST PROFOUND AND LEAST DISCUSSED reasons why we are still very far from that wedding between one of my grandchildren and a Sawsan, and from the tremendous social change I seek, became clear to me not long ago at a difficult meeting in the Galilee.

In 2007, I was invited to a public debate about an issue—admissions committees for Jewish rural communities, whose sole purpose was to "screen" Arab candidates. Most of the small villages in Israel are quite ethnic; the Jews live in their own neighborhoods and the Arabs in theirs. The Jewish villages are usually more affluent and therefore more attractive to Arab families who are looking to improve their lives. In order to prevent this "invasion," the Jewish settlers wanted a selection process to prevent the freedom of movement and housing, one based on "Zionist criteria." The discussion was very stormy, laced with shouting, shaking fists, and waving flags. At some point, one of the participants, whose body language had said from the start, "I don't agree with you," hurled very harsh personal comments at me, and then said, "The most meaningful moment in my life as an Israeli was when three Israeli fighter jets flew over Auschwitz."

Our two worlds apparently were reverse mirror images. He saw a positive connection between planes over Auschwitz and structural discrimination against people because of their ethnic origin, religion, or national affiliation. And I saw the exact opposite. I tried not to raise my voice, but I did not mince words: "To me it was a hollow moment, totally empty. A declaration of arrogance, nothing more. The people, Jews and others, murdered down below were not killed because they didn't have an air force, weapons, or were denied atomic bombs for mass destruction. They were murdered because other people—the Nazis and their associates—had no binding values of human rights, inalienable basic rights of equality among all people without compromise, despite the differences between them. Western Jews have no air force and no atomic bombs and no paratroopers, and still they are far less threatened than Israel and Israelis, because they have a safety net of a constitution and rights, like any other member of their society."

The evening did not end well, to say the least, because after those words there was a moment of silence in the hall. Then people assailed me from every direction for many minutes: "Let's see you living next to Arabs." The shouted questions were difficult, and my answer didn't really calm anyone down. "Listen, for me to be a Jew is not a genetic code of someone born to a Jewish mother. It's a value system that is in conversation with and open to those who enter it, while tolerant of those who leave. Genetic Judaism is pure racism, and Jews who are not completely committed to equality and human rights are no different than any other discriminatory racist." As I left, the shouts trailed my car as it moved into the night. We—Jews and Israelis—sanctify Jewish blood and genetics literally and not the value system that forms the basis of larger Jewish culture.

We are on the cusp of the first generation without living witnesses to the Holocaust. In my lifetime, or the lives of my children, the last victims will pass away along with the last perpetrators. There will be no more Germans or Jews of those days. Because the Holocaust will no longer be a personal experience, but one consigned to the tremendous annals of history. Many powerful forces are already vying to shape this moment. The deniers began their task of obfuscation even before the passing of the previous generation. The commemorators are divided into two camps, ours and theirs. Theirs shave their heads, wear swastika tattoos, and march by the thousands in the streets of Germany and Europe. The neo-Nazis and xenophobes are not about to disappear from the landscapes of our lives. They are active and committed to commemorating what they see as the greatness of the past, seeking to revive the romanticized hatred that was. And like them, in a dialectical and completely opposite fashion, there are those among us who yearn for a reality in which the Holocaust will never end, and that we will always and forever have a way to shape our existence through it, the experience of endless trauma.

Against them I wish to present my parents' spiritual and existential last will and testament. My sisters and I were born from Mom's snow, not from the blood and massacre. We received a pure, clean slate from our parents. We grew up in a miracle, in a home completely free of traumas. Mom's Hebron was destroyed before her very eyes, Dad's Dresden went up in flames, and still they created a calm and joyful human environment that was optimistic and trusting. And from these foundations a rarely powerful connection was made between my parents and my wife.

My father-in-law was a partisan in the Jewish underground in France. He fought the Nazis, and my mother-in-law was a young woman who volunteered to write letters to a partisan. After the war they met, and thanks to them we are all here. She knitted him socks, wrote letters, and sent him her chocolate ration right to the front lines. When the war was over, they returned together from the assimilating world to Judaism. But in contrast to others, they didn't return from the killing fields to the nationalist, isolationist, and traumatized extreme. On the contrary.

The miracle of World War II, they taught me, is not the fact that the Jewish people were saved, and that the State of Israel rose from the ashes. The real miracle is that humanity was saved because of the bravery of Righteous Gentiles. For dozens of years my dear father-in-law, a precious man, has been devoting all his efforts to finding and dec-orating Righteous Gentiles, those who risked their lives to save other human beings, Jews.

Many years ago, when I served in one of my public posts, the chair-man of the Jewish Agency (1995–1999), a group of young Israelis came to meet me. "We have an idea of first-rate historical and national significance," they told me. "We want to tell you about it, and if you're convinced, we'd like you to lead it."

"What's the idea?" I asked, with curiosity.

"Six million Jews were killed in the Holocaust, right?"

"Right," I replied.

"And there are six million Jews today in Israel, right?"

"Correct."

"And Israel is the heir to the Judaism that was destroyed, right?"

I didn't answer.

"We think that every Israeli should adopt a dead victim and tattoo on his arm the number of a Jew who was murdered there. And when that Israeli's days are done, someone else, maybe one of his children, will tattoo the same number. And that way, you see, they will never die, they will live forever. And the memory of the martyrs will never be forgotten."

I'm looking for another way. One that does not only orbit the past, reliving it again and again, unable to ever get out of there. Neither is it a way of life that is an indifferent, straight, and rigid line that moves to the future and leaves the memories of the past behind it as if nothing had happened. I'm trying to clear a path for myself and for us who re-member but are alive. A spiral of progress and memory, a synthesis of a line and circle, of continuity and change. I'm looking for the path that will take me from the memory to the lesson, from trauma to renewed trust in myself and in people in general, from what was mine and ours to what is supposed to be universal and belongs to all people wherever they may be.

For many, the Holocaust was and will forever be an incurable trauma; for others, it is a pure crystal around which the elements of their identity coalesce to form a whole. For both, the Holocaust is a tangible reality, present in whatever they do.

I wanted to take the legacy of my parents' home and turn it into an alternative concept to the culture of tragedy that guides our life here. I imagined the miracle that my parents created; they managed to transmit and inculcate in us many of the values of a world destroyed and vanished while preventing destruction and trauma from having any real contact with our lives.

The mass demonstrations in Jerusalem against reparations from Germany to Holocaust victims and survivors, against diplomatic relations with Germany, and even the Eichmann trial, did not come into our home. Just like the settlement enterprise and the renewal of Jewish settlement in Hebron, my mother's home town, which were kept outside our heavy wooden door. I don't recall even one conversation in which these issues came up and were discussed. So, it's no wonder that the whole Holocaust industry that has swept Israel in recent years was very alien to me. I'm not a psychologist and I don't know if Mom or Dad successfully repressed the horrors of their youth and the terrifying reality that wiped out their happy childhoods, or perhaps, like any normal young couple, they created their own reality for themselves and created a new world. Either way, I was never involved, emotionally or practically, in the "Holocaustization" that has become such second nature for us Israelis and Jews.

I N 2006, I TOOK A FASCINATING TRIP WITH OUR YOUNGEST son, Noam. Together we followed the footsteps of my late father to Germany. We traveled far, thousands of miles, but what I discovered was deep inside me. On the last day of the journey we were notified that our flight was delayed, and suddenly we had a few unplanned free hours. We left our luggage and strolled, like any ordinary father and son, along the paths of the Berlin Zoo. While Noam ran around looking at the many cages and unusual animals, I found myself sitting on a bench and peering at the captive monkeys behind the partition. All, except one, jumped energetically and mischievously from branch to branch. One hand holding a branch and the other stretched out for the next branch. Letting go, leaping into the air and moving forward, up and back. Over and over. Just one, the exception, sat alone, oblivious to his mates. I asked a zookeeper who passed by what that monkey was like.

"He's different," the German veterinarian answered me. "He can't climb and move forward because he's afraid to let go of the branch. When you hold a branch with two hands, you can't move. That's his fate," he added sadly. "He sits all day on the ground like someone in mourning, cut off from what's going on around him."

I thought about the poor monkey, and not only about him. I asked myself, is this the metaphor? Are we the monkey? Since the Holocaust, we have been holding tightly, our knuckles white, to the little we have, unwilling to let go. Clinging to memories and pain, and not letting go. Wallowing in the trauma and using it to justify everything. Sitting on the ground of the past, mourning, and not taking off to the heights of humanity and humaneness. When Noam came back from his tour of the zoo, my train of thought was interrupted. We went to buy ice cream and began the journey back home, and I forgot to ask the veterinarian if there was a remedy for the monkey's ailment, our ailment.

I HAVE NO IDEA IF THERE IS A GOD, I DON'T HAVE PROOF of his existence or non-existence, it's not important to me. One thing I'm sure of: if there is a Creator somewhere, she created the world through debate and disagreement. I believe that disagreement is the most important tool of human creation, which Jewish culture adopted and greatly improved. Because if I agree with you and you think like me, and we all agree about everything, then ultimately everything degenerates and dies. But if we disagree on something, sharpen our self-held truths, if we're precise and thoughtful, maybe something new will be born between us.

My arguments pertaining to the legacy of the Holocaust hurt my readers in various ways. More than anything, it is difficult for Israelis to face the mirror I hold up to them. "How dare you compare us to Germany? We are, after all . . . " I had carefully compared contemporary Israel to Germany between the Second Reich and the downfall of the Weimar Republic, not to the Germany of the grim and dark days of Nazi rule. But the very comparison of something Israeli to something German was enough to create an uproar. A response is necessary to the claim: why Germany of all places? The role of an analogy in a conversation or discussion is to be a reflecting mirror, and it is almost always problematic. If something in the analogy doesn't match 100 percent, immediately attention will turn to the aberration, not the substance. Still, there is no alternative to looking at the mirror facing us, even when it is not always clean, and even when the image reflected in it is not always flattering.

I have given great consideration to what would be the most accurate historical analogy. I thought of comparing our reality to the invasion by the white colonists of North America—"pioneers," refugees, immigrants, and religious reformers who ultimately brought a great tragedy of annihilation and erased memory to the members of the original indigenous people. I thought later a great deal about the history of France in North Africa in general, and particularly in Algeria. A painful occupation and disengagement full of tragedies, very similar to our reality in the Palestinian territories. In the end, I was left with Germany. Anyone in his right mind knows that the two works that were the most important and had the most influence on contemporary Jewry were Hitler's *Mein Kampf* on the one hand and Herzl's *Altneuland* on the other. What was there in the German environment then that produced two such prophecies, the prophecy of darkness and the vision of light?

Germany, as I knew it from observation and endless reading, contained an impossible race between two different and contradictory spirits. One spirit carried collective gusts—gray, sad, and angry—of national trauma. Because of the damage inflicted on Germany by the international community—the Germany that did not find its place in the sun during the great imperialist contest, that was vanquished and humiliated in World War I—it became the most hurt and insulted nation in Europe. At the same time, however, winds of freedom were blowing there like nowhere else. Winds of equality, creativity, freedom, brotherhood, and new and fascinating thinking. It was a race between pessimism and optimism, between hurt and hope, between trauma and trust. In the end, hurt rose to power, and the national trauma overcame hope and its spirit of progress, renewal, and humanity.

Such a race is also taking place in Israel. Between a painful and tangible national trauma and a new spirit of Jewish hope and Israeli esprit de corps. The race has yet to be decided. Sometimes trauma is ahead, and sometimes it is hope. And it is not at all clear who will win this race. I wanted to raise an alarm, a warning sign on the nation's path, telling it to pay attention. Sometimes trauma wins, and who but the Jewish nation knows better the implications and consequences of such a dark victory.

The storm caused by my attempts to sound a warning was accompanied by self-righteous fury in the press and the public that pushed me far outside the accepted circles and the Zionist consensus. They pushed and I willingly distanced myself. Their emotions were no longer mine. To my great sorrow, not too many years were necessary for my painful views to become a commonplace reality. The same thinkers, writers, journalists, and critics who attacked me have become the critics of contemporary Israel, as if their words were taken from my writings. They lament racist Israel, the shrill xenophobia here, the malignant occupation that seems irreversible, the repellant aggressiveness and collapse of the supporting pillars of democracy. These voices are being heard from all directions. And Israel, unwittingly and without acknowledgment, has become a polarized society whose rifts seem a long way from healing. When they get to the places where I had been in previous years, I've already moved on elsewhere. I'm already beyond despair, looking for new hopes, paradigms, and insights that are entirely different from those that have brought us to this pass, to this shock.

In 2007 I was interviewed by the *Haaretz* newspaper. It was an interview with plenty of shouting, and its climax was this exchange between me and the interviewer:

He: "Don't you understand that your positions endanger the State of Israel? There won't be an Israel. It won't exist."

Me: "Tell me something. How can it be that I have been a Jew for two thousand years, without a gun, without planes, without two hundred atomic bombs, and I never for a day feared for the existence and eternity of the Jewish people? And you—the Israeli—you've been armed to the teeth for sixty years, with troops and special forces, with capabilities the Jewish people never had, and every day you are scared, perpetually terrified that this day is your last."

He: "I don't have an answer to that."

He published the interview and ended it this way: "You can't take away from Avrum what he has. You can't take away his education or eloquence or ability to touch painful points of truth. Maybe for that reason he is so infuriating. A friend and a predator, a brother and a defector." He marked me and the border between us. He was inside, and I was outside. He was a patriot, and I was a defector.

On the morning the interview was published I went out as usual to bring in the newspaper. Before the first light of day I had read it. Not easy, but penetrating, sharp, and thought-provoking. With our first coffee, I brought the paper to my partner. She, who doesn't read newspapers and despises our cacophonous news, read it very quietly. When she finished reading she erupted in bitter tears, crying like she never had before, even in the most difficult moments of our lives. The kids, who were home at that moment, rushed into our bedroom.

"Why are you crying?" they wondered.

"I agree with Dad's every word, but I already see the reactions," she said with the pain of her experience. "I have no more strength for the hatred, the madness, the evil that is about to pounce on us."

Roni, my oldest daughter, thought for a minute and said warmly, "You don't have to cry, Mom. In fact, you mustn't cry, there's no need to cry." She argued that I was finally expressing what I held to be true, and that this truth is also her truth, of her generation, and that finally someone is speaking to it truthfully. This voice must be preserved, Dad's voice, she told her. He should be supported, he must be helped, because he is the only hope left here, in this lousy country.

It was a moment of clarity for the family. Everyone was right. My partner could not imagine how much her prediction would come true, the intensity of the resentment that has since become an inseparable part of our lives. And my daughter was very right in her intuitive assessment. It was the first time that I had confronted in such a clear fashion a generational gap.

Most of those I lost, or who wanted to do away with me, were of my age group, and their remarks to me and about me recurred in numerous ways: "Avrum, just when we finally have some peace and quiet you bother us with your questions? Leave us alone, for God's sake!" Their children, on the other hand, didn't stop coming. First, they came one at a time. Then they invited me to parlor meetings and gatherings, and now I'm also involved in building many of their futures. Many of them understood that along with my criticism of the current reality there is a proposal for an alternative spiritual and moral identity that is positive and constructive. Their message is loud and clear: we don't necessarily agree with you, but you are one of the few who allow us to ask the absolute questions that trouble us so much. In recent years, the existential and political conversation with them has become something entirely different.

A YEAR LATER, IN SEPTEMBER 2008, MY DAUGHTER RONI got married. I was flooded with happiness. My first daughter to get married, at home, in a small and intimate circle of friends and loved ones. She and Ariel chose me to officiate and bring them into the covenant of marriage. We went up together to the hill above our small house in the village; we put up a marriage canopy in the Judean Hills, on the outskirts of Jerusalem, and were very excited. The day after the wedding, the three of us, Roni, Ariel, and I, flew to Germany to run the Berlin Marathon together.

It had taken me a long time to return to Germany. I had been there many times, but none of my visits were easy or simple. My first trip abroad was at the end of high school. My parents said to themselves and to me that I must broaden my horizons before joining the army. I traveled to Munich to see the Olympic Games of 1972. The visit was aborted with unforgettable symbolism due to the murder of eleven Israeli athletes by Palestinian terrorists in Munich. Years later, I headed a parliamentary delegation to Berlin. We took off at dawn, and when we landed I realized that I was sick, feverish, and weak. That same evening, in the same plane, I returned home, and when I landed I was feeling healthy and hardy—another attempt to reach Germany that came up empty.

I had been in Berlin many times: during layovers between flights to distant destinations, as a member of Knesset and public figure, as Knesset speaker on the day the Bundestag moved from Bonn to Berlin, as an Israeli with his youngest son following his father and his world that had vanished. But I had never been to Berlin like this. I had never come to Berlin as a pariah at home in my country and I had never come to this defining city in pursuit of my love, running, and with my loved ones. Free of any agenda, liberated from emotions and excessive emotional baggage. So I thought.

I cried the whole forty-two kilometers. For one-third of them I cried in pain and sorrow. There was Oranienburger Straße, where my father would often pray. And from there you go to Grenadierstraße, where the Gestapo headquarters was, and then we passed very near the Alexanderplatz of the writer Alfred Döblin, and the finish, oh, the finish. Potsdamer Platz, under the boulevard of linden trees, the Unter den Linden, still bearing the imprint of the Nazi architect Albert Speer, through the Brandenburg Gate and the actual finish line. Once upon a time—during the Nazi era—there were other thousands here, they too cheered, but not for me, they too were full of joy for the body and for nature, without me. But then, in 2008, it was my time, and with my whole body and soul I felt that something different was happening here. Every street corner spoke to me, echoed and reflected familiar shadows of a past that I was never privileged to know, of a present that could have been mine. I ran and cried for Dad and for us and for myself and for the history that was, and all those who are no more. For another third I cried because it was hard for me. The kilometers added up, the muscles cried out, and age also asserted its claim.

In the last third I cried for joy. I was living in the most amazing Jewish generation ever. There was never a generation like this before. Jews running? Marathons? Jews running a marathon as equals? As athletes, not objects of persecution? There was no difference between me and the Danes and the Dutch and the Germans and the British and all the others around me, just as happy as I was. We were really all equal. Each one according to his ability, each one according to his wishes. Where was my dad, why wasn't he here waiting for me in the expanses of the Tiergarten, to see me grinning? Happy and believing in the happiness of my children? Dad, you were right, there is a different Germany, but Dad, you didn't know, there is also a different Israel.

All my life is a race, an endless marathon. I have come from an ancient history and I am focused on eternity. Meanwhile, I'm trying to grab some moments of reality and current events and understand them, to decipher the meaning of things. Now I'm on the Judeo-European track. So complicated and complex. So much potential and achievement, along with endless disappointments and innumerable victims. I'm not one of those who think that in the Holocaust saints were killed by animals. It was a horrific and unnecessary war and a brutal annihilation of people with no reason or purpose. People murdered people. The murderer was a German person, and he can't be relieved of responsibility as if he were a mad, mindless dog. The murdered Jew, gypsy, and homosexual was a human being, who must be remembered as such.

This is how it happened: the arrogant individual, full of feelings of inferiority, was pushed to immortalize his superiority through evil violence and the elimination of the one he saw as lowly and inferior. The first thing this violent human virus attacks is the concept of equality of all people. And the minute that one individual is worth less, the way to his elimination is easier. It happened to us in Germany, and it can happen to any nation, anywhere, in any situation.

It didn't only take me time to get to Germany; it took Germany time to get to me. I saw the fears and hesitations of the German interviewers and of other friends. "Herr Burg, it is difficult for us," they admitted to me. Only a few reached the last leg of my journey, the end of the marathon, the proposal to go together, Jews and Germans, sacrificers and sacrificed together, to all the places where people are still tied to the stake, bound to the altars of cruelty. To raise our voices together and say: "'Never again' is not only for the Jews. Never again! For any murder and destruction of any human being, whoever he may be." Because that is the universal lesson of the tragic relationship between the Germans and Judaism that we are trying to make a turning point. From "our Holocaust" to a better world, healed and humane, for all human beings in the image of God, in which there will be no Holocausts—for anyone. A different Germanism, Judaism, and humanism is my key to making a few necessary corrections in this world.

CHAPTER FOURTEEN

A TALE OF TWO MEETINGS

I N MY LIFE I HAVE MET THOUSANDS, MAYBE EVEN TENS OF thousands of people. Important and ordinary, well-known and anonymous. I remember many of them, and some of them might remember me. I met people who were talented, wealthy, foolish, brilliant, good, strange, wonderful, and bad. In the years when I was an important and powerful person, I didn't know how to enjoy this wonderful human wealth. In virtually all these meetings I was introverted, defensive. Trying to preserve an imaginary treasure that someone was trying to loot. That life was a large-scale barter bazaar. Sometimes I entered the rooms of others and wanted something from them, and sometimes they came to me and wanted something from me. Either way, I almost never had pure meetings; everything was tainted by interests.

Today I have different meetings. Not only are most of my meetings, contrary to the past, encounters that I want to have, but I am also much more relaxed, less defensive. I have much less to give, and I'm happy to share what I have. I'm much less threatened, and therefore more open and attentive, and thus able to receive more. Today I can also reconstruct many of the previous encounters and derive from them after the fact what I wasn't able to obtain in real time.

Of all those past encounters, two were doubtless responsible for the organization of my new life. The first became one of my exit points from the tough cynicism of political life, and the second was an entry to new worlds where there is still more darkness than light.

A T THE START OF MY TERM AS KNESSET SPEAKER IN 1999, I received a surprising letter. It contained a description of the sad fate of the contemporary Tibetan nation and a review of the non-violent doctrine of the spiritual leader of all Tibetans, ending with a request: "The Dalai Lama, leader in exile of Tibet, is coming to Israel. Would you agree to meet him?"

The entire letter was written in meek and apologetic language. How can you say "no" to this man? A representative of a small nation facing an aggressive giant, whose spirit, along with the spirit of his people, is far greater than all the spirits of his enemies and oppressors. Is there anything more Jewish than that? This was the most "Jewish" person I knew of—an optimistic exile, tormented but never in despair.

I gave my OK, and my staff started putting in motion the hidden cogwheels that turn a directive into reality. Plans, coordination, agreements, and logistics. Just a few hours after this agreement, the waters were muddied. As always in this life, what's good for one person is bad for another. I pushed the good button, and someone received a bad and unsettling electric shock on the other end of the Jerusalem halls of power.

"Someone wants to speak to you," my chief of staff told me.

"Tell him that I'll call back in the evening."

"He says it's really urgent."

"Put him through." The director-general of the foreign ministry was on the line.

"I must meet you immediately," he said.

"Come over." And he came. At his second sentence I was already sorry that I had agreed to meet him.

"You must cancel the meeting with the Dalai Lama," he demanded.

"Why not receive the Dalai Lama?" I wondered.

He: "You can't."

"Why?" I continued.

"It's contrary to Israel's foreign policy."

"Why?" I asked, pushing back.

"Because the week after the Dalai Lama's visit, the president of China is arriving in Israel."

"So what?" I still did not understand.

"The Chinese visitor is threatening to cancel his visit to Israel if you, as Knesset speaker, receive the Tibetan leader."

It turns out that the Dalai Lama, whose people were slaughtered and expelled by the Chinese communists, travels the world and tries to arrive everywhere ahead of the Chinese president or other senior officials of that superpower. Everywhere he goes, he tries to mobilize public opinion and raise consciousness of the injustice done to his people and homeland. Everywhere, Chinese diplomacy tries, in the name of the billions of Chinese, to threaten the host countries not to provide a platform for the high priest from Tibet. The Knesset podium seemed too big to them, echoing from Jerusalem to Washington.

"You must cancel the invitation," the man demanded gruffly. I was furious, but, still, I took a deep breath as befitting a person of my position, I counted to ten, and I replied in the calmest demeanor I could muster.

"The visit will take place, and I will try to publicize it as much as possible at home and abroad," I said. "If Israel's foreign policy is based on the interests of arms dealers doing business with the murderers of Tiananmen Square, I will not be a part of it. Though I didn't intend it, I would be the happiest person if the Dalai Lama's visit with me at the Knesset would open your minds a bit."

The quarrels and exchanges of letters went on until the last minute, but in the end life is stronger than everything. The Dalai Lama honored the Israeli parliament with his conciliatory and peace-seeking presence, and the international publicity was amazing. A week later the Chinese president visited the Knesset, as planned, and the foreign ministry was flooded by a wave of protests. And lo and behold: what was the official response that Israeli representatives abroad were directed to give to all the critics of the state that had invited the Chinese dictator? Don't forget to emphasize that a week before the Chinese visit, the Dalai Lama received the highest honor in Israel, a visit to parliament.

I frequently recall that meeting. Outwardly it was a meeting of two politicians, two public servants, one Tibetan and the other Israeli. Inwardly it was a tremendous collision between my Israeli and Jewish sensibilities. There were many people in the room. Parliamentary employees and Knesset members stood outside wanting to catch a glimpse of this iconic figure. I don't recall the content of the conversation, it was so formal and publicized, and there was no time in it for a heart-to-heart talk. But the atmosphere surprised me.

I expected someone submissive with bowed head, in keeping with his image. But there was no calm at all in the room. There was great aggressiveness, or, more accurately, power. He was well aware of the meaning of the image he projected, he understood the meaning of the visit, as if he had been briefed by the aforementioned director-general of the foreign ministry. He pressed all the buttons he had planned: Jewish history, morals as opposed to interests, he spoke to me and addressed Israeli public opinion. From Jerusalem, he sent ballistic messages to Beijing and Washington. There was a great deal of power in his weakness. A frail deference whose every move projected the same message: "I cannot be broken." In the intervals between his slow and measured words and those of the translators I was reminded of the annual school trip to Hula Lake, the freshwater lake stemming from one of Jordan's river sources in the northern part of Israel. Israel's early pioneers drained it as a "swamp" in 1951 and rechanneled the water to the faraway Negev desert. At the time, it was a fantastic Zionist achievement, which turned out to be a very mixed blessing.

It was in 1964 or so, we were little children, and we were very excited when the nature teacher showed us the cedar of Lebanon. "This is the tree from which the Temple was built," she said, adding some theology to the botany. "Once there was a swamp here," she added, piling on Zionist mythology. "But we drained it. The water was taken from here in the national water carrier to the Negev desert. That was Zionism! For generations, since our exile, this land was uncultivated because there were swamps here and the Negev soil went unplowed because there was no water. Then we Zionists came, drained the excess water and transported it there, and both places became a green and flowering paradise."

No one told that teacher and us that a few years later it would turn out that the frenetic Zionist effort to defeat nature—as well as human nature—would lead to environmental damage that would require generations to overcome. "Here is the lake and here is the reed. Maybe this is the primeval pond. You call it a bulrush. Who can tell me which is stronger: the reed or the cedar?"

"The cedar," we all replied in a chorus of shouts, as expected.

"Not at all." The teacher beamed with a smile that was all pedagogy, common sense, and the victory of her knowledge over our childish ignorance.

"Here comes a strong wind, an exceptionally stormy wind. And it blows and sweeps away and uproots everything in its path. And the cedar stands firm. Hardly moving. Stubborn and straight and proud. He is rigid, and the wind blows. Finally, from the heights of its upright position, it topples over, uprooted, and dies. And the reed in the lake, so small, humble, and devoid of arrogance," she said poetically, "bends in any wind, ordinary or exceptional. And the wind goes to other places, hurrying to meet the cedars that are right for it. And the reed straightens up and goes on with its life as if there had never been a wind in the area. So, who is actually stronger—the reed or the cedar?" And not one of us answered. Certainly not with a shout. "And that," the teacher said, returning to her favorite theological element, "that is precisely what the prophet asks: 'Is this the fast I desire? A day for men to starve their bodies? Is it bowing the head like a bulrush and lying in sackcloth and ashes? Do you call that a fast, a day when the Lord is favorable?'"

Oh, what a fine victory for the teacher, nature, and the Bible, so Jewish and also so educational.

In the end, she held a vote in the bus. "Who wants to be a cedar?"
she asked, and all hands were raised. "And who wants to be a bulrush?"
Not a hand went up. Thus, despite all the explanations and verses, the
swaggering Israeli cedar is much more seductive and attractive than the
pitiful reed, that diaspora Jew.

Today I'm ready to retroactively renounce some cedar moments in
my life for the opportunity to go back and be a bulrush according to
the doctrine of the Dalai Lama. "China will be uprooted like a great
tree exposed to wind," he predicted at the meetings, as if we had been
together on the school trip in fourth grade. If he had participated in the
vote on the bus, he would have likely not voted like everyone else. In
one moment of a buttoned-up official meeting I was again exposed to
the doctrine of my teacher from my distant childhood days, a doctrine
that I then considered ridiculous, and today turns out to be deep and
full of hope and faith, strength and power, consistency and change.

T HE SECOND MEETING THAT CHANGED MY LIFE WAS IN
Berlin, on the eve of Rosh Hashanah in 2009, when I met a man
different from anyone I had ever met in my lifetime—so different, but
at the same time so remarkably similar to the Dalai Lama. Until now
it isn't clear to me if he was a small reed on the bank of a large lake, or
the broken branch of a giant cedar that had collapsed. In the few hours
I was with him, I felt again for the second—and so far, the last—time
the same sense of a lone man containing power far greater than himself.
Just as I had felt with the Tibetan monk.

In this case, I wasn't limited in time and there weren't any official
representatives to interrupt us. I came specially to Berlin to meet him.
We had planned this meeting for a very long time. One day I received a
telephone call from a friend who asked whether he could give my email
address to someone, an Israeli living in Munich. "Of course," I replied.
After two weeks, I received an email message from him, in which he

asked whether he could pass along my email address to a friend of his, also the son of Israelis from Munich. "Of course." Two weeks later, another email: Can I give your address to my wife? "Certainly." And two weeks later, from her: Can I give your email address to my father? "Of course."

One morning I received the following in an email: "Greetings, Mr. Burg. My name is Helmut. My children bought me your book about the Holocaust. And I wanted to thank you very much for your words."

I answered him with the standard reply I issue to emails of this sort, and at the end added on impulse: "Dear Mr. Helmut, I greatly appreciate the special effort you have made—with your children and their friends—to find my address. I would be very happy if you could tell me a bit about yourself."

It took a few more days, and the answer that arrived did not surprise me: "I'm an ordinary German, actually I don't have anything to tell."

"There's no such thing," I responded immediately. "Everyone has something to tell. Every person is a story, and since we don't know each other, I'm sure that I haven't yet heard a story like yours." A few weeks passed and then another email arrived, with his resume attached. He had written it out over many pages by hand, and his daughter Irina translated the text for me from German to English. That reading produced an extended correspondence between us that ended with that meeting in Berlin. For the first time in my life I spoke with a Nazi. I had come for the Nazi, and was left with the great man inside him.

This is what he wrote to me:

> My name is Helmut, I was born in 1923 in a village near Nuremburg. I love nature, botany, geology, fossils, classical music, singing, dance, painting and other performing arts. My father was the principal of a school in Heidenheim, the village where I spent my childhood years. He was also my teacher. He became an artist and hated France. He considered France a sworn enemy. He admired the heroes of the First World War and was super strict. My mother was just like

*him. They both admired militarism and nationalism. We children
were educated in a strictly religious spirit. I don't remember that he
ever hugged me or gave me a kiss.*

*In Heidenheim there was a large Jewish community with a syn-
agogue. Many Jewish children went with me to the same school. I
remember names, like Solomon, Rorbach, Weinberg, and Gutman.
Especially the Gutman family. We had a special relationship with
them. Mrs. Gutman used to visit us, and on Jewish holidays brought
us a basket full of Jewish delicacies. We were happy, and to this day,
I like matza. When Mrs. Gutman had a son, she asked my mother
if she could call him Lothar, the name of one of my brothers who
died at a young age.*

*I remember exotic events from our childhood that were connected
to Jews. Their homes were on our street, and the synagogue was on
the other side of town. On Jewish Sabbaths and holidays, we children would watch curiously how the elegant Jewish men, with their
black hats, would march to the synagogue slowly and with dignity
behind the rabbi, who held the Torah with great respect. When they
entered the synagogue, we would sneak up behind them, hiding and
peering inside, in order to hear their singing and prayer. Oh, Avrum,
I loved it so much, the beautiful singing of the cantor.*

*At the start of the 1930s I started hearing more and more about
Hitler. In the family, from guests and other children. The few doubts
my parents had about Hitler disappeared fairly quickly. We saw
more and more marches of Nazi groups in our streets, and villagers
from out of town joined them. Everyone loved him. He was a man. A
hero, a fighter, not soft. He stood bravely against everything, everyone was saying. Hitler won the elections. Germany believed that with
Hitler all the problems would be solved. Finally we have a leader,
and he will bring us a better future.*

*In the summer of 1933 I was allowed to join the Hitler Youth.
Mom sewed me my first "brown shirt," I was given a nice black scarf
to wrap my neck in, and a cap for my head. In 1934, I marched*

on Nazi Party day in Nuremberg. We cheered Hitler and his colleagues in the leadership of the Nazi party. I loved the Hitler Youth, the friendship and camaraderie, the scouting in nature, the songs, and especially the patriotic songs and stories about the heroes. I wanted to join the army and be a soldier. I loved to identify myself as a fighter, a soldier, a hero. I wanted to die for the homeland as a hero fighting our enemies. To fight the sub-human, the untermenschen who do not deserve to live. We, the Germans were the superior "race." I was brainwashed. Avrum, my sense of guilt since those days weighs and will weigh on my heart like lead until the day I die. It is the shadow that is with me every day of my life, until the last.

Our high school, the gymnasium, was in Nuremberg. In those years, I was fascinated by airplanes and flight, and in the youth movement I was a young pilot. I learned how to fly gliders and loved it very much, that freedom and quiet in the air. I flew, and my parents officially joined the Nazi party. All our ties with our Jewish friends were broken off. I was forced to ignore them, the sub-humans. I was forbidden from shopping in Jewish stores. In school, we were forbidden to sit next to our former Jewish friends. The brainwashing of the youth movement inculcated with unbelievable power the belief that we are the superior Aryan race. On Kristallnacht in November 1938, synagogues were burned, along with the Jewish school and the shops of many Jews, including the Rorbach family store.

At the start of the 1940s I began working in the film industry in Munich. We documented special events with senior figures from the SS, who told stories from Russia about the inferior, terrible Russians who resembled animals more than people: "When you encounter one of them in battle, kill him immediately. Show no feelings or mercy. He simply doesn't deserve them." At Munich's main train station, I found myself one day at the station gate. The train arrived, and Hitler himself got off the train car, six meters from me, like a demon screaming and shouting. Hitler's soldiers, his bodyguards and all the teams were so busy that they didn't notice I was standing there off to *the side. I was in shock at the sight of this demon. I never had such images or thoughts about our leader, the führer. Later, when Hitler disappeared, I locked the feelings and shock inside me. At the end of 1941 I enlisted in the army. I fought in Russia and became ill. I returned to Germany, was posted in France, went through officer's training, and fought de Gaulle's partisans. I returned again to Germany and was sent from there to the eastern front, to Russia.*

In the beginning of June or July 1944 we fought in Minsk. The führer, Hitler, ordered us to defend the city like Stalingrad. But the Red Army captured the city and we were trapped inside. After nine days of heavy fighting, with the battle lines constantly shifting, it was all over. Most of our comrades were killed, many people died. After a few days, I met with my three closest friends. We stuck together for a few days. But during a heavy artillery battle at night I lost contact with them and got lost in a forest. I lost the three of them in a terrible swampy area. The nightmare became reality. I lost them and knew that soon I too would die. I tried to hide in a shallow river. I dived under the water, coming up for air from time to time. When I went back under water I heard voices talking Russian and people approaching the river. . . . I knew my end was near. Suddenly a hand grabbed me and pulled me out. The partisans beat me to a pulp, with fists, kicks, and rifle butts. Naked without a uniform, barefoot and covered with blood, I lay at the river's edge. Suddenly the men stopped beating me. A female partisan on a giant horse approached them. She was their commander, and she shouted orders at them to stop hitting me. They obeyed and immediately stopped. She jumped off the horse and leaned over me. She looked at me, knelt next to me, and carefully lifted my head and cradled it. She wore a brown cap, and her blond hair was in two braids. Her head bent over mine so that I couldn't see the sky, only her face.

She began speaking to me in German in a low and sensitive voice: "War is not a good thing, comrade. What are you doing here? You've come to destroy my homeland? Where the hell are you from?"

"*From Munich,*" *I heard myself whispering to her somehow. The partisan continued: "Hmm . . . it's a beautiful city, your Munich. Why didn't you stay there, you German Fascist?" Those words of hers, of that sub-human, hurt me more than all the blows from the men with their rifles, kicks and punches. Her words seared my soul. It was logical, my feelings of guilt. . . . I have no words to express my feelings in those moments. Here I was, a blue-eyed German, and this sub-human, the untermensch, helping me . . . to sit. She pulled my wallet out of my uniform pocket and looked at the pictures inside. "Your mother?" she asked. "Your father?" When I nodded my aching head, I heard her say, "Mom is crying if you stay in Russia." My mouth was completely dry, my lips bleeding. I could barely say a word. One of the partisans brought me a pitcher of tea and bread in a bowl. The partisan leader continued talking to me seriously: "Soon the war—kaput. Hitler—kaput. The Red Army will capture Berlin and the war will end. Everyone will go back home. I am a teacher, I teach schoolchildren the German language. To read German poetry. What beautiful music you have. We love Bach, Mozart, Beethoven, and Strauss, of course. I prefer to dance Strauss's waltzes than shoot German fascists in Belarus. Comrade, do you know this waltz?" And she began to perfectly whistle the "Blue Danube," and I cried and cried and cried.*

She got up and shouldered her rifle. "Drink more tea and eat more bread," she told me. After I followed her instructions, she ordered that I be given an old uniform and transferred the next day to the Red Army, which would hold me in a prisoner of war camp. She mounted her horse, and her last words to me were, "The war is over."

Out of the group of partisans a Russian fellow of Jewish origin was assigned to watch me. He spoke a type of Yiddish. When we stopped for a moment in our long journey, he ordered me to sit next to him on a block of wood by the side of the road. He looked at me, slowly pulled out an SS pistol and pointed it at me. He told me in Yiddish: "So, Fascist, do you know what this is?" and looked at the gun. "Yes," I replied. And he told me, "So, I can kill you with this weapon. I shot the commander of the Nazi unit and took his gun. But I won't shoot you. It would be too easy for you."

After many days with partisans, as a lone German among Russians, some of whom were Yiddish-speaking Jews, I was transferred to the control of the Red Army, and reality became difficult and repugnant. One tank commander shouted at me from the top of the turret, "An immediate execution is taking place. I will kill you near the village fence." My Russian-Jewish bodyguard translated the sentence to Yiddish. I knew that I was about to die. Here. The villagers, women and children, cried to the soldiers, "The officer does not have to shoot the young German just like that." The officer refused. He wanted to execute me, he wanted to kill. The officer pushed me to the wall. I stood there. As the officer was getting his gun ready, a young woman came out of the group of villagers that surrounded us. She pushed her body next to mine, raised her hands and shouted to the officer in Russian, "Don't shoot." A big commotion started. She shouted again, "Don't shoot." I felt how her body was shielding mine. Slowly I also felt that I was losing consciousness. I fainted.

The next thing I felt were strong but gentle slaps on the cheeks and cold water washing over my face. I lay on the ground and saw the blue sky. I'm probably dead, I said to myself. But then I heard the voice of the Jewish partisan, my bodyguard. He looked at my face and kept slapping me. He was so happy, he shook me. The first face I saw after my death was therefore a Jewish face. A Russian Jew who was so happy for me, that I hadn't been shot to death, and these were his words: "Comrade, you are alive. Comrade, you are alive." And he kept shaking me, "Everything is alright, you are going to a labor camp. The Red Army is in Berlin. Hitler kaput. When you return home, talk about us. So, comrade, you will never forget that Russian woman!" Where is she, Avrum? From July 13, 1944, until now that has remained my life's question.

A few days later I arrived at the prisoner of war camp. Tens of thousands of prisoners like me. Days with nothing to eat, and nights of bombardments by the German air force. We were moved from place to place in closed train cars, without water or drink in the sweltering summer days. Then came the Russian winter, and with it diseases and epidemics that killed hundreds and thousands of us. In every moment of my life there, in those horrendous conditions, I didn't stop saying to myself: that Russian woman did not save you so you could end your life here this way. No, no, no. I must survive in order to return to Germany and tell everyone about it. That sentence became my life's mantra during the next five and a half years in Russian captivity.

I would like to share with you one personal and intimate memory. Since my conscription and in all the twist and turns I have experienced I never parted with a metal spoon that Mom gave me when I went off to war. "Son," she told me, "in the war there will only be wooden spoons. Better to eat from a metal spoon." Many soldiers tried to steal my spoon. But I always managed to keep it. That way, unwittingly, it became what represented my life. The spoon was the only thing that I had left from my mother. I knew that if I lose the spoon, I will never return home. Interesting, in German there's a saying that goes, "To turn in the spoon," meaning, to die. The metal spoon was the only thing I took with me all the way to Russia and back to Germany. Avrum, when we meet one day, I will bring you my spoon. I will show it to you.

A simple metal spoon can tell so many unbelievable stories: in winter we had to shovel snow outside the boundaries of the camp. We left for work at first light and returned to the huts at night. The gates of the camp were closed and locked until the next departure at dawn the next day. One snowy evening I returned to the camp and felt my leg, I wanted to feel my spoon in its regular place, on my leg. But alas, the spoon was not there. I was shocked. I shouted hysterically, "My

spoon is gone, where is my spoon? It's gone!" I apparently dropped it
outside the camp when we were shoveling snow. "I must go out there!
I must look for it!" My comrades grabbed me tight, and one of the
guards asked if I had lost my mind, because the minute that the giant
camp gates were shut and the fence lighting went on, no one could go
out. Certainly not to search for a silly spoon in the snow. I cried and
protested. I knew that I would not return home, that I would die in
that place if I didn't find my spoon, the gift of my beloved mother.
The chief warden, "the black" we called him, a tall and black-haired
Russian Jew, came up to me and asked why I was screaming like
that, what was going on? I told him that I had lost my spoon. The
tall Jewish guard laughed, "So, no need to shout so much. You'll get
a new spoon."

"No," I begged him, "this is not an ordinary spoon. It is a spoon
from my mother." Suddenly he stopped laughing. "What, the spoon
was from your mamushka?" With my limited Russian and his bro-
ken German, we understood one another completely. "Come with
me," he ordered me. He ordered the guards on the towers not to shoot
me. The giant camp gates opened into the stormy night. I was so
scared. Honestly, I hadn't the slightest idea where to look. When the
guards called me to come back, all my hopes were dashed. I crawled
back. Right next to the gates something shined in the light of the spot-
lights from one of the piles of snow that we had shoveled in the day-
light hours. I retraced my steps, looking for the place where the shine
came from. I dug furiously and ... my spoon was back in my hand.
Unbelievable. I raised it in the air and screamed, "I have it." When
I returned to the camp, the Jewish guard, "the black," came over to
me and asked with curiosity and friendship, "Did you find it?" When
I showed him my spoon, he was so happy for me and said: "What
a guy. Great. He found the spoon his mother gave him. Fantastic."

I had other Russian miracles. In the camp I studied Russian, and
I especially learned from the children. I worked like that, as a pris-
oner among these sub-humans. And what did I discover? Goodwill,

warm conversations, without harassment, help without any hatred
at all. My full return to humanity began there. That's what I told
myself. I want to be friendly, I want to serve and help everywhere
that I can.

Helmut's life story unfolded across a few more pages soaked in blood and tears. The journey of a Nazi child from Bavaria to today's Munich, in which his daughter is married to an Israeli, and they have no children. The upheavals of an entire century on a few translated pages. For many months, I felt that I must meet him. First it was just curiosity. I have met many Germans and Austrians in my lifetime. Some are my friends, real friends. But none of them ever revealed the Nazi side of their families to me. The silent abyss of the past was always spread out at our feet, and I never really succeeded in crossing it and reaching them, hearing firsthand what happens in the family intimacy that comes from this past. Some indeed come from families that were always humane and socialist, and that is one of the roots of our friendship. And others, I have no doubt, were touched with evil. A father or grandfather, an aunt or sister. Someone there was part of the evil system, and a conspiracy of silence envelops them to this very day.

And here, suddenly, a man who is so honest and direct steps into my life. "Yes, I was a Nazi," he writes me. Between the lines, I think that he wants to meet me, no less than I want to meet him. I so much wanted to meet him, both to touch this experience with my own hands, but also to meet through him parts of myself. I wanted to feel what I really feel facing a genuine Nazi. It was not the Eichmann of my childhood, separated from reality by a glass cage in the courtroom. It was a man of flesh and blood, a small cog in a terrible murderous machine. One of those who made that giant and effective apparatus possible and so awful. Curiosity drew me to him, and I confess that I also had a very deep and existential fear, maybe a victim's fear of the victimizer, maybe a congenital Jewish trait.

Out of my emotional curiosity more complex thoughts emerged. The profound change he had undergone, with his simple honesty—linked to memories and pains as well as to hopes and responsibility—aroused my intense curiosity. Am I able, I asked myself, to understand Helmut's story as a key to healing the world? I hoped to find an answer to my wondering. If an individual such as Helmut could change and free himself of the brainwashing that drowned an entire German generation, and was able to turn the rigid legacy of militarism and nationalism of his parents into the inclusive universalism of his children—are societies and cultures able to do it? It's so "Jewish." The concept of repentance—regret of the bad past and accepting responsibility for a better future—is the deep inner foundation of Jewish renewal. If he can, so can others. Even I can change and improve. From my inner place I saw an elderly anonymous individual, a member of the previous generation, which I perceived to be ossified, with a key to the lock of part of my future. We set a meeting for late August 2010, and I made a special trip to Berlin. I from Israel, he from Munich, and Berlin, a neutral city between us. He came with his daughter Irina. We sat for hours and talked. In English, German, Hebrew, and anything in between. I recorded the whole conversation with him, and I listen to it often during long trips in Israel and abroad.

When he entered the room, I felt a certain disappointment. So short and fragile. I had expected that a tall, handsome Aryan, like a mythological god, would enter the room, fair-skinned and blue-eyed, who had just emerged from the Black Forest, as in the epic German Nibelung poem. I imagined him tall, strapping, meticulously dressed. Maybe not in uniform, but almost. Instead, a kind grandfather stood before me. Fragile. A great tenderness on his face. His fragility invites you to offer him support. And when we shook hands, a thought went through my head: "His touch, his skin, is not cold and frozen. Not like a poisonous snake. He feels completely human." And indeed, he was. I touched the Nazi, and nothing bad happened to me. Or more precisely, I touched the former Nazi, and a lot happened to me, for the better.

We went down for lunch. We each ordered, and when the platters arrived, he moved his hand slowly under his jacket, took out the spoon, wiped it gently and hesitantly with the tablecloth and began slowly eating his soup. I choked up, and was transformed.

CHAPTER FIFTEEN

BETWIXT AND
BETWEEN

SOME YEARS AGO, AROUND 2003, AT THE HEIGHT OF THE
bloody days of the intifada, someone took the trouble to cover
many bus stops in Jerusalem with graffiti that said, "God of Vengeance."
In the dead of night my youngest son, Noam, and a friend went out
with spray paint and covered those graffiti with a different one: "Lord
of Peace." Indeed, the Jewish God has many names and epithets, a
name for all seasons, an epithet for every existential situation. But only
some of them migrated to Israel with the rise of Zionism. Most of the
soft names, with overtones of compassion and mercy, were left behind
in the diaspora, embarrassed, as if left unwanted.

Meanwhile, the contemporary Jewish commonwealth, which is our
third Jewish sovereignty, the tough God, and many of his violent disciples, set the tone of identity and spirituality. The gentle, complex Jews
and their Judaism went elsewhere. It took me many years to understand the structural problem of the Zionist revival. A callous toughness
that rejects the soft components of historic Judaism. I was one of the
young children of this Judaism, and later one of its political leaders. I
gave so many speeches about the Holocaust and revival in my day that
I knew by heart every bend in the course of this river of our history and

rhetoric. A river full of Jewish blood, flanked by bloodthirsty wicked gentiles on its banks, constantly cheering the sight of our flow into the ocean of death. Although my conscious mind lived within the classic narrative of Passover—"Not just one enemy has stood against us to wipe us out. In every generation, there have been those who have stood against us to wipe us out"—my subconscious was already looking for another channel of history.

In my search for other directions I went back to Gershom Scholem's book, *Devarim be-Go*. There is a letter there to Hannah Arendt. On very frequent occasions in the past I had read Scholem's position regarding the Holocaust, delved into it and thought about it. From his letter to Arendt I tried every time anew to glean more ideas. I didn't know Hannah Arendt well enough, but I understood Scholem precisely. In the thick of my search someone drew my attention to the fact that Scholem— who was known for his personality, not the most pleasant, not the most deferential or ready to acknowledge another ego aside from his own—had erased Arendt's reply and left only his position for the annals of history. Such an act of intellectual violence immediately piqued my curiosity. What was so terrible about what she wrote that compelled this great historian to erase her from his book? I found her letter, and I also found, to my surprise, that very few of the writings of this important philosopher had been translated to Hebrew. It took the academic establishment decades to overcome Zionist doctrine in order to open some gates into the worlds of this original and courageous woman, her experiences and thoughts. With the letter I also discovered Arendt, and following her I also reached large parts of my hidden self.

With almost brazen courage she writes to Scholem, her faithless childhood friend:

> To come to the point: let me begin, going on from what I have just stated, with what you call "love of the Jewish people" or *Ahabath Israel*. (Incidentally, I would be very grateful if you could tell me since when this concept has played a role in

Judaism, when it was first used in Hebrew language and literature, etc.) You are quite right—I am not moved by any "love"
of this sort, and for two reasons: I have never in my life "loved"
any people or collective—neither the German people, nor the
French, nor the American, nor the working class or anything of
that sort. I indeed love "only" my friends and the only kind of
love I know of and believe in is the love of persons. Secondly,
this "love of the Jews" would appear to me, since I am myself
Jewish, as something rather suspect. I cannot love myself or anything which I know is part and parcel of my own person.*

Then she tells Scholem about a conversation she had with a senior
political figure in Israel, apparently Golda Meir, whose name was omit-
ted and gender changed at "his" request for purposes of publication
of the exchange of letters. Many said about Golda Meir at the time
that she was "the only man in the government." No wonder that Arendt agreed to alter her identity. But beyond the cruel and disparaging
humor, had I believed in God's direction of my personal life and intervention in current events, I would have considered my encounter with
this text a divine sign.

I ENCOUNTERED THE LETTER IN 2006, WHEN I WAS IN THE
midst of a journey into the depths, in the footsteps of my late father,
with Noam, my youngest child, the only one of my children who listened to me and did not travel with all his friends to the "March of
the Living" at Auschwitz (an annual educational program that brings
students from around the world to Poland, where they explore the
remnants of the Holocaust). On Holocaust Memorial Day (Yom

---

*Scholem's and Arendt's letters to one another were published in the January
1964 issue of *Encounter*; Arendt's letter to Scholem was reprinted in her anthol-
ogy *The Jewish Writings*, ed. Jerome Kohn and Ron H. Feldman (New York:
Schocken Books, 2008), 465–471.

HaShoah), thousands of participants march silently from Auschwitz to Birkenau, the largest Nazi concentration camp complex built during World War II.

I read Arendt's letter to Scholem on the morning of our Sabbath day in Berlin. I marked the place in the book, put it into a pack, and we went to pray at the new synagogue, the Neue Synagoge on Oranienburger Straße in Berlin. It is a beautiful and elegant building that I knew about from all the stories told by Dad, who walked the streets of this neighborhood before the destruction, just as he did during his repeated visits to the city in the last years of his life. We walked there with a written guide prepared for us by Hillel, my nephew, who is a son to me and a friend, as well as an editor of my books and a fellow traveler in life. Long before me, he sensed that his identity would not be complete without going through the Berlin station. And now we were following him.

It is an ornate synagogue, freighted with symbols and meaning. It's hard to understand the history of the Jews of Berlin without it. The peacock-like golden dome and other costs of construction were all paid for by the distinguished Jewish community of Berlin in the mid-nineteenth century. The building was a proud, aggressive declaration that said: "We can do it ourselves, openly." Within its confines the ancient rites were renewed, and adjustments were made between the lives of the Jews and the lives of Germans in general. Everything proceeded as usual until Kristallnacht of 1938. A Nazi mob gathered near this symbolic synagogue and tried to set it alight. A decent and brave police officer by the name of Otto Bellgardt arrived and confronted the inflamed Nazi mob alone. He ordered them to disperse, and stayed to protect the historical site. The synagogue was looted, but saved because of the bravery of that officer. What was saved from the Nazis was destroyed in an allied bombing by British air force planes. Over the years, the building was restored and returned to the Jewish community for religious and communal use. "Let's go there," I suggested to Noam. "Let's see a synagogue saved from the Nazis, and I'll show you the perimeter markers of the synagogue that existed until the British bombs destroyed it."

The prayer was sad and sparse. We didn't feel the heritage, the depth of the years, the weight of history. Just a coincidental collection of visitors like us who had gathered for a Sabbath prayer and were disappointed. At least the service was egalitarian, and didn't discriminate between women and men. During the prayer, I continued reading the exchange between those two professors, who once were friends and became so hostile toward one another. When the service was over, I asked one of the women there, one who seemed knowledgeable and connected and not a casual visitor like us, whether she would be ready to take us to the courtyard to see the boundary markers of the synagogue. "Certainly," she replied with a welcoming expression. We went up and down staircases, passed through narrow corridors between the different wings of the structure, and in the many minutes we spent between the current place of prayer and its destroyed predecessor we chatted a bit.

"Who are you?" she asked.

"My name is Avrum, and this is my son, Noam, and we are here on a kind of roots trip."

"Whose roots?"

"The roots of my father, and you?"

"My name is Hannah Arendt," she replied, and aware of the small drama attached to her name, she added after a pregnant pause, "not that one."

That day I found Hannah Arendt twice, and I didn't need any more. That is how the one-sided affair began between her, whom I never knew, and me, whom she will never know. In the end, I dedicated my book *The Holocaust Is Over; We Must Rise from Its Ashes* to that impressive woman who has influenced my life so much since. "To the late Hannah Arendt, who knew and understood before everyone, who dared and expressed it better than anyone." I sensed then, without thoroughly figuring it out for myself, that Hannah Arendt picked up for me where Yeshayahu Leibowitz left off. I wasn't completely done with him;

I am committed without reservation to his positions on the occupation and separation of religion and state. But over the years I have sensed a certain deception when confronting his rigid Orthodoxy. I don't want to be open like him to all corners of the world but closed airlessly when it comes to my Judaism and its normative system. I'm not Orthodox in any sphere. When it comes to the human sphere, I don't believe in one exclusive position. So precisely in religion, tradition, and faith, which are the most transcendent human creations (yes, yes, human and not divine), I won't allow other interpretive voices aside from the increasingly insular voice of Jewish law?

That is why Leibowitz's ideas have played a progressively smaller role in my life. But because there is something very close between him and Arendt, it was easy for me to move from him to her, to understand her defiant position, just like his, and identify with her. They both chose to look for the Archimedean point outside the conventional comfort zone in order to raise the Jewish humanistic world to new heights. And they both simultaneously refused to disconnect from the warm bosom of their identity as Jews.

I'm not in love with the collective, any collective, even though I don't argue with my being part of one. I feel very comfortable in the position that Arendt borrowed from Bernard Lazare: "the conscious pariah." She, who was one of the latest and most important of an impressive line of German Jewish intellectuals, scientists, and artists from a variety of fields, believed in all her heart that the conscious pariahs are "those who really did most for the spiritual dignity of their people, who [are] great enough to transcend the bounds of nationality and to weave the strands of their Jewish genius into the general texture of European life . . . those bold spirits who tried to make of the emancipation of the Jews that which it really should have been—an admission of Jews as *Jews* to the ranks of humanity, rather than a permit to ape the gentiles or an opportunity to play the parvenu."*

---

*Quoted in Arendt, *The Jewish Writings*, xliii.

In those days, I saw moment by moment how my ties were fraying and how I was becoming disconnected from everything that was familiar and comfortable to me: acceptance and public stature. In the days when I had no one except my family members as a rock of stability, I had Hannah Arendt. For many years, I had time to read her writings and try to understand some of her wisdom. I felt part of her mission, except that this time it was much more difficult. The German Jewish philosopher tried, through her doctrine and ideas, to propose the direct path to the integration of European Jews in the European fabric being renewed around them. Today my effort is on the one hand to integrate Jewish Israelis in the region that they despise and fear, and at the same time to spread our arms as wide as possible to prevent a final rift between Israeli Jews and the West. Unfortunately, Israel of the twenty-first century is no longer the front line of Westernism. Its value system has changed, the human fabric is different, and for too many of us the European West boils down to "Holocaust" and "anti-Semitism," while its American part is perceived as shallow, childish, seductive, and nothing else. Building this potential bridge between the point of departure to Israeli sovereignty from nineteenth-century Europe, and the goal of its arrival on the shores of the Mediterranean, is one of the most important challenges of our time.

When Lova Eliav, the prophet of peace of the previous generation, gave Golda Meir his defining book, *Land of the Hart*, Meir asked him, "Why did you write a book? Berl Katznelson has already written everything." I felt that Hannah Arendt had already written everything I had to say and far better than I, and I felt relieved. I had someone to lean on. With the deepening of the one-sided acquaintance between us I realized that what attracted me to her thoughts were her two magnetic poles. On the one hand her love of thought, as if life was a great riddle that needs a creative solution, a maze with a logic to its mistakes and vicissitudes, with a way out of its traps. I also like thinking. I'm not capable of reaching her heights and depths, but that doesn't mean that I can't think my own way through life. Just like running: I was never a

great athlete and will no longer become one, but that hasn't prevented
me from making running the main hobby of my life. The other pole of
her magnet excites me anew every time—how she can simultaneously
be inside and outside two worlds. Critiquing European culture, its suc-
cesses and failures, based on the heritage and modernity of Jewish culture, and as a respected German philosopher, standing outside Judaism
in order to improve the experience of Jews.

When I managed to listen to her frustrations, to genuinely feel the
tears of the abandoned friend and dispel the heavy cloud of cigarette
smoke that hid her pain like a thick scarf, I heard her whispering to
him, to Gershom Scholem, and I thought that I also want those words.
I want to shout them as an answer to all my adversaries and attackers:

> What confuses you is that my arguments and my approach are
> different from what you are used to; in other words, the trouble
> is that I am independent. By this I mean, on the one hand, that I
> do not belong to any organization and always speak only for my-
> self, and on the other hand, that I have great confidence in Less-
> ing's *selbstdenken* [self-thought, thinking for oneself] for which,
> I think, no ideology, no public opinion, and no "convictions"
> can ever be a substitute. Whatever objections you may have to
> the results, you won't understand them unless you realize that
> they are really my own and nobody else's.*

Well done, Hannah, that is precisely where I am with my thoughts,
which are always "betwixt and between." In the middle between so
many places, but they are genuinely mine, and I'm not ready to replace
them with any clichéd, hollow content. You may say that you are unconditionally inside, but actually you are "betwixt and between." I also
feel that way. Between Jerusalem and Tel Aviv, between sanctity and

---

*From Arendt's letter in *Encounter*, January 1964; quoted in Arendt, *The
Jewish Writings*, xlv.

liberty, between East and West, between Israel and Europe, between tradition and progress, between this place and the wider world, between loss and hope, and between Israeliness and Judaism.

N OT ONLY DID THE GREAT HANNAH ARENDT SHOW ME the way to that place "betwixt and between," my son Natan and my late parents left me signs on the way there. Immediately following the end of his military service in 2005, Natan traveled far away. Like so many of his generation of Israelis he went on a long trip to distant lands, knowing where he was departing from, but not knowing where he would get to. The rivers of the Amazon, the peaks of the Andes, the villages of Bolivia, and the forests of Brazil enveloped him. We didn't see or hear from him for many months. We were very concerned, but happy for him. We knew that after three years of military service he needed this; he required a long period of purification, internal cleansing, and renewal. Every so often we got regards from him, and in the pictures he sent from the road his face looked different. The tension was gone, the warm smile was a fixture again. When Natan returned from the big trek, a brown official envelope waited for him at home. On the front was a triangular military stamp, whose meaning is clear to any Israeli—you're being called up for reserve duty! The change in his body language was sudden and unequivocal. The tension returned, and the year-long trip was almost erased.

On his first leave from reserve duty we talked, and he was sadder than usual.

"What's the matter, son?"

"Nothing. Everything's okay."

"Come on."

"Nothing important. Something came up with some old Arab."

After a few minutes, his defensive wall crumbled.

"I was at a checkpoint at Tapuah Junction. You know where it is, a crazy place. On the one side Arabs, on the other side the worst possible settlers. And they're all going at each other all the time. The only thing they have in common is us, the soldiers. During one of our breaks I sat with my colleagues and we made a pot of coffee. We took out some cigarettes and cookies and chatted about our trips abroad. I told them about South America and they told me about India and the East. Suddenly an old Arab came up out of the gulley, about your age."

"Thanks for the compliment."

"Sorry. Anyway, he came up out of the *wadi* [ravine] and walked up to us. 'We're on break, go to the checkpoint,' we told him. But he didn't understand. He kept moving toward us and showed us his ID card. 'No need, no need,' we told him, '*mush lazem*,' we added in checkpoint Arabic. But he insisted that we look at his ID, to see that it's OK. It was like the conditional reflex of a trained animal. He sees a soldier, and takes out his ID card. When I was in South America, I would go to the most remote villages and look for old men like him to tell me about their traditions and identity. I would sit with them and listen for hours. And now I'm sitting, and he comes to me with his ID in hand, you understand. I'm on break and he's afraid of me. I want to get to know him and listen to him, but there's no chance that we will ever drink coffee together and have a conversation. And in that moment, I was caught 'betwixt and between.'"

I could relate to him so much. I'm betwixt and between all the time. His simple human story is typical of so many interfaces in our lives, of our being constantly trapped between our official and meaningful identity, between formality and feeling, between the boy that always remains in me and the old man who insists on crowding him out, between soldier and civilian, between a person and his neighbor. I thought for a long time about this place that is betwixt and between. I asked myself over and over again where I was. On one side? On the other? Between them?

Out of this abyss, the wadi of life betwixt and between, everything comes to me. Colliding, complementing, contradicting, pushing, seeking simultaneous release and refuge, serenity and commotion. A constant duality. And the more this internal tension is strong, tearing apart, the more keenly I feel the fact that I am a Jew. So much so that sometimes it seems to me that whatever is not composed of internal contradiction is not Jewish. This is one of the most important keys that I found on my search.

FOR A LONG TIME I HAVE BEEN TRYING TO FIGURE OUT what exactly this thing called the Jewish people is. It is clear to me that being Jewish is not something that comes from nature, like being a cat or a bird. I was created simply a human being. The kind of human being I became already belongs to other categories. I can't accept automatic membership, the obliging collective without thinking, without selection, without distinguishing between good and evil. Under no circumstances am I ready to accept the assumption that being Jewish is a genetic phenomenon or divine choice, and that people I have nothing to do with become at the moment of my birth, against my will, my brothers forever and ever. I'm not prepared to be stuck to that collective that Arendt is trying to dissociate from, and that I don't always manage to connect with. Before my automatic membership in a group I am a private citizen, and in fact I am an accidental Jew. I don't think that if I had been born to a Tibetan monk I would have chosen to circumcise myself at eight days, or even if I had been the son of Martin Luther King, that I would have asked my father, the Baptist minister, to let me put on tefillin at my bar mitzvah. Birth into a particular cultural environment is very much a matter of chance. The Christian is accidental, the Muslim is accidental, and so am I. But the moment I was born into my culture, it becomes the environment of my life. From it and with it I try to influence the world so it will be better. Judaism and Jews are a comprehensive cultural reality that can bring me closer to people who are very distant from me in their origin, place of residence, and experiences—as long as they are made of the same value materials as mine.

On the other hand, I sometimes gaze at some acquaintances from my own people and cannot understand what we have in common. They are warmongers, and I am a peace-lover and conciliator. True, we share a common weekly agenda that centers on the same Sabbath. True, we speak the same language and draw from the same wells that contain the sources of Jewish identity. But in practice, we are so different, to the point of genuine enmity.

Someone told me once that Archbishop Desmond Tutu said in one of his sermons that the Dalai Lama has a place of honor in heaven even though he never believed in the Holy Trinity or Jesus the savior. And that anyone who doesn't think so belongs to "a different Christianity," a real idolater. On so many occasions I find myself so close to Desmond Tutu and the Dalai Lama that I want to touch and hug them like my wife, my sister, my brother-in-law, and my children. In contrast, I am all too many times embarrassed and sometimes actually hostile to the positions, actions, and existence of some of those who are defined as my Jewish brothers and sisters. My Judaism, like the Christianity of Tutu, is open, conversing, granting, and receiving. It is the complete antithesis of the alienated insularity that characterizes most of contemporary Judaism, especially its Israeli version.

Precisely for that reason I can't but wonder at what is there in my small and restless nation, in all its components, that has roiled the global agenda for thousands of years. I wonder what the Jewish DNA is. Not the biological one, the composition of cells and genetic chain, but the cultural genome that brings Jews time and again to the forefront of the world stage.

There are so many peoples active in different arenas of the world. Most of them are much larger than us. Many have long and distinguished histories like ours. But only a few of them receive the attention, both positive and negative, that the Jewish people receive. If there is a nation admired across borders, it is my people. And if there is a nation that has received heaps of scorn, anger, resentment, and fear, it is the very same people, mine. The easy solution is to cast blame on the opponents, haters, anti-Semites, and critics of Israel. The fascinating challenge is to dig deep into the Jewish universe and find there, in the bowels of identity, the fertilizing and disrupting materials that characterize the Jewish people and its relations with itself and with the nations and cultures within which it is active.

The simplistic explanation on which I was brought up in the general and religious schools of my childhood was "the chosen people." God chose us, and therefore the jealousy of other people is almost built in to the process that distinguished, chose, and set us apart from all the rest. I fear the perception of chosen-ness and reject it. The twentieth century saw the chosen race in Germany, the chosen class in the Soviet Union, and the enmity of many people across the world toward us, the "chosen people." Every such chosen-ness has so far caused far more harm than good. The chosen race was vanquished, the chosen class collapsed. The time has come to also calm down the chosen people. I don't believe in being chosen; I don't accept the assumption that God chose me or anyone in general, in order to elevate him above any other person or above any other people. I would add that during my long years of acquaintance with the ills of Israeli democracy I learned that under no circumstances is it possible to maintain full democracy for all citizens equally and fairly as long as one population—the Jews—is convinced that God chose them and raised them above everyone. Because equality and chosen-ness stand in painful contradiction.

So, if it is not being chosen by God, what still distinguishes Jewish culture so much and makes it, and us, so prominent in the global conversation? A good part of the explanation is in simple history. What happened to our previous generations positioned us in a special place in the fabric of human histories. Not divine chosen-ness and not our own special history. That is how things happened. And at the end of the process we were transformed from a people and communities who were outside many other societies into an icon of relevancy.

When I once asked—in a café in Berkeley, California—this question of the historian Yuri Slezkine, he referred me to a passage from his book, *The Jewish Century*: "There is a special closeness between the Jews and the modern era. No matter what the measure—rationalism, nationalism, capitalism, professionalism, . . . literacy, democracy, hygiene, alienation, or the nuclear family—it appears that the Jews were there first, did it first, understood it best. . . . The identification between the Jews and the forces shaping the modern world was one of the few things that most European intellectuals . . . were able sometimes to agree on."*

Benjamin Tammuz, one of the most accurate and eloquent Israeli narrators and documenters, compares the Jewish existential tension in one of his stories to people sitting in a plane, when suddenly the pilot tells them over the PA system:

> "Ladies and gentlemen, we have engine trouble and we can't land in the neighboring airport because of fog, and we have about half an hour's worth of fuel. If we're lucky we'll get to the nearest airport, and if not, pray and ask for God's mercy." And then, ladies and gentlemen, in that moment on the verge of annihilation, of farewell, people will appreciate the one value that has no name, that alone makes life worth living. At that moment people will touch the margins of culture. And for this reason, ladies and gentlemen, I reiterate that the Jews were closer to this divine spirit more often, and they hold on with more strength to the edge of the spirit. Because the Jews have been travelling in this very plane for three thousand years. A people in the sky, literally. More than any other nation they hear the voice of the pilot saying: be prepared, your moments are numbered. There is no place ready to accept you, and you are suspended in mid-air. There is no place that wants you, you are strangers, aliens, condemned to die, abandoned between heaven and earth. You are about to die.
>
> And for this reason, I go as far as to say: since the Jewish nation had a greater connection to the spirit than any other nation,

_____

*Translation mine; compare with Yuri Slezkine, _The Jewish Century_ (Princeton, NJ: Princeton University Press, 2004), 60.

there is no reason in the world that prevents me from drawing the following conclusion: anything that is spirit and anything that is culture is actually Jewish. And for this reason, Mozart is Jewish, as well as Bach and Rembrandt and a few more good people too numerous to name.*

There's a great deal of sad humor in Tammuz's allegory, but it also has kernels of truth about the passion of the Jews, holding fast to life and not willing to let go. And all this is done with a great deal of melancholy, cynicism, and common sense. The Jewish encounter, like the encounter of the passengers of the crashing airliner, is a very purified encounter between man and his essence. And the Jewish people—Tammuz says through the mouth of the protagonist—has been at this moment so many times that it has become the most refined and precise collective. All of life is temporary, and for the Jew this is eternal temporariness. Creativity and lust for life stem from it, the constant frenetic motion, with waves of paranoia, from Woody Allen to Benjamin Netanyahu.

Heard through the conversation of many Israelis, the Israeli reality appears fairly shallow, one whose complexity is disappearing. There are designated "bad guys" and automatic "good guys." Most people think the same about most important issues. Israeliness has greatly simplified Jewish complexity. Judaism through the generations lived its whole life in a complicated duality, full of serious internal contradictions that were fertilizing and fascinating raw materials. A nation of the world spread out wherever there were people, and still aspiring to concentrate together. Individuals and communities that adjusted to the boundless wealth of the societies in which they lived, while preserving a separation and difference from those same societies. Many languages, and

---

*Benjamin Tammuz, *ha-Pardes* ; *Mishle baḵbuḵim* ; *Pundaḵo shel Yirmeyahu* [Orchard, Bottle Parables, Jeremiah's Inn] (Tel Aviv: Yedi'ot aḥaronot: Sifre ḥemed, 2008), 170–171.

one holy tongue. Prayer for complete redemption, and utter passivity when it came to promoting it. Moderation and extremism, openness and insularity, assimilation and conversion. All these tensions created a lively and up-to-date culture, attentive to itself and conversing with its external environment. Many of these elements passed away with the Israeli revival. And that is precisely what I seek: the fertilizing middle ground between the poles.

The Jewish culture that was is that kind of culture. A culture whose secret was its will and ability to contain internal contradictions as a worldview. In the place where I grew up there was only one correct worldview, and I never connected with it, though I never knew how to formulate properly for myself my repulsion from orthodoxy. Ever since childhood I sensed that there were other worlds, other opinions and truths, but I was not permitted to touch them. Across the street there was a "different" synagogue, Conservative, but "we don't go there."

Once I was suspended from the yeshiva where I studied because I lost my schoolbag and told the teacher that "even God doesn't know where it is." "God is omnipotent," I was scolded, and sent home with a stern note to my parents. And I knew then already that it simply can't be, that there must be other thought about the place of God in the world, one that doesn't impose on him the petty management of the scattered schedule of a fourteen-year-old youth. The expression "people like us" became a restraining and restrictive framework that defined our family's attitude to the world of others and completely contradicted the spirit of intellectual curiosity that my parents fostered in us from the day we were born. Everything was permitted except changing religious outlook. "That's the way it is" was a binding worldview. "That's the way it is" is not an offhand response of a parent to a particularly annoying child. "That's the way it is" is a complete outlook with binding axioms regarding matters and issues that have no other explanation. I learned it almost from my first moment in the worlds of thought.

"But Mom, 'that's the way it is' is not an answer. You always say that to me."

"Right, son, but 'why' is not always a question."

I assume that such exchanges exist in every home in which there are misunderstandings between opinionated adolescents and parents with a worldview and outlooks like my parents'. "When Dad gets back he'll explain it to you." That was the secret weapon in their arsenal. Mom worked on the tactics, and Dad was responsible for the strategy, she for blocking my erupting youth, he for channeling the defiance to channels of knowledge and curiosity. She dealt with the here and now, he with the long-term and historical. One day Dad came home and taught me one of the most beautiful Talmudic lessons, which is with me almost every day of my life. This lesson fixed our culture as a culture of disagreement, a culture of constant contradictions, betwixt and between.

> For three years there was a dispute between the school of the scholar Shammai and the school of the scholar Hillel, the former asserting, "Jewish law is in agreement with our views" and the latter contending, "The law is in agreement with our views." Then a divine voice declared: "Both views are the words of the living God, but the law is in agreement with the rulings of the school of Hillel." Since, however, both are the words of the living God, what was it that entitled the school of Hillel to have the law fixed in agreement with their rulings? Because they were kindly and modest, they studied their own rulings and those of the school of Shammai, and were even so humble as to study the words of the school of Shammai before theirs. (Babylonian Talmud, Tractate Eruvin, Folio 13b)

For many years, that dispute divided Jewish society, including the Pharisees of the Second Temple era. Three years without a decision, which exacted a price of blood from the disputants. Human tribunals could not reach a decision and recommendation on whom to favor: the traditional, precise, and stricter school of Shammai, or the more lenient, though not lightweight, school of Hillel. Finally, the narrative says, there was no alternative to divine intervention. A "divine voice" declared: "Both views are the words of the living God." I don't know what that voice is, and whose voice it is, but it is clear to me that the narrator meant an intervention and decision by the highest authority, which asserts: "Both views are the words of the living God." That is a wonderful sentence, a verdict like no other. If there is one God and he has one truth, how can it have more than one real interpretation? Isn't there only one truth, and no other? Unless there's a God of multiple truths and contradictions, which means that there is no one correct and straight view that is God's view, but several. God is multifaceted, with a truth that has several legitimate interpretations. Only together are they a complete spiritual and pluralistic reality that assumes that the truth, wherever it is, has more than one authentic and credible source.

The arrangement between the disciples of Shammai and followers of Hillel actually laid the groundwork for the Jewish pluralism of contradiction. Although there are dogmas and absolute statements in Jewish culture, there is also complete acceptance of the opposite opinion. About everything. Or almost everything. I try to imagine a particular moment in Jewish history, the moment of the first meeting of sages who gathered in Yavneh. Jerusalem had been destroyed because of the internal rivalries and violence that tore apart the city of the Temple. You could feel the grief in the air. Many people had lost loved ones; they had property in the smoldering city and memories that went up in smoke. Everyone had already done their own soul-searching about their share of responsibility and the fault of their neighbors. The Temple had been destroyed for all of them, and there was not one person in the room who did not understand that the Jewish state was finished for many years to come.

From the trauma of the destruction, bereavement, and personal loss, they made the most natural but also most astonishing decision: they would never let disputes over ideas and ideologies tear apart and destroy. Civil war before the destruction brought forth the culture of disagreement that followed, a culture that subsumed all sects and factions and brought them all in. The halls of study and their penetrating debates shaped the Jewish soul for a great many years. A soul that is no stranger to contradictory voices and colliding ideas. On the contrary. Out of the destruction a new Judaism was born, which has lived on until our time. I think that is the secret magnetism of Jewish culture, which has pushed and pulled Jews to opposite places precisely because of their Judaism. The greatest communists and capitalists, tough pioneers, genteel bourgeois, complex intellectuals, artists, and people of action. A human kaleidoscope full of contradictions and disagreements in which everyone—lover or hater—can find a hook on which to hang one's hat.

It appears that not only Arendt and my son at the checkpoint were betwixt and between. My father and mother, as well as their God, came from there and went there. That is my wadi, and these are the old people coming out of it toward me, and I'm very comfortable here, in the warm culture of Judaism as the homeland of internal contradiction.

EPILOGUE

THE DAWN AFTER
THE LONG NIGHT

I N 2013, I PARTICIPATED IN A MASS GATHERING IN VIENNA, a city that in recent years has become a kind of distant second home for me. In the commotion of the tens of thousands of people who packed the place, I "corresponded" in my head with the late Stefan Zweig, the prominent Jewish writer who wrote *The World of Yesterday*, a great lamentation for his beloved Europe that the Nazis had destroyed, and who, a day after he sent the manuscript to his publisher, took his own life in Rio de Janeiro.

> *Greetings, Mr. Zweig,*
>
> *I'm sitting here, leaning on a tree, on the edge of Heldenplatz in Vienna. I'm writing the last lines of this book and thinking of you. Before me lies the expanse of the Heroes' Square. There from the balcony, Hitler announced the Anschluss seventy-five years ago, the annexation of Austria to Germany. He stood there at the other end of the square, and the throngs cheered him enthusiastically. Maybe one of them leaned on my tree, just like me. Now separating me and the lofty balcony, between that nightmare and this reality, stand tens of thousands of Viennese who came here to mark the anniversary of*

the end of the Nazi occupation and to express their revulsion against Nazism and its values.

Too bad you're not here. Here on the grass next to me is a Turkish family. The mother and big sister are wrapped in the traditional headscarf, and the youngsters are running around chattering in Viennese German after a ball with the logo of the Rapid Vienna soccer club. On a mat on the other side are a few same-sex couples. They are in love, judging from the way they touch each other, and like me they are enjoying the last rays of the sun of the "blue hour," the hour of the beautiful Viennese sunset. There are also many Jews assembled in the crowd. I know some of them, some are identifiable by their traditional garb, others are no different from the rest. Disabled people in wheelchairs move everywhere freely because of means of access available to anyone. And I can identify in the crowd members of the gypsy people, the Roma. In this wonderful human mix, it is hard for me to avoid the thought that all those whom Hitler wanted to destroy—the Jews, the disabled, the homosexuals, the gypsies, the foreigners—are now celebrating our victory. It took many years, too many, and claimed many victims, too many as well, and still we reached this day. The news these days is very disturbing, Europe is shaking, the economy is fractured, the immigrants and nationalists are staking out territory, and benighted fanatics threaten world peace from near and far. And still, I am happy and full of hope. A minute ago, I heard two people saying to each other, "Today the Second World War has ended." And I believed them. It won't happen again, not here, not to us, not to anyone else across the Western democracies.

In 2017, with Donald Trump and Brexit and Marine Le Pen and Geert Wilders and Nigel Farage on the rise, people are concerned again. It would not be accurate to say that I am without worries; I am very concerned about the future of freedom. Yet I am full of confidence and trust that it will eventually prevail. The strengths of the free human spirit will overcome. I believe that people will not go back voluntarily to the confinement of fewer rights and fewer liberties. As much as modernity, secularism, and progress require many updates, corrections, and fine-tuning, they are still the superior paradigm. We have to work very hard, sometimes fight for it, but the victory is ours.

I look around me, in Israel, in Europe, and all over the United States, and I see social responsibility expressed like never before; impressive civil societies, humbling volunteers, persuasive activists. There is almost a formula: the worse the government, the better the civil society. There dwells our true human security; from there comes to the world the enhanced and improved pluralistic and diverse social models. All of these fantastic, devoted people were not around to stop your beloved Europe from perishing. Now they are, we are, with the promise, "never again." Just listen to Angela Merkel, of all people, the German chancellor, Time magazine's 2015 Person of the Year, who said, "If Europe fails on the question of refugees, then it won't be the Europe we wished for. If we now have to start apologizing for showing a friendly face in response to emergency situations, then that's not my country."*

And, Mr. Zweig, if you ask, desperately like she, how Europe can make space for thousands of refugees and migrants, the answer is so Jewish: "We will cope."

I think about you with sadness and gratitude. With sadness, because with all the lovers of peace and freedom that are here, your suicide is much sadder. You wouldn't believe it, but we won. Who am I to preach to you, but I don't believe that it is permitted to despair, ever. The good human spirit is much stronger than the evil human spirits. And between committing suicide and patience, between despair and happiness, I am always patient, waiting for the happiness to come. I'm sad because had you been alive, you would have stood on the stage today, and before the concert you would have built a

---

*Roland Nelles, "The Real Merkel Finally Stands Up," *Der Spiegel*, online English edition, September 16, 2015.

bridge for the crowd between the good Vienna that was and the good Vienna that exists, and together we would have crossed the river of roiled waters of the years of terror and hatred.

And I also think of you with great gratitude. In the last few years I have written the pages of this book. Many of them were written in your shadow, with your inspiration. In the last few years I have read your books and the books of other Jewish writers here in Vienna, writers who were people of this city. I finished reading Radetzky March *by Joseph Roth in the Schönbrunn Palace, where the final plot takes place, and there the empire also ends. I read* The Capuchin Tomb *in Café Mozart around the corner from the Imperial Crypt. And I read your* The World of Yesterday, *again and again all around the city.*

The book made a strong impression on me. Some have characterized it as a kind of biography. As I read the book more times, I thought that you were not writing about yourself at all. That if you had been asked to write an autobiography, it would have looked entirely different. In The World of Yesterday *you did a great favor to many people like me. You opened the windows of your life to give me, the reader, a glimpse of the world in which you lived and from which you parted so tragically. You lent me your private photo album so that I would understand the human reality that you abandoned when you reached the conclusion that it had abandoned you. I don't know if there is such a discipline, but for myself I define* The World of Yesterday *as an "autobiography of a period." As if the period itself had written its memoir and used your windows to do it.*

How did it begin? It's really strange. I have no real connection to places. I love beautiful landscapes, but I'm not addicted to them. I love my homeland without sacredness and without meaning simply because I was born there, and these are the people, the language, and the places that I am used to. I love nature, but like the homeland, I don't need ownership to feel good in it.

That's why my feeling in Vienna was so odd and strange to me. A city in which I feel at home more than in many other places. I don't like cities, and there is no place in the world that I love more than our small and isolated house in the Judean Hills. And still, in Vienna something else happens to me. Our first acquaintance was not good. I didn't know you and the city you were born in. I arrived in the middle of the night from Naples. I appeared before an audience of intellectuals in the old and inspiring home of Chancellor Bruno Kreisky. I lectured there about my book The Holocaust Is Over; We Must Rise from Its Ashes, *which had been published at the time in German. The next morning I was supposed to head off to another place, to meet other people in a different language. At night, when it was all over, Gertraud went home alone, and I went out of the hotel to walk around the city for a bit. There weren't people on the Graben pedestrian mall. The Viennese coffee shops were closed. A thin fog wrapped the city on a cold November night. Light chills accompanied me on the night walk, but not chills from cold. I had the strange feeling that from every doorway, from every alley leading to the church square, there were eyes peering at me. Only once before in my life did I have that feeling, in Prague. The murkiness of that beautiful and mysterious city wordlessly explained to me the existential mood of Kafka, a native of the city.*

The next day I left Vienna with the feeling that I would not return there again, at least not in the near future. And I was very wrong. I have returned to the city since then many times. I was invited to various and fascinating gatherings as part of the Bruno Kreisky Forum, a medium for international dialogue that attracted me. With time, and over the many times I visited Vienna, deeper layers of the city were revealed to me, and I was taken with her charms. During a routine taxi ride I chatted with a young local friend by the name of Hielfried, and he opened the door for me to the secret cave.

"I'm so impressed with you Viennese," I told him.

"Really?" he replied with the cynicism of a local who has seen everything.

"Yes, you are so cultured. Everyone has read the latest books, this one was at a concert yesterday, that one at the opera, and tomorrow

*they all meet for a culture weekend at the Burgtheater. The whole
conversation is saturated with all the varieties of culture."*

"The city was really once like that," he said. "The capital of an
empire. A cosmopolitan city to which all the sounds and voices, ideas
and expressions of central Europe flowed, where they collided and
created the most wonderful and terrible manifestations of the twentieth century.

"We are still living on that energy. Many of the creators of
that Viennese culture and its carriers were Jewish," he added
matter-of-factly.

That was a piece of information that I knew, but was not conscious of. In our German Jewish background, Berlin was the center of the world. The city to which Moses Mendelssohn went in the
mid-eighteenth century and where he opened with his own hands
the gates of the West and of Judaism. Vienna was on the fringes of
consciousness. Hielfried's remark pushed me to know more about
this city. And from there I quickly reached you and the people of
your generation.

In 2012, I met Professor Steven Aschheim of the Hebrew University. He let me read his reflections on Vienna. Even before the first
line, in the title, everything fit into place. He wrote about "Vienna:
Harbinger of Creativity and Catastrophe." And suddenly I understood the mystery of my attraction, and why precisely in this city I
could reach the places to which my writing took me. What a magnetic city. A few years ago, I was in Leipzig with my youngest son,
my beloved Noam. We sat on the patio of a pizzeria near a church
where Johann Sebastian Bach, the Kapellmeister, would conduct,
where he is buried. "Dad," Noam said, interrupting my thoughts, "do
you think that Bach once walked on this street?" Since he asked that
question I think differently about streets that existed in history. To
think that there were days that in these very streets of Vienna, Freud,
Herzl, and Hitler walked, and maybe even tipped their hats to each
other. The city where in those days both pan-Judaism, which became*

Zionism, was born, along with pan-Germanism, which became its
great misfortune, Nazism. The city in which the most emotionally
disturbed person walked freely, along with the greatest emotional
healer.

What do I see in the Vienna of today? It's not clear to me. Many
things are still blurred blots, not a clear and accurate picture. A kind
of Rorschach test that doesn't have an incorrect answer, just different
answers with different meanings. Sometimes I see the terrible past
poking out among the cracks, refusing to blend in with the walls. In
politics, in facades, in graffiti on the walls, in tattoos of the younger
generation. At other times, I see the decline of the empire. How this
city, like a black hole, absorbed all the languages and cultures, names
and memories of all the peoples and tribes linked by nothing but
the energy of imperial Vienna. And when the historical centrifuge
reached peak speed in World War I, all the peripheral areas were
detached, leaving Vienna alone to carry the multiculturalism that
was the concentrate of the twentieth century. According to Aschheim,
Vienna was the harbinger of creativity and destruction, the cradle of
psychoanalysis, the center of advanced experimentation in painting,
literature, and modern music, and the place where the first molds of
mass politics and incitement were cast, in which the forces of myth
and irrationality entered the life cycles of individuals and society.

It took this city a long time to take up its current place after the
dramas and traumas of the previous century. But now it is there. The
same city, with the impressive ring boulevards, the great imperial
buildings, the institutions, the gardens, and the names. The same but
so different. The fascinating mix of languages. Muslim women covered from head to toe shop with scantily clad young women in erotic
lingerie stores. Many international and local paths of statesmanship
and diplomacy, open and secret, cut through the breadth and depth
of the city. Serbs and Croats, Turks and Jews, Catholics and Protes-
tants, intellectuals and businesspeople—all pour new content into
the vessels of the old memories.

Sometimes I feel that Vienna is a model very similar to Israel. Many cultures folded into one place. Sometimes colliding with powerful insensitivity. That same secret of a black hole sucking in energies that once burned and are now dimmed. And at the same time, I feel that something new is seeking to erupt onto the respectable surface.

What seeks to erupt, Mr. Zweig, is you. When you ended your life in distant Rio, you became a pupa that went to sleep for a few generations. And today, decades later, it's time for the butterfly to emerge. When you explained your act of desperation, you wrote: "Every day I learned to love this country more, and I would not have asked to rebuild my life in any other place after the world of my own language sank and was lost to me, and my spiritual homeland, Europe, destroyed itself." And you ended this way: "I send greetings to all of my friends: May they live to see the dawn after this long night. I, who am most impatient, go before them."*

Indeed, you went too soon. The dawn broke, patience pays off, and I wish to be one of your friends and followers of your path. In every place, especially in the place of the Jews, in Israel. In my own way, which does not have the spiritual strength that drove you and your generation. But I am trying very hard.

---

*Stefan Zweig, suicide letter, February 22, 1942, Stefan Zweig archive, Archives Department, National Library of Israel. A digital image and partial English translation of the letter are available online at http://web.nli.org.il/sites/NLI /English/collections/personalsites/archive_treasures/Pages/stefan-zweig .aspx.

INDEX

Andrea Krogmann

Avraham Burg was born in Jerusalem in 1955 to one of the most prominent families in Israel. His father, Dr. Joseph Burg, was a Holocaust survivor who escaped from Germany to Palestine in September 1939 and went on to lead the National Religious Party and serve as a minister in the Israeli government from 1948 to 1988. His mother, Rivka, was a seventh-generation resident of Hebron and the daughter of the local community rabbi. Avraham Burg first took on a public role during the first Lebanon War in 1982, when he was a leader of the anti-war protests. He went on to serve as advisor to Prime Minister Shimon Peres, a member of the Israeli Knesset, the chairman of the Jewish Agency for Israel and the World Zionist Organization, and the Speaker of the Knesset, among other public positions. Since his voluntary retirement from public life in 2004, Burg has become an outspoken leader of the Israeli left wing. He is the author of numerous books, including (in English) *The Holocaust Is Over; We Must Rise from Its Ashes* (Macmillan, 2009) and *Very Near to You* (Gefen, 2012). He lives in Nataf, just outside Jerusalem.

The Nation Institute

Nation.

Founded in 2000, **Nation Books** has become a leading voice in American independent publishing. The inspiration for the imprint came from the *Nation* magazine, the oldest independent and continuously published weekly magazine of politics and culture in the United States.

The imprint's mission is to produce authoritative books that break new ground and shed light on current social and political issues. We publish established authors who are leaders in their area of expertise, and endeavor to cultivate a new generation of emerging and talented writers. With each of our books we aim to positively affect cultural and political discourse.

Nation Books is a project of The Nation Institute, a nonprofit media center established to extend the reach of democratic ideals and strengthen the independent press. The Nation Institute is home to a dynamic range of programs: our award-winning Investigative Fund, which supports ground-breaking investigative journalism; the widely read and syndicated website TomDispatch; our internship program in conjunction with the *Nation* magazine; and Journalism Fellowships that fund up to 20 high-profile reporters every year.

For more information on Nation Books, the *Nation* magazine, and The Nation Institute, please visit:

www.nationbooks.org
www.nationinstitute.org
www.thenation.com
www.facebook.com/nationbooks.ny
Twitter: @nationbooks